François Neveux is the leading medieval historian in France and has written numerous books on the Normans. He is Professor of History at Caen University.

Titles available in the *Brief History* series

A Brief History of 1917: Russia's Year of Revolution
Roy Bainton
A Brief History of the Birth of the Nazis
Nigel Jones
A Brief History of the Circumnavigators
Derek Wilson
A Brief History of the Cold War
John Hughes-Wilson
A Brief History of the Crimean War
Alex Troubetzkoy
A Brief History of the Crusades
Geoffrey Hindley
A Brief History of the Druids
Peter Berresford Ellis
A Brief History of the Dynasties of China
Bamber Gascoigne
A Brief History of the End of the World
Simon Pearson
A Brief History of the Future
Oona Strathern
A Brief History of Globalization
Alex MacGillivray
A Brief History of the Great Moghuls
Bamber Gascoigne
A Brief History of the Hundred Years War
Desmond Seward
A Brief History of Medieval Warfare
Peter Reid
A Brief History of Misogyny
Jack Holland
A Brief History of Medicine
Paul Strathern
A Brief History of the Private Lives of the Roman Emperors
Anthony Blond
A Brief History of Science
Thomas Crump
A Brief History of Secret Societies
David V. Barrett
A Brief History of the Age of Steam
Thomas Crump
A Brief History of Stonehenge
Aubrey Burl
A Brief History of the Vikings
Jonathan Clements

A BRIEF HISTORY OF

THE
NORMANS

The Conquests that Changed
the Face of Europe

FRANÇOIS NEVEUX

In collaboration with Claire Ruelle
Translated by Howard Curtis

ROBINSON

RUNNING PRESS
PHILADELPHIA · LONDON

In memory of my teacher,
Lucien Musset (1922–2004)

Constable & Robinson Ltd
3 The Lanchesters
162 Fulham Palace Road
London W6 9ER
www.constablerobinson.com

L'Aventure des Normands (VIIIe – XIIIe siècle)
by François Neveux
© Éditions Perrin, 2006

English language edition published in the UK by Robinson,
an imprint of Constable & Robinson Ltd, 2008

A copy of the British Library Cataloguing in
Publication data is available from the British Library

UK ISBN: 978-1-84529-523-3

1 3 5 7 9 10 8 6 4 2

First published in the United States in 2008 by Running Press Book Publishers

US Library of Congress number: 2007936635

US ISBN: 978-0-7624-3371-1

Running Press Book Publishers
2300 Chestnut Street
Philadelphia, PA 19103-4371

Visit us on the web!

www.runningpress.com

Printed and bound in the EU

CONTENTS

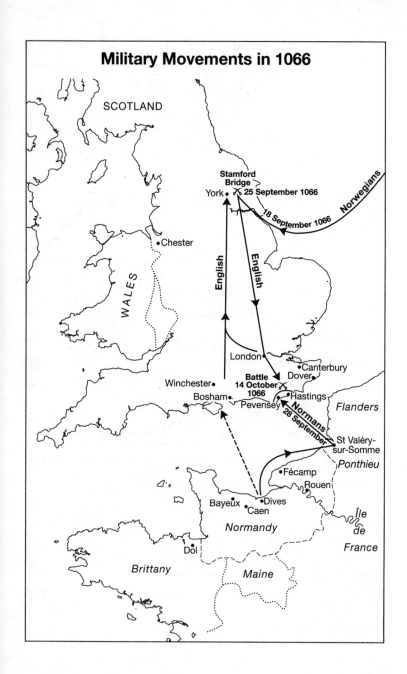

Military Movements in 1066

SCOTLAND

Stamford
Bridge
York · 25 September 1066

Norwegians

18 September 1066

Chester ·

W A L E S

English

English

London ·

Winchester ·

Bosham ·

Battle
14 October
1066

· Canterbury

Dover ·

· Hastings

Pevensey ·

Normans

28 September

Flanders

St Valéry-
sur-Somme

Ponthieu

· Fécamp

Rouen ·

Bayeux ·
· Dives

· Caen

Normandy

Île
de

France

Dol ·

Brittany

Maine

Battle of Hastings

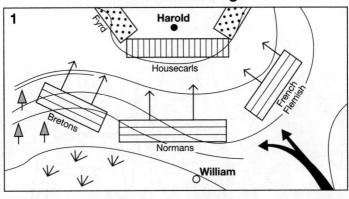

1

Fyrd

Harold

Housecarls

Bretons

Normans

French Flemish

William

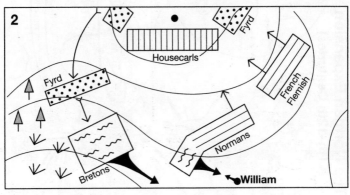

2

Fyrd

Housecarls

Fyrd

Fyrd

Bretons

Normans

French Flemish

William

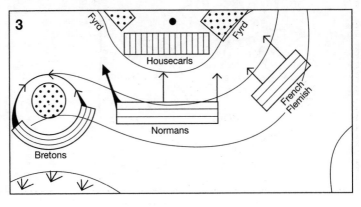

3

Fyrd

Fyrd

Housecarls

Bretons

Normans

French Flemish

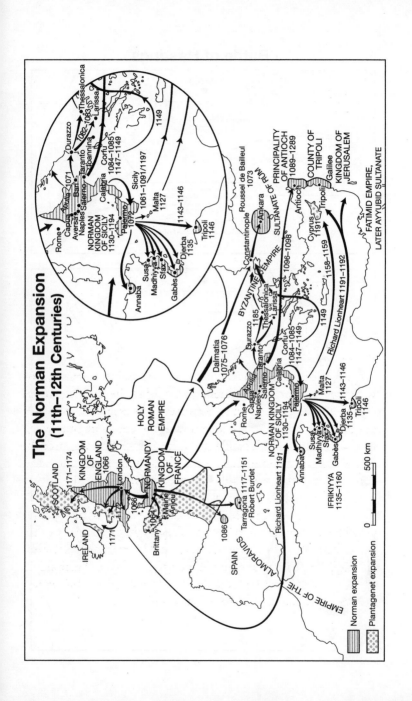

The Norman Expansion
(11th–12th Centuries)

SCOTLAND
1171–1174

IRELAND

KINGDOM
OF
ENGLAND
1066

London

1066

Maine

Brittany

NORMANDY

1064

KINGDOM
OF FRANCE

Anjou

HOLY
ROMAN
EMPIRE

Tarragona 1117–1151
Robert Burdet

Richard Lionheart 1191

SPAIN

ALMORAVIDS

EMPIRE OF THE

1086

Rome

Capua
Aversa
Naples
Salerno

Apulia

Bari

Taranto

Calabria

Corfu
1084–1085/
1147–1149

NORMAN KINGDOM
OF SICILY
1130–1194

Palermo

Annaba

IFRIKIYYA
1135–1160

Susa
Madhiyya
Sfax

Gabes

Djerba
1135

Malta
1127

Tripoli
1146

1143–1146

Dalmatia
1075–1076

Durazzo

BYZANTINE
EMPIRE

Thessalonica

Larissa
1185

Corfu
1084–1085/
1147–1149

Constantinople

Roussel de Bailleul
1073

Ankara

1096–1098

SULTANATE OF RUM

SULTANATE OF
PRINCIPALITY
OF ANTIOCH
1089–1289

Antioch

Cyprus
1191

1149

1158–1159

Richard Lionheart 1191–1192

Tripoli

COUNTY OF
TRIPOLI

Galilee

KINGDOM OF
JERUSALEM

FATIMID EMPIRE,
LATER AYYUBID SULTANATE

0   500 km

Norman expansion

Plantagenet expansion

Rome

Capua
Aversa
Naples
Salerno

Apulia
1071

Bari

Taranto
1063

Calabria

Corfu
1084–1085/
1147–1149

NORMAN KINGDOM
OF SICILY
1130–1194

Palermo
1072

Sicily
1061–1091/1197

Malta
1127

1143–1146

Tripoli
1146

Djerba
1135

Susa
Madhiyya
Sfax
Gabes

Annaba

Durazzo

Thessalonica

Larissa

1149

1127

Durazzo
1081–1085

PROLOGUE

12 May 841

A Viking fleet appears at the mouth of the Seine, commanded by Asgeirr. Reaching Rouen on 14 May, he and his men plunder the city and put it to the torch. The Scandinavians sail on up the Seine and on 24 May attack the abbey of Jumièges, which they also plunder and burn. The next day they approach the monastery of Fontenelle – but the monks know they are coming, and the two sides come to an agreement: the monastery is spared in return for a ransom of 6 *livres*. On 28 May the monks of the abbey of Saint-Denis, near Paris, also negotiate, obtaining the release of sixty-eight prisoners for the sum of 26 *livres*. On 31 May, Asgeirr and his men set sail again; with them are captives, who will be used as slaves. Their ships are laden with precious objects of gold and silver: the expedition has proved very fruitful. They will return.[1]

14 October 1066, 8 a.m.

During the night, King Harold of England and his army have taken up position at the top of Senlac hill, the only option left them by William Duke of Normandy, whose early arrival had enabled him to choose the field of battle.

The English are firmly entrenched on the hill. Facing them, William draws up his army in three groups: on the left, the Bretons; on the right, the Flemish and the French; in the middle, the largest group, the Normans. The cavalry are in force, at least 2,000: able to manoeuvre as one, they constitute a formidable fighting force. On the slopes of the hill is a vast clearing where the cavalry can deploy. William is hoping that they will help him gain the upper hand over the English army, which is composed entirely of foot soldiers.

Riding out in front of his troops, Duke William addresses them in a loud voice, exhorting them, at this decisive moment, to fight 'manfully but wisely',[2] telling them that if they win, they will enjoy glory and riches; if defeated, they will be slaughtered or taken prisoner by a cruel enemy.[3] They have no choice but to win the day. His words are repeated by heralds who carry his message to the men in his army, some 8,000.

Then, raising his arm, William gives the arranged signal for the first assault. It is 9 o'clock in the morning. The battle of Hastings has begun . . .

Christmas Day 1130

Dressed like a Byzantine emperor, Roger II of Hauteville, Duke of Apulia, Calabria and Sicily, long-haired, with beard and moustache, makes his entrance into the cathedral of Palermo, a former mosque converted into a church. His robe is sumptuous and he carries the ends of his cloak over his left arm. His belt and pallium are decorated with gold and precious stones, a magnificent garment made in the palace workshop by the Muslim women of his harem.

Pope Anacletus II has granted him the title of king, but he has not made the journey himself, since in Rome his authority is being disputed. It is the Archbishop of Palermo who places the crown – made by the city's goldsmiths – on the new king's head. This coronation is his day of glory, a reward for the efforts he has made over a long period to take control of all the territories conquered by the Normans in southern Italy. In the struggle against the often rebellious barons, his army, largely composed of Muslim soldiers, had been his vital ally.

One of Roger's followers, George of Antioch, the 'Emir of Emirs' of the new Kingdom of Sicily, decides to immortalize the event. He orders a mosaic for his own foundation, the church of the Martorana. But in this mosaic, it is Christ himself, not the archbishop, who with his right hand places the crown on King Roger's head …

These three episodes have been chosen from among many others to illustrate the extraordinary Norman adventure of the eighth to the thirteenth centuries. This adventure first led the Vikings out of Scandinavia eastwards to Russia, and westwards, to where they created Normandy. Later, a new adventure led the Normans from Normandy to England and Sicily. That is the subject of this book.

I

SCANDINAVIAN BEGINNINGS

The 'Normans' began as 'Northmen' – that is how they are referred to in Western sources. Christian authors also used names such as 'pagans' or 'Danes'. The Danes were in fact the earliest of the Nordic peoples to become organized, and from the eighth century were the most easily identifiable neighbours of the Kingdom of the Franks. They were seen as pagans, at a time when conversion to Christianity was the obligatory route to acceptance within the Frankish world. In this book, the word 'Normans' will be reserved for those Scandinavians who settled during the tenth century in what had been Neustria, where they founded the Duchy of 'Normandy',[1] although the word was soon used to apply not only to the Scandinavians but to all inhabitants of the duchy, whatever their origin. In other words, from the tenth century onwards, most Normans (i.e. inhabitants of Normandy) were in fact Franks. The word 'Scandinavians' will also be used here when talking about the 'Northmen', to refer to the inhabitants of Scandinavia, specifically those whose language is Germanic, in other words, those who feature in this book, but excluding the Finns, the Lapps and other native populations. The Scandinavians came into contact with the West during the eighth century when they embarked on naval expeditions which were as much to do with trade as with war. It is traditional to speak of 'Scandinavian invasions', which gives these expeditions a very pejorative connotation. That is a reflection of the pessimistic vision of Frankish, Anglo-Saxon and Irish clerics, who in thus describing them were expressing the point of view of the victims. Modern historians have tried to examine these events within the general context of the period, and it has become more common to talk of 'migrations' rather than 'invasions'.

Two words have come to be accepted as designations of the Scandinavians who appeared in Western Europe: Vikings and Varangians. The term 'Varangians' is reserved for those who travelled eastwards, especially from Sweden. They went through what is now Russia and Ukraine until they reached Constantinople and the Byzantine Empire, and were first known as *Rhos* (in Greek) or *Rus* (in the Slavonic languages). Later, this name was extended to all the inhabitants of what is now Russia. Historians prefer the term 'Varangians' (*vaeringjar* in Old Norse), which was originally used to designate those Scandinavians who were employed as mercenaries by Russian princes and Byzantine emperors. These Varangians played an important role in the remarkable story of the Scandinavians; but this book will deal specifically with those who are generally called 'Vikings'.

The term 'Viking' only became common currency in the nineteenth century. There is some dispute about the origin of the word. It may derive from the Old Norse *vik* (bay) or the Latin *vicus* (town), whose Germanic equivalent is *wik*. The term is found as early as the seventh century, in an Anglo-Saxon context, in connection with maritime activities, especially piracy,[2] and it is this meaning that became more general later – in other words, the Vikings are first thought of as pirates. The same word was also used, more broadly, to denote all the Scandinavians who conducted expeditions to Western Europe between the eighth and eleventh centuries.

The Vikings only became well known from the point at which they came into contact with westerners, who used writing. For the previous period, it is necessary to refer to other sources, all of them problematic.

The sources

The written sources concerning the Scandinavians during the period of the 'invasions' almost all come from outside Scandinavia. Those from the Christian West are written in Latin by clerics. There are also sources in Arabic, from the Muslim world, and in Greek, from the Byzantine Empire, but they mainly deal with the East. These sources have the advantage of being contemporary with the Viking migration, but they have one major disadvantage: they express a point of view that is clearly hostile to the 'invaders'.

The oldest written sources from the Viking world itself are runic inscriptions.[3] This system of writing appeared in the Germanic world in about the first century AD, probably in imitation of Latin script, and spread throughout Scandinavia, where it was used until the fourteenth century. Runic inscriptions are carved on stone, wood or bone. They have given us a great deal of information about everyday life in Scandinavia and about some of the Viking expeditions.

Another historical source is Scandinavian literature. The earliest examples are the poems written by *skalds*, court poets who, like Celtic bards or African *griots*, were given the task of praising the great deeds of those who protected them and their ancestors. These skaldic poems derive originally from oral literature and present historians with immense problems of interpretation.[4] A similar observation can be made about another source, the sagas.

The sagas were also transmitted orally before being written down, starting in the twelfth century, and especially in the thirteenth and fourteenth centuries (mostly from 1150 to 1350).

Some sagas come from Norway, but most are from Iceland. Iceland seems to have been an extraordinary conservatory of Scandinavian institutions, literature and history, and much of what we know of the Viking world we owe to the Icelanders: Régis Boyer has quite rightly called this 'the Icelandic miracle'.[5] The most important of the sagas are the royal sagas, especially those collected under the title *Heimskringla*, written by Snorri Sturluson.[6] These are epic stories based on historical events. Some depict figures such as the Norwegian kings Olaf Tryggvason and Olaf Haraldsson, the latter also known as Saint Olaf.[7] While it is undeniable that the sagas are works of great quality, many of them genuine masterpieces,[8] the fact that they were written so long after the events they depict has aroused suspicion in historians, who have questioned whether they can truly be considered historical documents. In many cases they seem to have more to do with legend than with history. Moreover, the authors of the sagas were men of their time, and the principal aim of their stories was to sing the praises of a particular family or clan of the period at which they were writing. That is unquestionably true of Snorri Sturluson, who played an extremely important political role during his lifetime. The sagas tell us more about the period during which they were written than the period, centuries earlier, which they were supposedly describing. They remain, as Régis Boyer has written, 'a tremendous mine of information in every field, provided we learn to read between the lines'.[9]

It may be that we have become excessively critical of these sources. The same could be said of Scandinavian laws, which were written down relatively belatedly (some two centuries after the Viking period). It has often been stated that these laws did not really apply during the period of the 'invasions'. More recently, however, this negative view has been revised somewhat by historians of law, who have demonstrated that, although they certainly show the influence of both Roman law and biblical scripture, they have their origins in an older period, Scandinavian legislation being unquestionably conservative in nature.[10]

The most fruitful source remains archaeology, which continues to provide us with new information. The tombs of the Viking period have yielded much material, and in particular the ships discovered at Gokstad and Oseberg in Norway. Other ships from the end of the Viking age, the eleventh century, have been found at Roskilde and Skuldelev in Denmark. These have been extensively studied and the reconstructions of Viking ships have provided us with a great deal of information.[11] In addition, many trading centres have been excavated,[12] and a remarkable series of fortified camps has been studied, all of them located in Denmark, at Trelleborg, Odense, Aggesborg and Fyrcat.[13] More recently, archaeologists have taken an interest in purely rural sites. Anne Nissen-Jaubert, for example, has singled out five particular regions of Denmark – Thy, to the north of the Limfjord, the region of Arhus, the centre of the Jutland peninsula and two regions on the island of Sjaelland – and, by putting together the information gained from excavations and the written sources, has been able to study shifts in population and living conditions over a long period, from the third to the twelfth centuries.[14]

A second kind of source, place-names, should also be taken into consideration. In the absence of other reliable sources, much emphasis has been placed on this kind of study as a means of estimating the density of Scandinavian settlement in particular areas, especially in England – above all in the northeast, the Danelaw – and in Normandy. In the latter case, it has been noted that Scandinavian place-names were particularly common in the Pays de Caux and Cotentin, less so in Bessin and on the Caen plain. These findings should, however, be treated with caution. Place-names based on the names of people may show that an area was under Scandinavian domination, but not necessarily that there were many Scandinavians living there. In this respect, it is interesting to look more closely at the names of smaller, more defined areas, which may give a better idea of the degree of rural colonization. But it is not easy to distinguish purely Scandinavian place-names from Saxon place-names – reminders of a previous wave of occupation. In addition, in Normandy's case, there were sometimes mixed settlements that could be called Anglo-Scandinavian. Like the literary sources, both place-names and personal names reveal the emergence of a common language, which seems to have been a vital link between all Scandinavians.[15]

Language

The old language of the Scandinavians is usually referred to as Proto-Norse (*urnordisk*). Gradually, starting in the eighth century, the various dialects became differentiated, an evolution that continued until the thirteenth century, by which time there were two groups of languages: western Nordic (the basis of Norwegian and Icelandic) and Eastern Nordic (the basis of Danish and Swedish). It should be noted that there was never a very marked separation between these languages: even today, there is mutual understanding between the inhabitants of the three countries. Icelandic, however, is a separate case. As with institutions, Iceland was extraordinarily conservative with language; hence modern Icelandic is still very close to the Old Norse spoken 1,000 ago throughout Scandinavia. The relationship of Icelandic to the other Scandinavian languages has been compared to that between Latin and the Romance languages, with one major difference: Icelandic is still spoken today.[16]

In the sagas, this common language is called *donsk tunga*, which means 'Danish language', even though it has no specific connection with the Kingdom of Denmark. All Scandinavians at that time understood each other perfectly well. They could also communicate easily with speakers of other Germanic languages, of whom there were many around the northern seas, from the Frankish Empire to Anglo-Saxon England. This is undoubtedly one of the keys to their success as traders. And it was trade that led them to other ways of appropriating goods.[17]

Scandinavian society

The Scandinavians were primarily farmers and shepherds. They supplemented these basic activities with hunting and fishing. Given their respective climatic conditions, the Norwegians concentrated on the rearing of livestock, whereas in Denmark and the south of Sweden arable farming had long existed. Archaeological excavations have revealed that agriculture expanded significantly after the beginning of the eighth century, with the cultivation of barley and the beginnings of crop rotation. There were also advances in the use of tools, such as the replacement of the swing plough by the heavy plough. In Sweden and Norway, settlements were generally scattered, as was also the case in Iceland after colonization in the eleventh century. In Denmark and in the fertile regions of the south and east of Sweden, Östergotland and Uppland on the other hand, archaeological excavation has revealed houses grouped in settlements, one of the best known of which is Vorbasse in Jutland. This settlement seems to have moved site several times from the sixth century, though remained fixed from the eighth to the twelfth centuries. It comprised a number of farms spread out along a central street. The buildings of each farm were laid out in the same way, within a large enclosure, which suggests that all the farms were planned together. In each case, the main building is a 'long house', 10 to 30 metres in length by a few metres in width. The walls were made of stone, without mortar, and were usually sloping. The roof was curved, and was noticeably higher in the centre than at the ends. This large building was most often surrounded by much smaller annexes. Similar observations have been made on other sites, which suggests that this was a general development, at least in those regions where arable farming predominated.[18]

Trade had long existed within Nordic society, and intensified in the eighth century. The Scandinavians were able to offer foreign merchants the products of their hunting (skins and furs), fishing (amber and walrus ivory) and gathering (wax and honey), as well as crafts, especially jewellery. In return, they acquired more sophisticated products from the worlds of the Franks, Byzantines and Arabs: fabrics, weapons, glass and ceramic objects, and wine. At first, trade was conducted through barter, but precious metals were also used, especially silver (measured by weight). The first coins, known as *sceattas*, seem to have been minted in Scandinavia in the eighth century, not in Frisia,[19] though it was with Frisia, as well as with the countries of the Rhine and with Anglo-Saxon England, with which this trade was conducted, as is shown by the presence of such coins on sites in these different regions.

This commercial activity led to the birth of the first towns, which were in effect trading centres. The oldest seems to have been Ribe, in the south of Jutland, founded at the beginning of the eighth century. In all probability, it was there that the *sceattas* depicting Odin, or a bearded king, on one side and a monster on the other were minted.[20] Other towns soon followed: Hedeby (Haithabu) in the south of Denmark, in the middle of the same century, Birka in Sweden, and Skiringssal (Kaupang) in Norway. These towns are named in texts of the period. Others have only become known through archaeological excavations.[21] All were built of wood and included harbour facilities, at the very least a wharf, and they were often surrounded by ramparts of earth. Their creation is part of the vast wave of urban development that took place throughout Western Europe in the eighth and ninth centuries. These 'new towns' were traditionally given the name *portus* (Latin for 'port'), as they were always either by the sea or on a navigable river. Examples are such well-known sites in the Frankish world as Quentovic, on the Canche estuary, and Dorestad, on the Rhine estuary.[22]

In the course of the eighth century the Scandinavian world was clearly developing rapidly, and the sources allow us, for the first time, to gain an idea of its social organization.

Accounts written after the event, such as certain poems of the *Edda* and especially the *Ringthula*,[23] depict a Scandinavian society composed of three social groups: the slaves, the free peasants and the jarls (*jarlar*). The philologist Georges Dumézil saw this as an example of his trifunctional hypothesis.[24] But we need to be cautious. This threefold division of society is based rather on myth: these writers may have been inspired by the Western model – peasants, warriors and clerics – which itself was equally mythical. Certainly there were slaves in Scandinavian society, and they may well have been especially numerous during the Viking period. Régis Boyer distinguishes two sorts of slaves. The first were considered as mere merchandise and sold just like hides and furs: there is no evidence that such slaves existed in Scandinavian society. The second were prisoners of war, who could buy their own freedom – their lot was far better than that of slaves in the Roman Empire or even in the Frankish world.[25]

The vast majority of the inhabitants of Scandinavia belonged to the category of *boendr* (singular: *bondi*). These were free men who enjoyed full political and social rights. The *bondi* had a fixed abode and at least partly owned the lands he farmed. He took part in public affairs and sat in the assembly known as the *thing*, which meant that he could both judge and bear witness and, more generally, give his opinion on all the questions debated at these assemblies. He was also involved in drawing up laws. If he were offended, he and all his family were fully compensated. Last but not least, he bore arms: he was a warrior in the full meaning of the word. When the Viking expeditions began, the Scandinavian armies were largely composed of *boendr*, since at that time there was no such thing as a professional army in Scandinavia.[26]

Contrary to what has often been stated, Scandinavian society was not egalitarian. There were important differences between men, mainly based on wealth and land ownership. In Iceland, there were three categories: the *smaboendr*, the *boendr* and the *storboendr* – or small, medium and large *boendr*.[27] This was clearly a strongly hierarchical society, even though all the *boendr* enjoyed the same basic rights. Most free men were farmers (either raising livestock or cultivating the land), who also practised other supplementary activities, such as fishing and trade. Some, however, exercised a specialized profession as 'lawspeakers', priests and healers.

The lawspeakers were men who know the spoken law by heart and were capable of reciting it at the *thing* or during trials. This profession has its equivalent in Frankish society: the *rachimbourgs* of the Merovingian period, or the *échevins* (*scabini* in Latin) of the Carolingian period. The two other categories – the priests and the healers – have no equivalent in the Frankish world, being more or less directly connected with the old religion. The healers were called *laeknir*, a word that means both doctor or surgeon and magician. As for the priests, it is by no means certain that they existed as such in Scandinavia, since sacrifices and other religious acts were performed by kings or heads of family. Even though there are priests in the sagas, this may have been a case of grafting on to the older society the biblical and Christian models in use at the time of writing.[28]

Another myth that needs to be put in perspective is the place of women. Women are said to have enjoyed great freedom in old Scandinavian society. But this was not really the case, at least officially. Legally a *bondi*'s wife was her husband's inferior. She could not appear in court and had no share of his inheritance. Marriage was an agreement between two families, and the word used for it is telling – *brudhkaup*, or 'bride price'. The bride's family gave the bridegroom's family a dowry (*heimanfylgja*), and in return the bridegroom's family granted a dower (*mundr*).[29] These are fundamental customs, found in many so-called 'traditional' societies, especially in Africa. 'Arranged marriages' were not so exotic: they were common practice in middle-class European families until the beginning of the twentieth century. Marriage law was deeply rooted in the mentality of the Scandinavians who conquered Normandy. It was later incorporated into Norman law, which continued until the French Revolution, although it underwent major changes under the influence of Christianity, in particular the imposition of monogamy as the official line.[30]

Polygamy was accepted in the Scandinavian world – as long as it benefited men! Female adultery was severely punished, whereas men were entitled to bring one or several concubines (*frilla* in the singular) into the house. Of course, the official spouse retained an authority over the other women, the symbol of that authority being the bunch of keys that she wore at all times. As long as she observed the taboos, the Scandinavian woman was respected and was considered the guardian of the home. She performed a number of tasks, such as cooking, washing, working in the fields. She was responsible for bringing up the children and had to supervise the servants. She also possessed secret knowledge, related to magic and sorcery, although in this field she was in competition with the healers (who were men). Overall, it is clear that a wife had genuine authority within the house, while her husband reserved all outside activities for himself. Women's authority was reinforced during the Viking period by the fact that many husbands were away on expeditions to far-off lands.

The father remained the head of the family and had absolute power over his children. It was he who gave the newborn child a name, often that of a forefather or ancestor. A clear distinction was made between a legitimate child, who was entitled to the inheritance, and an illegitimate child, the offspring of a concubine, who was excluded from it.[31] But if men had a monopoly over political activities, the woman nevertheless played an indirect part, since she was the guardian of the family honour. It was she who perpetuated the memory of ancestral exploits, who reminded her father or son of their duty of vengeance, or who might become a soothsayer and predict an adventurous future for the men of her household.[32]

As far as political organization is concerned, we are again dealing with a myth, that of a perfectly democratic society, practising a kind of direct democracy. The fundamental institution was the assembly, the *thing*, which gathered together the *boendr* of a region. The *thing* met in the open air in a suitable location. All *boendr* had a right to participate in the *thing* and give their opinions. In reality, not everyone's opinion carried the same weight. We find in the *thing* the same strict hierarchy we have already noted in groups of free men. Gradually a higher category of local chiefs was formed, who exercised power and constituted a genuine aristocracy. These men derived their power from the land they owned, the armed entourages they maintained (the *lidh* or *hirdh*), and the protection they granted to a certain number of dependants. They were given different names depending on the countries: *hersar* in Norway, *godhar* in Iceland, *jarlar* in certain regions. In this regard, too, the example of Iceland (late in the period but well known) is of great interest. The *godhar* were at once powerful heads of families, lawmakers and religious dignitaries (practising ancestor worship among other things). It was they who had pride of place in the local *thing*, and later in the *Althing*, which gathered together the free men of the whole island. Each of them drew their influence from a court of dependants. They held power collectively, there being no king in Iceland.[33]

Outside Iceland this aristocracy played the role of intermediary between the *boendr* and the higher authority, which might be embodied, depending on the country and the region, in a *jarl* or a king.

Genuine *jarlar* (singular: *jarl*) were rare. The only ones known to us are the *jarl* of Möre, the *jarl* of the Hladhir in Norway and, later, the *jarl* of the Orkneys. But the emergence of powerful local figures can be observed in many regions. In the absence of reliable texts, archaeology has been of great help in this area, with excavations at sites that were manifestly centres of power – Gudme and Lejre in Denmark, Borg in Norway and Gamla Uppsala in Sweden. These sites include large halls where political and religious ceremonies were held, and the high-quality furnishings show that they were residences of important leaders. Such centres become more and more common the further we advance in time. They are the signs of a concentration of power, from which the Scandinavian royal families were gradually to emerge.[34]

The emergence of royal families

The first Scandinavian kings are little known, their stories the stuff of legend. The question may in any case be asked as to what was meant by the word 'king'. In many cases, they were figures who exercised power within a particular region, a power perhaps only slightly greater than that of the *jarlar* and the other regional chiefs. In this respect, the early Scandinavian kings might be compared with the many Irish 'kings' whom the Vikings had to face in the ninth and tenth centuries. In addition, the kings were not necessarily attached to one territory only: the texts mention 'kings of the sea', at least until the eleventh century.[35] Clearly these were leaders of maritime expeditions, but the fact that they were given the title of king suggests that the word did not have the same meaning for the Scandinavians as it had for the Franks.

To be a king in Scandinavia, it was first necessary to belong to a lineage that was considered royal. Régis Boyer observes that the word *konung* (*könig* in German, *king* in English) derives from the word *kyn*, which means kinship.[36] Nevertheless, there was no real heredity, and power struggles between the various pretenders were often fierce. It sometimes happened that when a choice could not be made between two brothers or two cousins, they were allowed to rule jointly – until such time as the stronger of the two managed to eliminate the other.

In all cases this was an elected monarchy, on the Germanic model, and it did not entirely disappear from the Frankish world until the end of the tenth century (and well beyond that in Germany). The king was chosen by the aristocrats – in other words, the great *boendr*, or the *hersar* in Norway – although we do not know exactly how these elections were carried out. The role of these aristocrats was not limited to elections: they reserved the right to have a say in the affairs of the king, and even to overthrow him if need be. As late as the beginning of the eleventh century, according to Snorri Sturluson, the Swedish king Olaf Sköttkonung was obliged by the *boendr* to make peace with the Norwegian king Olad Haraldsson (Saint Olaf). To support their claims, their spokesman, the great *bondi* Thorgnyr, mentions in his speech a historical (or perhaps legendary) episode: at a *thing* held in Muli, five kings behaved arrogantly towards the *boendr*, who rebelled and killed them by throwing them in a swamp.[37] This model of a weak king, dependent on the important men of his kingdom and exercising only limited power, seems to have prevailed for a long time in Norway and Sweden. The same was not true in Denmark, where the monarchy was older and more established.

In Scandinavia as in many other societies, from the Germanic monarchies of the West to the old monarchies of Africa, monarchy had a sacred character. The king was first and foremost a priest responsible for the most important acts of worship towards the gods, including sacrifices. Ernst Kantorowicz's theory about the 'two bodies' of the king can be applied to the Scandinavian kings.[38] Apart from his mortal body, the king is endowed with an immortal body, which makes it possible for him to play the role of intermediary (and intercessor) between men and gods. Contrary to received opinion, the Scandinavian kings were not primarily war leaders, although they might often have to conduct military operations. Above all, the sacred king was the person responsible for the fertility of the land and the fecundity of women. It was he who could keep the climate favourable to the rearing of livestock and the growing of crops by maintaining a good relationship with the gods. In this particular respect his role was comparable to that of the African kings. A far as possible, war had to be avoided in favour of economic activities, agriculture and trade, which would bring wellbeing to his people. The king was the guarantor of peace and prosperity.[39]

The earliest kings appeared in Denmark. The first was Ogendus, who is mentioned in the *Vita Willibordi*, and who is supposed to have lived in the first half of the eighth century.[40] Subsequently, a King Sigfred is mentioned in the 780s. This was the period when Charlemagne conquered Saxony and for the first time reached the borders of a Scandinavian country. Later, in 808, King Godfred invaded territory belonging to the Abodrites, who were allies of the Franks, and found himself in conflict with Charlemagne. What happened after the assassination of Godfred in 810 is a good example of the fierce power struggles common in Scandinavia. Godfred's sons were pushed aside in favour of Hemming, who made peace with Charlemagne. When Hemming died, there was a struggle between two clans. The victors were two brothers, Harald Klak and Reginfred, themselves soon driven out by Godfred's sons, who had returned from exile in Sweden. Harald found refuge at the court of Louis the Pious. After 827, only one of Godfred's sons managed to assert his authority: this was Horik I, who remained sole King of Denmark until his death in 854.

The other Scandinavian monarchies came later and were more fragile. The kings of Norway are only known through later sources, especially the *Hemskringla* of Snorri Sturluson. The first king we know about for certain is Harald Harfraga ('Finehair') who reigned somewhere between 870 and 930. He succeeded his father, who had been king in Vestfold,[41] and asserted his authority by defeating other kings and chiefs at the battle of Hafrsfjord.[42] Some writers believe that Harald was never king of the whole of Norway, but only of one region in the south-west of the country, either Rogaland or Hordaland. As far as Sweden is concerned, we know through *The Life of Ansgar* the names of two kings, Björn and Olaf, who were established in Birka in the ninth century, though we do not know the full extent of the territory over which they exercised authority. Of the two constituent parts of the population of Sweden, the Svear and the Götar, they certainly ruled the Götar,[43] and may have ruled the Svear as well.

The kings of Norway tried to inflate their own origins by claiming to be descended from the Ynling dynasty, the issue of the god Freyr. This use of divine genealogies was common in the Anglo-Saxon kingdoms of England. The Svear kings of Sweden also boasted of this semi-divine provenance – a clear demonstration of the connections between the Scandinavian monarchies and religion.

The Scandinavian pantheon

The religion of the Scandinavians has links with ancient Indo-European sources, and many comparisons can be made both with the religions of India and Iran and with Greco-Roman polytheism. Our knowledge comes, of course, from texts written later, during the Christian period, which may have been influenced by Christianity. One of the principal sources concerning religion, the most reliable because the oldest, is the poetic *Edda*, some of which was probably written in about the year 1000.[44]

In the beginning there is chaos and emptiness, with the two antagonistic worlds of darkness and light (or fire). From the confrontation between these two worlds is born a hermaphroditic giant, Ymir, who couples with another primeval creature, Bestla. From this union the first gods are born: Odin and his brothers Vili and Vé, who soon kill Ymir. Then Odin, helped by Hoenir and Loki, creates men, using as 'raw material' the stumps of trees washed up on the seashore. Many other gods were added to form the Scandinavian pantheon. They were divided, perhaps at a later date, into two groups, the Aesir and the Vanir. The gods were said to live in the centre of the world (*Asgardhr*, literally 'the domain of the Aesir'; on the periphery *Utgardhr*, 'the outer domain', live the giants. Man's place is between the two, in the *Midhgardhr*, 'the middle domain').[45]

The cosmos is seen as being in a state of constant confrontation between the forces of order (the gods) and disorder (the giants). Mankind is both the protagonist in and the object of this confrontation. The aim of religious practices, particularly sacrifices, is to maintain the fragile balance between these antagonistic forces, in order to ensure the survival of the world. But the world is not seen as eternal. According to the *Völuspá*, a poem in the *Edda*, a final confrontation between the Aesir and the Vanir will bring about the end of the world, the *Ragnarök* or 'twilight of the gods', famously illustrated in music by Richard Wagner. This apocalypse will be followed by a rebirth, incarnated in a human couple who have been miraculously spared. It is possible, however, that this last transformation shows the influence of Christianity.

The few gods really venerated by the Scandinavians were endowed with strong personalities. Foremost among them is Odin, whose name derives from the word *ódhr*, meaning 'fury'. He is a god who leads some men into a state of trance: the god of magicians as well as of poets and warriors. His kingdom is called *Valhöll* (the Germanic *Wallhalla*). The valkyries have the task of taking dead warriors there after a battle. Thor is the god of thunder, the noise of which is produced by his chariot, drawn by oxen. He is represented by a hammer (*Mjölnir*) which symbolizes thunder. A mischievous deity, Thor is depicted with a red beard and is endowed with a formidable appetite. He is a first-rate fighter and conducts an effective struggle against the giants. He supplanted his rival Odin as the chief god in Norway and Iceland. Odin and Thor can be seen as a pair of complementary deities.

The same could be said of two more peaceable deities, who form a real couple: Freyr and his sister Freyja. Belonging to the family of the Vanir, they are the god and goddess of love, fecundity and fertility. They are extremely popular deities. Others, such as Heimdall, Baldr and Loki, are much less popular.

At a lower level, there are demigods, such as the elves and trolls who have survived in the collective imagination: traditional stories about them are told to this day in the Scandinavian countries.

Last but not least, the 'souls' of the dead play a considerable role in the lives of the living. The separation between the two worlds is far from being as hard and fast as in Christian or Western beliefs. Ghosts intervene in the world of the living, often in a malign way. Conversely, a man may change into a *hamrammr* (shape-shifter) and temporarily take on the appearance of an animal, a wolf, a bull or an eagle, for example. The living may communicate with the dead, especially with their own parents or ancestors, through dreams and apparitions. They also use magic in order to force both the supernatural powers and the ancestors to realize the desires of the living. Magic is practised in various forms, the most common being divinatory or shamanic practices, including trances and ecstasy. The dead are also objects of worship, along with the chief gods.[46]

In the old religion, worship was mainly a family matter. It was the head of the family who led the worship of ancestors and the principal gods of the pantheon. At a higher level, there were more important ceremonies, celebrated by the local chief. Finally, there were great collective religious rituals, held in the main political and religious centres, such as Uppsala in Sweden and Lejre in Denmark, and presided over by the king, who was primarily, as we have seen, a 'priest'. These ceremonies are remarked upon by Western authors such as Adam of Bremen and Thietmar of Merseburg, both of whom mention sacrifices of animals and humans. Although their testimony is somewhat questionable, since they may well have been influenced by their Christian prejudices, the possibility of human sacrifice cannot be ruled out, at least in the earliest period. Sacrifices were followed by great communal dinners, at which a lot of beer was drunk and the flesh of the sacrificed animals was consumed – horses, according to Western sources, or pigs, according to Scandinavian sources.[47]

There were different forms of funeral, depending on the region. In much of Sweden, the dead were exclusively cremated, whereas in Denmark and Norway, as well as in the south of Sweden, cremation coexisted with burial. The appearance and size of tombs was very variable, depending on local custom and the social rank of the dead person. The most spectacular took the form of a raised stone, a turtle in the shape of a boat, or a huge tumulus. The tombs of Norwegian chiefs in which the dead man was buried with his ship, as at Gokstad and Oseberg, have already been mentioned. The richest are the royal tombs, such as those at Jelling in Denmark. Family animals, especially horses, were occasionally buried with the dead man. According to the Arab traveller Ahmad ibn Fadlân, a female slave sometimes chose to die voluntarily by the side of her master.[48] All tombs included objects that could allow the dead man to survive in the other world. This other world could take different forms: *Hel* for ordinary people, or the much more prestigious *Valhöll* for warriors killed in combat, who alone were judged worthy to participate in the *Ragnarök*. The funeral ceremony was followed by a certain number of rituals: the 'inheritance beer' (*erfiöl*) was drunk by everyone, the new heir was enthroned, and then there was a funeral banquet, during which invocations were made to the memory of the dead.[49]

United by a common language and civilization, the Scandinavian world was characterized above all by a religion that pervaded all individual and collective acts. It was a polytheistic religion, dominated by a certain number of well-known deities, most importantly Odin and Thor.

The Scandinavian economy was based on the rearing of livestock and on arable farming in certain favourable regions. Hunting and fishing were secondary activities everywhere. The sea was never very far away, and many Scandinavians were experienced sailors. Thanks to these skills, they were able to trade with both the Frankish and Russian worlds. In so doing they discovered rich but poorly defended countries, which soon encouraged them to move from trade to plunder. So it was that, at the beginning of the ninth century, one of the most extraordinary human adventures of the Middle Ages got under way: the Viking migration.

2

THE FIRST VIKING RAIDS

Until the end of the eighth century, the Scandinavians stayed within their region of origin. Political contacts with the outside world were limited and mainly involved certain 'southern' areas, like Denmark, already a kingdom and confronted with Frankish expansion. On the other hand, all the indications are that trade underwent a real expansion, giving rise to trading centres such as Ribe, Hedeby and Birka. Relations between the Scandinavians and their neighbours to the west (the Franks and the Anglo-Saxons) and the east (especially the Slavs) seem to have been entirely peaceful. This was to change rapidly at the end of the eighth century, however, when the Northmen started to attack coastal regions, seizing their abundant riches by force and sowing terror in their wake. We are dealing here with a large-scale movement of people that would stretch over three centuries – from the ninth to the eleventh – and cause widespread upheaval, both in the countries 'visited' and in Scandinavia itself. It brought about major shifts in population and is now qualified as a 'migration'. This was an extraordinary adventure, which would take Vikings and Varangians to the very edges of the known world, the Caspian Sea and the Mediterranean at one end and the American shores of the Atlantic at the other. The obvious question is why the Scandinavians of the eighth century went in a few years from being peaceful farmers, hunters, fishermen and merchants to being dreaded pirates. It is a question that has intrigued historians for more than a century.[1]

One of the first reasons traditionally put forward is overpopulation. This is not a new idea: far from it, since it was already advanced as early as the sixth century by the Gothic author Jordanes in his *Getica*.[2] Obviously, he was not talking about the Vikings, but about the first great 'invasions' of the Roman Empire, which stretched from the third to the fifth centuries. Even so, he regarded the island of Scandzia (Scandinavia) as, to use his image, the *vagina nationum* ('womb of nations'), and claimed that it was from there that most of the invaders of the Roman Empire came.[3] This same explanation has often been put forward with regard to the Viking migration. It is true that Scandinavia has little truly fertile land and a harsh climate; but there is a great deal of available space and a relatively small population. While there are no precise data for this, it has been estimated, for example, that at the end of the Viking period Denmark had about 700,000 inhabitants. Archaeological excavations have shown that the Scandinavians had no hesitation in moving home when they needed to, the likeliest reason being to farm new land. In addition, as we have seen, there was a great deal of progress in farming methods from the 700s onwards. It can be stated with confidence that the overpopulation theory has been totally discredited by archaeological discoveries.[4]

It is more interesting to look for explanations in the very structure of Scandinavian societies. As we have seen, power struggles were fierce. Forced into exile, the losing candidates often embarked on far-flung expeditions. More generally, it was a way for the *boendr* to acquire prestigious property and thereby improve their status within the social hierarchy. Either way, the intention was to reinforce their honour, a basic value in Scandinavian society. Religious explanations have also been put forward: participation in an expedition may have been a kind of initiation for a young warrior.[5] There were also, of course, the great collective enterprises led by regional leaders, *jarls* or even kings, which were particularly common in Denmark.

The fundamental causes of the Viking migration, however, are to be sought outside Scandinavia. The Scandinavians were quite naturally trying to increase their wealth. At first, some were able to achieve this through normal trade. In doing so, they became aware that some foreign countries were poorly defended and plagued by unrest, even civil war. The local rulers, whether kings or aristocrats, were often weak, their power challenged by rivals. As excellent sailors and warriors, the Vikings were frequently asked to intervene in local disputes. This was true in Russia and the Byzantine Empire, where they formed the famous 'Varangian guard', and it was also true in Anglo-Saxon England and even in the Frankish kingdoms. It should be noted, too, that when the need arose the Vikings, as mercenaries in the service of foreign powers, had no hesitation in fighting each other. Given all this, it was quite 'natural' for the Scandinavians to start acting on their own behalf – and to do so on a large scale. Ultimately, then, the main cause of the Viking migration was the weakness of the states with which they came into contact. If any proof were needed, we only have to advance a contrary argument. The Vikings always retreated when faced with strong regimes. This was the case during the first raids, during the reigns of Charlemagne and Louis the Pious.[6] Later, at the height of the migration, the Vikings were forced to withdraw by the determined resistance of Robert the Strong.[7] The same thing happened when they fought Louis III, who defeated them at Saucourt on the Somme[8] in 881: a victory celebrated in an epic poem, the *Ludwigslied*.[9] Of course, these triumphs by certain

Frankish leaders were short-lived and proved powerless in stopping the Vikings in the long run, although in the same period, a Saxon king, Alfred the Great,[10] did succeed in standing up to them. As we see, then, whenever they were faced with genuine resistance, the Vikings let things drop. They preferred to go elsewhere, in search of more favourable opportunities. In regions where there was a strong ruler, they became traders again. The Scandinavians were well able to combine two activities that to us seem contradictory: they were pirates whenever possible, and merchants the rest of the time. They could quite easily go to a port or a market and sell the products of their plunder – sufficiently far away to avoid problems. Their aim was to become rich, and to achieve this all means were acceptable. The Scandinavians are usually considered aggressors but, in some cases, they themselves felt threatened by foreigners. It should be remembered that at the end of the eighth century the Franks were expanding fast and Charlemagne had set about conquering Denmark's immediate neighbour, Saxony. This Frankish advance coincides with the first Viking raids, which could be seen as a kind of reprisal. Clearly, this is not enough to account for the whole of the Viking migration, but it does show how complex the causes were. The Viking expansion can only be understood if we consider it as a conjunction of many things, in particular those favourable circumstances which the Scandinavians exploited to the full.

Yet they needed the means to realize their grand ambitions. Having significantly improved their shipbuilding techniques, they now had a very effective instrument at their disposa: the ship was one of the principal sources of the Viking achievement.

Viking ships

Viking ships have become increasingly well known thanks to archaeological discoveries and recent research.[11] Older excavations in Norway, which have already been mentioned, revealed ships in the tombs at Oseberg (dating from about 850) and Gokstad (from about 900).[12] More recently, underwater excavations – at Roskilde and Skuldelev in Denmark, and at Hedeby, now in Germany[13] – have revealed a whole series of ships from the tenth and eleventh centuries. At Roskilde, the Viking Ship Museum doubles as a centre for marine archaeology, where research is carried out into how these ships were made and used.[14]

We know now that the Viking ship did not appear suddenly during the period of the great expansion,but was the end result of a long maritime tradition in the Nordic regions, going back to prehistoric times. This type of ship was gradually improved, and by the turn of the ninth century had reached such a peak of perfection that it was not surpassed for a very long time. It had become a formidable war machine which would prove its effectiveness on all kinds of seas and rivers, from the North Sea and the Baltic to the Atlantic and the Mediterranean.

A damp environment favours the preservation of wood. Underwater excavations, especially in the fjord of Roskilde, and research in marshy areas have revealed much about the history of navigation in Scandinavia. At Hjortspring, on the island of Als in the south of Denmark, the remains of a boat without a deck were found in a marsh. The vessel, 19 metres long by 1.9 metres wide,[15] was built in the fourth century BC using techniques that were already very sophisticated. Chronologically, the next boat found dates from the fourth century AD, in other words, about six centuries after the previous one: this is the famous Nydam ship, also discovered in a swamp in Denmark, in 1863. Measuring 23.7 metres by 3.75 metres, it may have had a team of thirty rowers. It was built using the techniques of the Viking age: planks and iron rivets, propulsion by oar and a lateral helm.[16] Boats of this kind, driven by oar, were widely used during the first 'great invasions' (third to fifth centuries), particularly by the Danes' immediate neighbours, the Saxons. During the High Middle Ages, it became the preferred means of transport of the

Frisians, who were already navigators, traders and occasional pirates. This type of boat underwent considerable improvement during the Viking period. A mast and a square sail were added, which allowed the sailors to take advantage of the wind, while retaining the option of using oars. There were different kinds of boats, depending on whether they were used for transporting goods or for military operations. Above all, larger and larger ships were built, true giants of the seas by the standards of the time. The basic techniques, however, remained the same.

The basic technique was the clinker system, whereby planks joined by iron rivets partly overlapped, making the hull extremely solid. Recent excavations, especially those in Skuldelev, and the ensuing reconstructions have given us a greater understanding of the way these boats were built. The method of construction called 'first plankage' was used, that is, the hull was built first, before fitting the ribs, which stiffened it. They began with the keel, which was not very deep (60 to 85 centimetres), then laid the bottom planks, so as to give them the desired shape. Then they placed the floor plates to maintain the planks. Finally they fitted the transversal elements (the beams and the bitt), to ensure the solidity of the whole. Ships built in this way were capable of sailing the high seas, but could also sail up rivers and penetrate deep inland. They could withstand the storms of the northern seas and the Atlantic swells. Technically, they were unquestionably superior to Roman ships, the planks of which were simply pointed and caulked.[17]

The Scandinavians had a very extensive maritime vocabulary, traces of which remain in most modern European languages. The word 'board' as in 'on board ship' comes from the Old Norse *bordh,* meaning plank. The word 'bitt' comes from the Scandinavian *biti* (beam), the French word *varangue* (floor plate) from *(v)rang* (curve) since this piece ensures the curve of the hull. Many words still have the same meaning as the Old Norse terms from which they come: *étrave* (French for stem) from *stafin*, 'keel' from *kjoll*, *tillac* (French for upper deck) from *thilja*, floor. There are many other examples. The richness of the vocabulary is just as striking when it comes to the names of the different types of ship. On this subject, the essential source is the sagas, although it is not always easy for researchers to know exactly what kind of boat the many words used correspond to.[18]

The basic ship was often called *snekkja*, which can be defined as a boat containing twenty benches (for some forty oarsmen). The word was in such common use that it passed into medieval Latin and into the Norman dialect, in the form of *isnechia* (1053–5), then *esnecca* and *esnèque* (twelfth century), or into Old English as *snacc* (1052 and 1066).[19] Warships were long, which allowed them to move very fast: they were more correctly called *herskip*, but were also known as *langskip* (long boat). The largest of these ships, comprising more than twenty-five benches, were also given a specific name, *skeidh*, which in England became *scaegdh* (1008) and in Normandy *eschei* (twelfth century).[20] Unlike the warship, the merchant ship was called *kaupskip*. This is a much wider vessel, able to store large cargos. It was propelled by both sail and oar, but used a reduced crew, fewer oarsmen in particular, and moved at a correspondingly slower speed. There were several kinds of merchant ship, each with its own name, the most common being *knarr*, which passed into Old English (*cnearr*), Middle Irish (*cnarr*), Medieval Latin (*canardus*) and Norman dialect (*kenar*).[21]

Among all these names, the one that is never found is *drakkar*: this word was not generally used in the Middle Ages to designate a Viking-style ship. On closer examination, however, we find that the word is not completely absent from the sagas. It is indeed a Scandinavian word: *dreki* in the singular, and *drekar* in the plural, itself related to the Greek *drakon* and the Latin *draco*, meaning dragon. In the Viking world, it was primarily used for the figures carved on the prow and stern of the ships, which often represent dragons. According to the *Saga of Saint Olaf*, King Cnut the Great 'owned a *dreki* so large that it had sixty thwarts'.[22] If this example is anything to go by, *drekar* seem to have been very large warships, which makes it less surprising that the word was revived in the nineteenth century, in the corrupt form of *drakkar*, to denote Viking ships in general. Be that as it may, the Viking ship was, from the ninth to the eleventh centuries, the most effective means used by the Scandinavians to see their warlike enterprises through to a successful conclusion. Because of it, they enjoyed an unquestionable naval superiority. The Vikings soon had control over the seas, at least in the whole of Northern Europe, from the Baltic to the Atlantic. It was one of the vital factors in their success, since, in other respects, they had no particular technological advantage, as can be seen from a study of their weaponry.

Axe and sword

The weapons of the Vikings were not very different from those used by their contemporaries, especially the Franks. The main weapon was the double-edged sword, with a blade some 85 to 90 centimetres long. Many swords of this type have been found during the dredging of navigable rivers, especially the Seine and the Rhine. They were very similar to Frankish swords, which themselves had an excellent reputation and were much traded: the Carolingian monarchs became so alarmed about this trade that they forbade the sales of arms to foreigners. These measures seem to have had little effect, and the Scandinavians certainly took advantage of these exports.[23]

Other offensive weapons included the spear and the javelin, which have often been found in tombs in Sweden and elsewhere. The bow and the knife were also used, but the weapon peculiar to the Vikings was the large battle-axe. Held in both hands, it was a formidable weapon and could wreak havoc in the enemy ranks.[24]

To protect themselves, the Vikings wore helmets, often conical, although other shapes were also used. They carried round wooden shields, of which the boss was often made of iron (and is therefore the only part found intact in excavated tombs). During naval expeditions, these shields were fixed on the high sides of the ships, thus protecting the oarsmen from arrows fired by the enemy. The body does not seem to have always been protected. However, in excavations at Birka, clothes covered with iron plates were found, and in Norway at least one coat of chain mail from the end of the period (the tenth century) has been discovered.[25]

The Viking fought on foot, but used horses to move about once they had left their ships. The easiest solution was to find horses on the spot, either by stealing them, which was not so easy, or by buying them. Once again, the Frankish monarchs were forced to intervene. In 864, for example, at the height of the 'invasions',[26] Charles the Bald, King of West Francia, forbade the sale of horses to the 'Normans', that is, the Vikings, on pain of death.

At first, Viking forces were small, composed of the armed entourage of a war leader. Later, in the 860s, the Vikings were able to put together much larger contingents of several hundred fighting men. It has often been supposed that such expeditions were organized by kings, especially Danish kings. These 'great armies' were made up of troops brought together for the occasion from various sources. Their cohesion depended on the personality of their leader, but also on the success of the expedition: if this failed, the army dispersed and each group was left to try its luck elsewhere. It was only at the end of the period that things became better organized. In the tenth century, the kings were powerful enough to order a naval levy (*leding* or *leidhangr*). This was how the great Danish expeditions to England were able to take place.

Overall, the Viking armies had no superiority over their adversaries in the field of weaponry. The main reason for their success was the speed of their boats, which gave them the advantage of surprise. They would arrive unexpectedly, before their adversaries had time to react. In Western Europe they were greatly helped by the fact that the military structures in place were powerless to confront such incursions. The Franks had no permanent army, and the *ban* (the summoning of vassals for military service) took place only once a year. Unrest and civil war prevented the Frankish monarchs from finding military solutions adapted to the new situation. Whenever the Vikings were confronted with a large, determined armed force, they used the same assets of speed and mobility to escape any unequal combat that might have turned to their disadvantage.

These methods were used at about the same time in the whole of the Nordic area. However, it was precisely at this period that Scandinavia started to divide into several entities, from which the modern-day countries derive. Not all the Vikings intervened in the same regions, even though forces of different origins sometimes encountered (and even fought) one another.

Most of the time, Danes, Norwegians and Swedes made an effort to avoid competition by each concentrating on a particular area of action. These were dictated by geography. The Swedes crossed the Baltic and moved eastwards, through what is now Russia and the Ukraine. The Danes mostly headed west and south-west, towards England and the Frankish world. The Norwegians, having the most northern of these countries, mainly moved north-west and out onto the open sea. The first archipelago they encountered was the Shetlands, which they colonized during the ninth century. Next came the Orkneys. Moving south, they visited the Hebrides, the Scottish coast, and finally Ireland.[27]

Celtic Ireland was not a unified country at that time. It was composed of many small kingdoms and five larger kingdoms. The divisions among the Irish allowed the Scandinavians to settle on the east coast. Here, the Norwegians were to find themselves in competition with the Danes, which was also the case in more southern areas. In Ireland, as in Russia, the Scandinavians created the first towns. These started out as fortified outposts built to protect them from Irish attacks, and developed into trading centres. In 841, the Vikings established the first settlements, Dublin and Annagassan. Later they also founded Wexford, Waterford and Cork on the eastern and south eastern coasts, and Limerick on the west coast, on the river Shannon. These towns only became fully established at the end of a long process. Dublin, for example, was much disputed between Irish and Scandinavians. It only truly became a town after it was finally recaptured by the Vikings in 917.[28]

From the Shetlands, the Norwegians also set sail across the Atlantic towards the unknown lands out to the west. In so doing they proved to be remarkable navigators and daring explorers. The first lands on which they set foot were the Faeroe Islands. They arrived there some time before 825, according to the Irish monk Dicuil, whose geographical treatise is one of the most interesting sources about these expeditions. Continuing westwards, they then discovered Iceland, in about 860. This island may not have been entirely uninhabited. If Ducuil is to be believed, the first Vikings found Irish hermits already living there. Be that as it may, they quickly began to colonize both the Faeroes and Iceland. According to Ari Thorgilsson in his *Íslendingabók*, the colonization of Iceland began in 870, and was completed sixty years later, in 930. At this date, the Icelanders founded their basic organ of government, the *Althing* or general assembly of all Icelanders. The island's institutions would retain their own special character throughout the Middle Ages. While recognizing the distant souzerainty of the King of Norway, Icelanders did not allow a local monarchy to emerge, since theoretically, their government remained 'democratic', although in reality it was oligarchic: at the assembly, power really belonged to the *godhar*, the richest of the *boendr*, who would soon divide the island among them. In 965, four 'quarters' were created, each possessing its own local assembly and sending an equal number of representatives to the *Althing*.[29]

In about 985, a man named Erik the Red was banished from Iceland for obscure reasons and embarked on a hazardous expedition to the unknown areas to the west. He left with twenty-five boats, of which only fourteen would complete the voyage. This expedition led to the discovery of a new land which Eric the Red, presumably to attract colonists, called Groenland ('Green Land'). Today, we think of Greenland rather as a land of ice, but the name 'land of ice' was already taken by Iceland. In addition, it could well be that the climate of the region has changed since the tenth century. The southern and western areas, where the Scandinavians settled, were suitable at that time for rearing livestock. To anyone arriving in high summer, they may well have seemed like a green land. The Scandinavian colonies would in any case be abandoned when the climate cooled during the fourteenth and fifteenth centuries in what is sometimes called the 'little ice age'.[30] Some fifteen years later, in about the year 1000, Erik the Red's son Leif is said to have travelled even further west and to have discovered a new land which he called Vinland ('Land of Wine') – again, a name chosen for propagandistic purposes. The identity of its discoverer is not entirely certain. Although the *Saga of Erik the Red* credits its hero's son, the *Greenlanders' Saga* names Bjarni Herjólfsson. What is known for certain is that there were several Scandinavian expeditions in that direction at the beginning of the eleventh century. What was the land they discovered? It seems likely to have been the coast of the American continent, which would make the Vikings the first Europeans to have set foot on the soil of America, nearly 500 years before Christopher Columbus. Much ink has flowed regarding this episode, and traces of a Scandinavian presence on the new continent have been eagerly sought. The quest has proved disappointing. Only one site can be attributed for certain to the Vikings, L'Anse aux Meadows, on the north coast of Nova Scotia. Even though there was no lasting settlement in Vinland, we do know that the Scandinavians spent time on the east coast of Canada and established trade contacts with the native populations. On an Indian site in the state of Maine in the United States, a coin showing the Norwegian king Olaf Kyrre (r. 1066–80) has been unearthed.[31]

The Norwegians did not limit themselves to these distant expeditions, which brought them more prestige than wealth. Their presence in Scotland and Ireland has already been mentioned. From there, some of them went further south. Traces of their settlements have been found in Cotentin, as well as in Aquitaine and even in Spain. In all these areas, they were in direct competition with the Danes.

The Danish Vikings naturally turned their sights on the regions to the west and south-west, which they knew from long-established trading contacts. The first victims of their acts of piracy were the west of England and the Frankish Empire. England was particularly vulnerable at the time, being divided into several small kingdoms, the most powerful of which was Mercia. As early as 789, three Danish boats landed on the coast of the Kingdom of Wessex. Its occupants killed the royal provost who had come to meet them.[32] Some years later came the first great raid against a monastery, Lindisfarne in Northumbria, on the north-east coast of England.[33] From 792, King Offa of Mercia set about putting in place a system of coastal defence in his kingdom, but he died in 796. The period of anarchy that followed would favour the Danish enterprise.[34]

The Danes also set their sights on Ireland, where they and the Norwegians combined their efforts. But the Scandinavians would encounter strong resistance from the Irish. A similar pattern emerged in the Frankish world at the turn of the ninth century. The first raids on the coasts of the Carolingian kingdom took place in 799. Charlemagne's response was rapid and vigorous. Before leaving for Rome to be crowned Emperor in 800, he toured the North Sea and Channel coasts and put in place a system of defence. These measures proved effective: there were no large-scale attacks until the end of his reign. Charlemagne's successor, Louis the Pious, successfully pursued the same policy. In 820, when thirteen Viking ships tried to attack, first in Flanders, then on the Seine, they met with genuine resistance. The difficulties did not begin for the

Franks until the 840s, when internal unrest paralysed their efforts at defence.

From that point onwards, the number of Viking raids increased on both sides of the Channel. Their routes were dictated by the presence of rivers, which were the ideal way to penetrate inland, as had already been proved in Russia. In England the Danes first sailed up the Thames, and in France the Seine, the Loire, the Garonne and later the Rhöne. In 841, the town of Rouen was razed. Rochester and London were attacked in 842. Next the Scandinavians sailed around Brittany, and in 843 landed on the island of Noirmoutier, which had been abandoned by its monks, then at Nantes and on the Loire. In 844, they reached Spain, and penetrated as far as Andalucia. In 845, the Danes again attacked the Seine valley and reached Paris. They would often return, especially in the years 856–62, when a 'great army' remained in the lower Seine. Between 858 and 862 there were Vikings in the Rhone valley and in Italy.[35] The second half of the ninth century marked the climax of Viking attacks in general, and Danish attacks in particular. After 865, another 'great Danish army' held sway in England. It numbered between two and three thousand men, a considerable force for the period.[36] Only the Danes could muster so many troops. The local monarchs, often warring among themselves, proved incapable of resistance.[37] It was in England that the Danes would succeed in establishing lasting states. But these only came about at the end of a long process, when all other methods had ceased to be profitable.

From attack to settlement

Wherever they intervened militarily, the Vikings had one objective: to accumulate as much wealth as possible. The means to achieve this had to be constantly adapted according to circumstance. The historian Lucien Musset has distinguished three successive phases in the actions of the Vikings in any particular territory.[38] The first phase consisted of pure plunder, and applies to those regions where raids were mounted for the first time. The Scandinavians launched what were generally surprise attacks on towns and, especially, monasteries, and simply plundered them. The victims most often reacted by fleeing, as recorded for example in the famous *Journey of the monks of Noirmoutier*.[39] Located as it was on an island close to the estuary of the Loire, the abbey of Noirmoutier was very exposed. The monks abandoned the abbey in 836, taking with them the relics of their founder, Saint Philibert, and sought refuge in several of their dependencies. They first settled in Déas (now Saint-Philibert-de-Grand-Lieu),[40] but, still not feeling safe, they set off again some years later and settled in Cunault on the Loire.[41] But the Vikings went upriver again in 853, and in 862 the monks had to flee as far as Messais in Poitou.[42] Their journey finally took them to Tournus in Burgundy, where they founded a monastery that is famous to this day.[43]

Obviously, this method had its limits. The Vikings could not return twice to the same place: they had to go further and further inland to find new, undefended riches. The second phase, therefore, was the imposition of Danegeld (literally 'Danish gold'), a tribute demanded of the region's inhabitants by a Scandinavian force in return for its departure. This method was utilized in areas which had become unsuitable for plunder, either because they had already been plundered too much, or because they could not be ravaged easily. The conception of such tribute was primarily an initiative of monks and kings, or their representatives. Recorded in Frisia as early as 810, it became general in the second half of the ninth century. In the Kingdom of West Francia, for example, King Charles the Bald was forced to pay Danegeld in 845, 853, 860–1, 862, 866 and 877. The effects of this kind of levy were not entirely negative. It allowed precious metals to be recycled, instead of being hoarded, and made it easier to bring the Scandinavians into the economic life of the regions involved. After all, they had to spend the money they had accumulated, and they could only find the goods they desired in towns that were centres of trade, most of them in the very lands they had plundered. This method, too, had its limitations, however, since some states were too impoverished to be able to pay Danegeld.[44]

The Scandinavians then moved on to the third phase: actual occupation. In this phase, they took possession of a territory, ruled it and exploited it to their advantage. The ninth and tenth centuries were to see the birth of a certain number of Viking states. As early as 826, the exiled Danish ruler Harald Klak was granted the territory of Rüstringen by Louis the Pious. Other concessions of the same kind followed: Walcheren was granted to Hemming (before 837) then to Harald, and Dorestad to Rorik (840–50).[45] These, however, were special cases, the territories concerned being more in the nature of 'benefices' or 'privileges'.[46] Scandinavian states appeared in Ireland in the middle of the ninth century, but these proved short-lived. The Viking rulers were all thrown out of the country in 902. They returned, however, in 914 and reestablished their states, including the Kingdom of Dublin. Other Viking states were created by the Danes in England in the last third of the ninth century. 'The great army' mentioned above seized York in 866, then brought about the collapse of the Anglo-Saxon kingdoms of Northumbria and East Anglia (from 866 to 869).[47]

The only Anglo-Saxon power remaining was the Kingdom of Wessex. In 871, in the middle of this dramatic period, the kingdom acquired an ambitious and dynamic young king, Alfred the Great. Having created the Kingdom of York in 876, the Danes were defeated by Alfred at Edington in 878. Two other Viking states were created in England at the same time, the Kingdom of East Anglia and the Kingdom of the 'Five Boroughs', covering the territories of five Mercian towns, Lincoln, Nottingham, Derby, Leicester and Stamford.[48] These three states made up the Danelaw (*Danelag* in Danish), in other words, the lands 'under Danish law'. The Vikings had to be content with these areas in the north and east, the rest of the territory being firmly held by Alfred the Great, who increased his defensive measures.[49] In addition, the three Scandinavian kingdoms were divided among themselves. This lack of unity among the Danes greatly facilitated the Anglo-Saxon reconquest, carried through by Alfred's successors, principally Edward the Elder, who recaptured East Anglia and the Five Boroughs in 917, and Athelstan, who seized York in 927. There was, however, a strong Scandinavian retaliation, led by the King of Dublin. The Kingdom of York was not finally recaptured by the Anglo-Saxons until 954. The reconquest had taken three quarters of a century.[50]

Meanwhile, other states were established in the Kingdom of France. The most successful was Normandy, founded in 911.[51] Nor should another attempt be forgotten, made by the Norwegians in the estuary of the Loire: they seized Nantes in 919 and crushed the Bretons in 931. But they were defeated by the Breton Count Alan Wrybeard, with the help of King Athelstan. This short-lived state had lasted only eighteen years, from 919 to 937.[52]

The 930s saw the end of the first wave, as defined by Lucien Musset. The interval would last some fifty years, until about 980. The Viking 'invasions' were not over, however. A second wave began, with its own particular characteristics. It involved the Danes almost exclusively, and the main object of their attacks was England. It would lead to the conquest of the kingdom, first by Sven Forkbeard in 1014, then by Cnut the Great in 1016. The Danish domination of England lasted until 1042. This episode marks the final end of the Viking migrations. It should be remembered, though, that the Vikings were not the only 'invaders' of Western Europe. Almost simultaneously, other regions – Italy and the south of France – were attacked by the Muslims, also taking advantage of the weakness of the Frankish states. Some unlikely encounters took place between Vikings and Saracens, who occasionally found themselves in the same areas, around the Mediterranean. But this was the exception. By and large, each people avoided encroaching on its rivals' 'hunting grounds'. This was also the case with the Hungarians, the last invaders to enter the

Frankish world by land from the east, from 895. The Hungarians' attacks focused mainly on Germany, but they also entered France, pushing as far as Orléans. The monks of Noirmoutier, who thought they had escaped the 'Viking invasions' by fleeing to Burgundy, were unable to prevent their refuge being affected by these Hungarian incursions.[53]

The Viking migration left a lasting mark on the history of the West. It made possible the establishment of a vast trading area in Northern Europe, which would prosper throughout the Middle Ages. It also led to the exploration and colonization of a number of far-flung territories, from Iceland to Vinland. Indirectly, the Vikings contributed to the strengthening of the western kingdoms, at least those which had managed to resist them. Such was the case – temporarily – with Anglo-Saxon England, and to a certain extent Carolingian and Robertian France. It was in this context that the one long-lasting state founded by the Vikings appeared: Normandy.

3

THE FOUNDING OF NORMANDY

After the unrest of the Merovingian period, the Kingdom of the Franks was ruled with a firm hand by the Carolingian kings. Pippin the Short, who reigned from 741 to 768, was succeeded by his son Charlemagne, who reigned until 814. They succeeded in establishing a strong state which continued to expand until it included almost all the Christian West: Gaul, Germany and, after 774, Italy. The most notable exceptions were England, Ireland and Muslim Spain. In the East, Charlemagne defeated the Saxons and moved the eastern border as far as the Elbe. In 800, at the age of fifty-three, he was crowned Holy Roman Emperor by the pope.[1] But it was precisely at this moment of triumph that the Carolingian Empire was threatened by the first Viking raids. When he inspected the coastal defences before his journey to Rome, Charlemagne may well have visited most of what was to be Normandy, a territory that had no autonomous existence at that time but was only a small part of Neustria, one of the kingdoms that had gradually been established by the

Merovingians during the seventh century. With its capital in Paris, Neustria included the whole of north-west Gaul, from the Loire to the Rhine estuaries, an extensive coastal area along the Channel and the North Sea, and all or part of the ecclesiastical provinces of Rheims, Sens, Tours and Rouen: Rouen was the only one of these provinces to be entirely within Neustria.

The borders of these ecclesiastical provinces were the same as those of the old Roman provinces, established in the fourth century. The province of Rouen corresponded to the second Provincia Lugdunensis, a name which recalls the fact that the Roman provinces had grown out of the break-up of Celtic Gaul, a vast area with its capital in Lugdunum (Lyons). The capital of the second Provincia Lugdunensis was Rotomagus, which was to become Rouen. It was composed of seven cities, that is, seven towns and their territories: Rouen, Bayeux, Évreux, Lisieux, Sées, Coutances and Avranches. When Christianity was established in the region in the fourth and fifth centuries, the bishops settled in these towns and made them episcopal seats, while the territories became ecclesiastical districts, called dioceses. Over the course of the fifth century, the administrative structures of the Roman Empire disintegrated, but the ecclesiastical structures remained. So it was that the second Provincia Lugdunensis survived in the form of the ecclesiastical province of Rouen. It would serve as a matrix for the new 'Normandy'.

In the Merovingian period, Neustria was a major centre of power, competing with the eastern part of Gaul, known as Austrasia. Things changed in the Carolingian period, when the kings resided between the Meuse and the Rhine and the province of Rouen became marginalized. It remained, however, a prosperous region, with a number of rich ecclesiastical benefices – such as the bishopric of Rouen and the abbeys of Fontenelle[2] and Jumièges[3] in the Seine valley – which the monarch often reserved for his favourites. For example, Charles Martel's nephew, Hugh, held concurrently the bishoprics of Paris, Rouen and Bayeux. Since the other bishoprics were vacant at the time, Hugh was the only bishop in the province. In spite of this strange situation, he was considered a saint. Later, during the reign of Pippin the Short, Charles Martel's son (and the king's uncle) Remi became Archbishop of Rouen. In this period, the Carolingian monarch restored the full functions of the archbishop, and so Remi found himself at the head of a revived province of Rouen. He was able to exert his authority over the other bishops, the other bishoprics having also been restored. In about 785, Gervold, chaplain to Charlemagne's mother, received first the bishopric of Évreux, then the abbey of Fontenelle. In 816, Emperor Louis the Pious appointed Eginhard, the famous author of the *Vita Caroli Magni* (*Life of Charlemagne*) to the same post.[4] At about the same time (825–8) the emperor chose as Archbishop of Rouen Gilbert, who also exercised the function of *missus dominicus*, or lord's envoy.[5] Another *missus* of Louis the Pious, Paul, occupied this seat from about 849 to 858.[6]

These bishops and abbots were politicians who spent little time in their dioceses and had no great interest in spiritual matters. One exception who should be mentioned, though, was Freculphus, Bishop of Lisieux from 825 to 852. This diocese had not had a bishop for a long time, and its religious situation left a lot to be desired. On his arrival in Lisieux, Freculphus was not even able to find a complete copy of the Bible. This piece of information comes from his correspondence with Abbot Rabanas Maurus of Fulda,[7] one of the greatest figures of the Carolingian Renaissance. Freculphus was a true intellectual, author among other things of the *Universal Chronicle*, which he dedicated to Charles the Bald, King of West Francia.[8]

Such a situation is hardly surprising, since the Carolingian monarchs considered bishops above all as government representatives. The archbishops of Rouen at this period did not have the extraordinary privileges that had been granted to Saint Ouen by the Merovingian king Theuderic III in the seventh century. The bishops were no longer alone in ruling their dioceses: they had to reckon with the counts. counts and bishops were both representatives of the monarch, one on the temporal plane and the other on the spiritual plane, and they exercised power jointly. The diocese did not completely correspond to the *pagus*, for which the count was responsible. In the province of Rouen there were a dozen *pagi*:[9] Talou (in the north of what is now Seine-Maritime), Caux, Roumois (*pagus* of Rouen), Évrecin (*pagus* of Évreux), Madrie (between the Eure and the Seine), Lieuvin (*pagus* of Lisieux), Bessin (*pagus* of Bayeux), Hiémois,[10] Avranchin (*pagus* of Avranches), Corentin (*pagus* of Coutances)[11] and North Contentin (*pagus Coriovallensis*).[12]

The Carolingians, first kings then emperors, made an effort to increase the efficiency of the administration. Until the 820s, they succeeded fairly well in this. Charlemagne appointed envoys called *missi dominici* (lord's envoys) to go on missions of inspection, with full powers to punish abuses and pass judgement on appeal. Their authority was higher than that of the local powers, whether counts or bishops. The *missi* generally moved about in twos – a count and a bishop – and had to visit a specific territory, the *missaticum* (plural *missatica*). The boundaries of these *missatica* are of great interest, since they give an idea of regional entities as they were at the time, rather than being based on the old administrative divisions that had long fallen into disuse. It is clear that the Seine was considered an internal border. To the north of the Seine, the diocese of Rouen was part of a *missaticum* that also included Picardy and Flanders. On the other hand, what is now lower Normandy, as well as the diocese of Évreux, was in the same *missaticum* as the vast diocese of Le Mans (corresponding to the modern-day *départements* of Sarthe and Mayenne). It was for this territory that in 802 Charlemagne chose as *missi* Archbishop Meinhard of Rouen and Count Madelgaud. The centre of power being situated to the north of the Seine, it became common, around the 830s, to call the inhabitants of these lands beyond the Seine (that is, between the Seine and the Loire) *Ultrasequanenses* or

Transsequenenses. Gradually, the old name of Neustria became restricted to this region between the Seine and the Loire.[13] Comprising lower Normandy, Maine and the banks of the Loire, it was a marginalized region, but it attracted the attention of the authorities when it was threatened both by Viking incursions and by the rise of the Bretons.

The rise of the Bretons

In the Roman period, Brittany, known as Armorica, was completely integrated within the empire. During the administrative reform, it was included in the third Provincia Lugudensis, whose capital was Tours. Armorica attracted immigrants from Britain, especially Cornwall and Wales. This migration cannot be precisely dated – it may have lasted from the fourth to the eighth centuries – but by the end of the period, the immigrants had gained the upper hand over the local populace and imposed their own language, a Celtic language closely related to Welsh. This language was spoken in a large part of Brittany, as far as the present-day *département* of Ille-et-Vilaine, well beyond what is now 'Breton-speaking Brittany', as can be seen from a study of place-names. The west of Brittany, however, resisted, and continued to use a Roman dialect derived from Latin, called Gallo.[14]

Bearing these circumstances in mind, it is not surprising that the Frankish kings, both Merovingian and Carolingian, had great difficulty in imposing their authority over the Bretons. To protect his kingdom from Breton incursions, Charlemagne established the so-called 'Breton march', which for a time was entrusted to Roland, the unfortunate hero of Roncevaux. The unrest that subsequently swept through the Carolingian Empire encouraged the stirrings of independence among the Bretons. In about 833, at a time when he was in conflict with his son Lothair, Emperor Louis the Pious granted the Breton leader Nominoe the County of Vannes, in return for an oath of loyalty. He also made him his representative for the whole of Brittany. At the time of his death in 851 Nominoe was at war

with Charles the Bald, King of West Francia.[15] He was
succeeded by his son Erispoe, who inflicted a new defeat on
Charles, who was forced to grant him the royal title. The
Bretons continued to advance under Salomon, who reigned
from 857 to 874. In 867, Charles the Bald granted him the
County of Cotentin (we may assume that Salomon was already
in possession of Avranchin).[16] Charles, however, would not
accept the division of the ecclesiastical province of Rouen, and
retained the bishopric of Coutances.[17] One of the consequences of this advance was that Mont-Saint-Michel came
within Breton control, under an abbot named Phinimontius.
The Bretons settled in the territories conceded to them, as can
be seen from a study of names in the area. Names of Celtic
origin such as Juhel, Rivallon, Rualoc and Harcouet can be
found in Cotentin.[18] The Breton lords who received lands in
the region remained there after the Norman conquest in the
tenth century. Moreover, the Breton occupation did not stop at
the administrative borders of Cotentin and Avranchin. There
are traces of their presence in Bessin and in other parts of what
was to become Normandy.[19]

From the point of view of King Charles the Bald, the influx
of the Bretons into this region had its advantages, since they
took charge of defending it against Scandinavian raids – the
king himself had great difficulty in trying to protect the vital
areas of his kingdom, especially the valley of the Seine.

The Vikings on the Seine

The Seine, a large navigable river, was naturally attractive to the
Vikings. They were not, however, able to enter it as long the
Frankish defences proved effective. In 820 came the first
incursion into the lower Seine, but it was repulsed by coastal
guards. There were no further attempts until 840, when the
death of Louis the Pious led to a grave succession crisis and a
civil war: naturally, the Scandinavians seized the opportunity.
The civil war came to an end in 843 with the signing of the
treaty of Verdun, which divided the empire between the three

sons of Louis the Pious: Lothair, Louis the German and Charles the Bald. The Kingdom of West Francia, which fell to Charles, included a long coastline, which stretched from Flanders to Spain. But the new king proved incapable of defending his territory against ever more enterprising aggressors. In addition, the rivalry between the brothers prevented them from uniting against the common danger. The reign of Charles the Bald therefore coincided with the height of the 'invasions', and for the next few years the Seine became the principal route by which the invaders entered the kingdom.

We know the chronology of the raids from Frankish sources, which of course express the viewpoint of the victims. The main sources are the official annals (*Royal Annals*), the unofficial annals (*Annals of Saint-Bertin*), and the annals of the great monasteries (*Annals of Fontenelle*, for example).[20] After 841, the raids became more frequent. In 845, a Viking chief named Ragnar sailed up the Seine as far as Paris. King Charles the Bald proved incapable of repulsing this incursion by force and had to negotiate with the aggressors. He obtained their departure on payment of a tribute of 7,000 *livres*. This is the first example of Danegeld being paid by a king, and was a decision of major political significance. In the short term, Charles the Bald achieved his object, as the Vikings put to sea again; but they had no hesitation in returning at the first opportunity and demanding another tribute. Charles found himself in a vicious circle.[21] The raids of 820–45 corresponded to the first phase, that of simple plunder, and the raid of 845 corresponded to the second phase, the imposition of a tribute. In 851 a Scandinavian force wintered on the Seine for the first time.[22] A fleet commanded by a man named Asgeirr entered the estuary of the Seine. Asgeirr apparently went on to exercise his talents in other regions, including Aquitaine (with Bordeaux). Returning to the Seine, he attacked the abbeys of Fontenelle and Saint Germer-de-Fly and the town of Beauvais.[23] In all, he wintered on the river for nearly eight months, from 13 October 851 to 5 June 852.[24]

His example was followed by many other Vikings. In October 852, a force commanded by Sidroc and Godfred entrenched themselves in an *oppidum* situated on the bank of the river.[25] For once, the Carolingians joined forces: Lothair and Charles the Bald besieged the Vikings in their lair. But the two kings did not see things through to the end and began negotiations. They finally authorized the Vikings to settle in Jeufosse, between Vernon and Mantes.[26] From there, the Vikings were obviously able to launch many raids with complete impunity. In 856, Sidroc was again in the Seine valley, this time in association with a chief named Björn. They wintered on Oscellus, an island on the river, near Jeufosse, and launched a raid on Paris in December. The following year, confronted with a rebellion in Aquitaine, Charles the Bald was unable to retaliate. The Vikings, of course, knew all about the political and military upheavals in the kingdom and took advantage of them. They sailed up the Eure and its tributary the Iton and ravaged Évreux and Chartres. The following year, 858, they moved westwards and attacked the town of Bayeux, killing its bishop, Baltfridus.[27]

During the summer of 858, Charles the Bald finally intervened and laid siege to Oscellus. The action met with failure, due to disunity among the Franks. A number of prominent figures, led by Robert the Strong and Archbishop Ganelon of Sens, were in rebellion against the king and had no hesitation in asking Charles' brother Louis the German, King of East Francia, for help. Learning that his brother was invading his kingdom, Charles was forced to raise the siege of Oscellus on 23 September 858, without having achieved anything. In 860, with matters still unresolved, Charles made another attempt to dislodge the Vikings from the Seine, by appealing to a Viking named Veland. Veland increased his demand from three to 6,000 *livres*. Charles finally obtained the departure of the Viking force from Oscellus, but authorized it to winter on the Seine, while he himself settled at Saint-Maur-des-Fossés on the Marne.[28] In 862, the Vikings sailed up the Marne and sacked the town of Meaux but, in retaliation, were attacked by Charles and forced to sail back down the Seine and disperse. So ended this difficult period from 856 to 862, which marked the climax of the Viking invasions on the Seine and its tributaries.[29] The king and his representatives finally decided to react by putting in place a whole series of defensive measures.

The Frankish reaction

We have already seen that the first defensive measures taken by Charlemagne and Louis the Pious were fairly effective, but the system then put in place had fallen apart during the unrest of the years 830–40. Charles the Bald tried to implement some of those same measures, which had proved their worth. In 845, he again set up guard posts along the coast, and in 852 he had barriers set up on the Seine. These measures proved insufficient to face the great wave that now engulfed the region.

After 860, the king undertook to block the waterways taken by the Vikings by building fortified bridges. In 862, he urgently fortified a bridge at Trilbardou[30] to intercept the Vikings who were on their way back from the attack on Meaux. Having managed to stop them, he decided to repeat the experiment. Several bridges were fortified in this way on the Seine, the Marne and the Oise, notably at Charenton and Auvers-sur-Oise.[31] The important thing was to stop the invaders at an early stage, in other words as close as possible to the sea. The width of the Seine at its estuary, however, made it impossible to build such defences anywhere before Rouen. The principal bridge was built upriver from the town, at PŒtres,[32] at the confluence of the Seine and the Eure. It has become better known now thanks to the research and excavations carried out by Brian Dearden and Caroll Gillmore.[33] The site was chosen because the Seine divided here into two branches. The bridge straddled the river and was protected at each end by a fort. The north one was situated at Igoville and the south at Pont-de-l'Arche.[34] The stones of this south fort were later re-used to construct the perimeter wall of the town, which developed around the bridge. Charles must have been determined to persevere with the building of the bridge at PŒtres, since the work took nearly fifteen years. It was interrupted in 865–6 because of further Viking incursions, but resumed once the danger was past. The king was able to mobilize the ecclesiastical institutions, who provided the finance, as well as freemen, who made up most of the workforce. He may also have brought in other people to settle there, in order to defend the work by force of arms. Last but not least, Charles entrusted the command of the region to one of his loyal followers, Nivelon, whom he made Count of Vexin.[35]

After half a century, it had become clear that fortifications were still the best protection against the Viking raids. There had been hardly any until then, apart from the walls of the old Roman towns and a few *castra* going back to the Merovingian period, but many of these fortifications had been dismantled during the period of the 'Carolingian peace'.[36] As late as 859, Archbishop Ganelon of Sens, asked the king for authorization, which he obtained, to partly destroy the walls of Melun in order to use the stones to rebuild the town's church. This was the last example of this kind of concession. Everywhere else, the Viking threat led to the restoration of town walls and *castra*. In 869, Charles the Bald asked the inhabitants of Tours and Le Mans to fortify their towns.[37] The same thing may well have happened in Rouen and Bayeux, among other towns in the future Normandy.

These official fortifications were joined by many 'private' fortifications, built without royal authorization. Charles the Bald waxed indignant about this in the edict of Pîtres in 864, which is a clear indication that they were proliferating. In the texts, these fortifications are called *castra* or *castella* (castles). The largest were vast enclosures capable of protecting towns of some size, such as the *castrum* of Saint-Lô, built on a rocky spur overlooking the valley of the Vire, or the *castrum* of Eu, later mentioned by Flodoard.[38] Other 'castles' were more modest affairs, being simple motte-and-baileys, earth mounds topped by a wooden keep and surrounded by a ditch and a wooden palisade. Jacques Le Maho has identified a number of these structures in what was to be Normandy, at Mont-Haguais, in Quettehou, Radicatel, near Lillebonne, and Mont-Gripon, at Beaubec-la-Rosière.[39] We need to exercise caution on this point, however, since, in the absence of written sources, these *castella* are difficult to distinguish from those built in the twelfth century, during the period of the dukes.

The Frankish reaction was not purely a defensive one. King Charles the Bald undertook a massive overhaul of the administration, the aim of which was to strengthen the ability of the territories to resist the advance not only of the Scandinavians but also of the Bretons. At the local level, as noted by Jean-Pierre Brunterc'h,[40] the old subdivisions of the *pagi*, called 'hundreds', disappeared. They were replaced by *vicariae*, controlled by *vicarii* (vicars), subordinates of the count, whose functions were as much legal and administrative as military.[41] At the same time, new *pagi* appeared, such as Otlinga Saxonia, previously part of the County of Bayeux. Similarly, the old *pagus* of Oximensis (Hiémois) was subdivided into three new *pagi*: Exmes, Sées and Corbonnais.[42] In every case, the intention was obviously to tighten control over the population and facilitate the mobilization of men.

Charles the Bald went further and created a large military command in the region between the Seine and the Loire, the area particularly threatened by the Vikings and the Bretons. His model was clearly the vast Duchy of Maine, which had been created by Pippin the Short for his illegitimate brother, Grifo, and which was still remembered a century later.[43] This command was entrusted to the head of an aristocratic family with possessions in the region, Robert the Strong. In 852, Robert, already Count of Tours, received from the king the title of marquis, along with a whole series of new possessions situated on the Loire, the counties of Angers, Blois and Orléans. As was the custom in the Carolingian period, Robert was also lay abbot of the largest monasteries in the region,

Saint-Martin de Tours and Marmoutier.[44] In 856, he rebelled against the king, probably because Charles tried to place Neustria under the guardianship of his son, Louis the Stammerer. But Robert was too good a soldier to be dispensed with. In 861, he regained his command, and apart from a brief interruption kept it until his death.[45] He was killed at Brissarthe[46] in the autumn of 866 while fighting a combined force of Scandinavians and Bretons. Robert the Strong has come down to us as the archetypal Frankish leader daring to risk his life in the struggle against the Vikings. He symbolizes the turning point of the 860s, marked by a new spirit of resistance against the aggressors. His heroic death earned him immense prestige, from which his descendants – the Robertians, forerunners of the Capetians – were to benefit.[47]

The death of Robert the Strong emboldened the Bretons, which may have been what persuaded Charles the Bald to yield Cotentin to King Salomon.[48] Robert the Strong's sons, Odo and Robert, were too young to succeed him immediately. Both were sent to live with their relatives in Germania, and did not return until they were adults. The command of Neustria passed to other prominent figures. Robert's immediate successor was Charles the Bald's uncle, Hugh the Abbot, a member of the Welf family, who would hold these possessions for nearly twenty years, from 866 to 883.

After the death of Charles the Bald in 877, a difficult period began for the Kingdom of West Francia. Louis the Stammerer reigned for only two years, from 877 to 879, and was succeeded by his two sons, Louis III and Carloman. Great hopes were aroused by the young King Louis when he gained a victory at Saucourt-en-Vimeu in 881,[49] but he himself died in 882, as did his brother the following year. The kingdom reverted to Emperor Charles the Fat, who proved incapable of defending it against the Vikings. The old Neustrian command was at least partly assigned to Renaud, 'Duke of Le Mans', and Count Henry.[50] In 885, Robert the Strong's son Odo became Count of Paris. In 886, he was able to recover his father's possessions in the valley of the Loire. By the side of Bishop Joscelin, he won fame during the famous siege of Paris of 885–6. Soon after, in 887, the discredited Charles the Fat was deposed by the German barons. Wreathed in glory from his recent victory, Odo was chosen as King of West Francia in 888. He then ceded to his brother Robert the family possessions situated between the Loure and the Seine. Odo was the first Robertian king. Members of a powerful family with connections to other aristocratic families,[51] Odo and Robert extended their alliances with the Counts of Vermandois, Herbert I and Herbert II, through marriage. These families shared power in the region between the Seine and the Loire. During the reign of Odo, at the end of the ninth century, the leading figure seems to have been the king's bother, Marquis Robert. Powerful as these men were, much of their territory was subjected to repeated attacks by the Vikings, while others seemed to resist their authority, like the valley of the Seine upriver from Rouen.

For more than half a century (from 845 at least) the Seine was the chosen route for Scandinavian incursions,[52] containing as it did one major city, Rouen, but also great monasteries, situated close to the river, such as Fontenelle, Jumièges and Saint-Ouen de Rouen.[53] In addition, there were a large number of small ports on the banks, many of which were within the dependency of one or other of these monasteries. As the richer monasteries were often plundered or burnt down, the monks eventually left to take refuge in better protected regions, making similar journeys to that made by the monks of Noirmoutier.[54] The first to leave, in 858, were the monks of Fontenelle, whose exodus led them north to Flanders, Montreuil-sur-Mer and Boulogne.[55] The monks of Jumièges followed in the 860s. They first stopped at the abbey of Saint-Riquier,[56] then at Haspres,[57] in the Cambrésis region. As for the monks of Saint-Ouen, who left at about the same time, they first took refuge in Gasny, on the Epte,[58] then, after the great incursion of 876, at Condé-sur-Aisne.[59] This departure of the monks does not mean that they deserted the region. From their refuges, they continued to maintain relations with their representatives in the lower Seine.[60]

Rouen itself was not entirely abandoned. Some activities continued, and the mint was still functioning. However, the city seems to have been undefended, and the Vikings entered it without difficulty in 885. The archbishops themselves, following the example of the monks, had long since left the town. In the 860s, Archbishop Ganelon had found refuge at Andely on the Seine,[61] on one of his estates. This did not keep him safe from the Viking fleets, however. In 876, his successor Archbishop John withdrew even further, to his estate at Braine, near Soissons.[62] There he was joined by his canons, so that Rouen was now devoid of any religious supervision. The political situation changed after the siege of Paris and the accession of King Odo in 888. Chased out of the Paris region, the Vikings turned their attention to Cotentin and besieged the 'castle' of Saint-Lô. The entry of a large Scandinavian force into this region led to a huge exodus of the religious communities. From 888 to 890 many of them took refuge in Rouen. Bishop Lista of Coutances was killed when Saint-Lô was seized, and his successor, Raguenard, settled in Rouen with his clergy. King Odo granted him the church of Saint-Sauveur, which would soon be renamed Saint-Lô and remain the seat of the Bishop of Coutances until the middle of the eleventh century. Other clerics from Contentin and Bessin followed the migration, including the bearers of the relics of Saint Leo of Coutances, Saint Germain le Scot and Saint John (from the abbey of Deux-Jumeaux).[63] As for the monks of Nantus,[64] they settled in Émendreville, on the left bank of the Seine.[65]

The historian and archaeologist Jacques Le Maho has carried out many excavations in Rouen. Following the results of his findings and clues in the few available texts, he has suggested that the city underwent a 'complete reconstruction', which may have taken place during the 890s. The walls were repaired. New streets were built, which did not follow the lines of the old Roman streets. The inhabitants rapidly became more densely packed within the walls, which suggests a substantial increase in the population. This reorganization seems to have been authorized by King Odo, who no longer had any rival within the city. The property of all those who had abandoned the city, whether clerics or members of great families, had been added to the royal estate. We know that this was the case with the monastery of Saint-Sauveur, and may also have been true of the monastery of Saint-Amand, situated *intra muros*, to the north of the cathedral.[66] Rouen had become a city of refuge like Chartres, Angers and Rheims at the same period. The development of Rouen was part of a more general evolution which affected much of the kingdom. Jacques Le Maho insists, however, on the fact that Rouen was almost uninhabited when it was taken over by the king.[67] To repopulate it, Odo forced the inhabitants of the small towns along the Seine to come to settle in the city.[68] This transfer of population is likely to have taken place in the years 888 to 890. The newly deserted river ports on the Seine now became the temporary home of refugees from Cotentin. Some settled in a place called Saint-Paul with the body of Saint Clair,[69] in the port of Jumièges with the body of Saint Peregrine, and in the port of Saint-Vaast with the body of Saint Hameltrude.[70] These clerics were unable to stay in the area for very long, because the Vikings had resumed their raids, and this time had decided to settle here permanently. The Scandinavians found the conditions highly favourable. The banks of the Seine were almost uninhabited and it was a perfect place to practise their traditional activities, fishing, maritime trade – and piracy.[71]

This major shift in the population of the lower Seine at the end of the ninth century is not mentioned in any text, but a study of place-names may give us some useful clues. Lucien Musset began studying the question in 1980.[72] He noted that Scandinavian names were no more common in the lower Seine region than in other regions such as Pays de Caux or Bessin, on the coast.[73] Nevertheless, the names seem quite different from those usually found in agricultural areas. They were not based on the names of Scandinavian leaders, replacing those of the former Frankish masters as was the custom. Rather, they reflected economic activities, especially those connected with the river, and were used for ports and fishing villages that had barely been inhabited before the arrival of the first Vikings. Most of these names are descriptive, for example, names ending in 'vic' (from the Old Norse *vik*, meaning bay), 'bec' (from *bekker*, stream), 'fleur' (from *floi*, gulf or estuary), 'clif' (from *kliff*, cliff), 'beuf' (from the Old Danish *both*, cabin), and 'tuit' (from the Old Danish *thwet*, clearing the ground).[74]

Going up the Seine, we find the following localities with names of Scandinavian origin.[75] On the right bank, Sanvic[76] may well have once belonged to the abbey of Saint-Denis, just as Harfleur had belonged to Montivilliers.[77] Villequiers was a former dependency of the abbey of Fontenelle.[78] Caudebec-en-Caux was the site of the former convent of Logium. Conihout,[79] near Jumièges, should be mentioned, as should Sagurs, part of the estate of the church of Bayeux.[80] On the left bank, we find Honfleur, Crémanfleur and Fiquefleur,[81] situated by streams leading to the estuary, Risleclif[82] at the confluence of the Seine and the Risle near Cionteville, and Quillebeuf, a port which probably belonged to the monastery of Jumièges.[83] Traditional river crossings also bear Scandinavian names, such as Twit-Port (now Vieux-Port)[84] and Bliquetuit,[85] opposite Caudebec-en-Caux. Finally, mention should be made of Brotonne, a former Merovingian royal estate, Couronne, Elbef and Caudebec-lès-Elbeuf.[86]

How are we to interpret this multiplicity of Scandinavian place-names? The most plausible explanation is that there was a large Nordic population in the area, as the English historian David Bates wrote in 1982.[87] It was traditionally believed that such an influx could only have taken place after the treaty of Saint-Clair-sur-Epte in 911. Jacques Le Maho, however, suggests that it took place in the last years of the ninth century and the first decade of the tenth, and that it was related to the arrival of Rollo, the founder of Normandy.[88]

The arrival of Rollo

The story of Rollo is known through the work of Dudo of Saint-Quentin, canon of the collegiate church of Saint-Quentin (Aisne). Soon after 987, Dudo was sent by Count Albert of Vermandois as an ambassador to the Duke of Normandy, Richard I, to ask him for help against the new king, Hugh Capet. The duke kept him on at his court and asked him to write a history of Normandy. Interrupted briefly by the death of Richard I, the project was resumed under Richard II.[89] Dudo's work was mainly written between 1015 and 1026. It consists of four biographies. The first is that of the Viking chief Hasting, depicted as the archetype of the bloodthirsty Viking, while the others are of the first three Dukes of Normandy.[90] Despite his work at the ducal court, Dudo continued to exercise his functions at Saint-Quentin, where he died as dean of the collegiate church in 1043.[91]

Dudo writes in a literary language, inspired by ancient models. He is nevertheless a serious historian, using written sources and oral traditions to construct a coherent historical narrative. Although his work has been severely criticized by historians,[92] for some years now medievalists of various disciplines have challenged their opinions and re-examined the texts. Dudo made errors, of course, but it is important to place him in his context and understand his project, which was 'a response to a desire for history', to quote Pierre Bauduin, one of the modern historians who have begun the necessary re-examination of Dudo's work.[93] The work of Pierre Bouet, a Latinist specializing in authors who wrote about Normandy, should also be mentioned.[94] This rereading of Dudo is all the more essential in that he is the only writer to have provided us with a coherent narrative of the beginnings of the duchy, so that even those most critical of Dudo have had no choice but to refer to his work.

Rollo's origins remain obscure. According to Dudo, he was one of the *Daci* (the Daces) which he himself identifies with the *Dani* (Danes). The name he gives him, Rollo, is a Latinization of the Old Norse Hrolf. According to the Icelandic sagas, written in the thirteenth century. Hrolf was the son of a *jarl* from Möre, in the west of Norway. In short, Rollo was a Norwegian chief commanding a force composed mainly of Danes,[95] but with a number of Anglo-Saxons, since Rollo had spent long periods in England.

Dudo gives us very few dates. He situates the arrival of Rollo in 876 – a year marked by a major Viking incursion on the Seine – but this is dubious, to say the least: it would mean that Rollo settled in the region thirty-five years before the treaty of Saint-Clair-sur-Epte.

Again according to Dudo, Rollo participated in the siege of Paris in 885–6, and later captured Bayeux. This event is not dated, but may be situated between 886 and 890, the date of the capture of Saint-Lô by a large force of Vikings.[96] This force was finally defeated by the Breton duke Alan the Great. It withdrew to the north of the kingdom and wintered in Noyon. After that, the lower Seine area seems to have enjoyed a few years of relative tranquillity.[97] There do not seem to have been any new Viking incursions in the region until 896, when a fleet commanded by Hundeus appeared on the Seine. Hundeus knew all about the conflict between the Robertian king, Odo, and his Carolingian rival, Charles the Simple. In 897, he went to see Charles in Lotharingia, where he was living in exile, and agreed to be baptized in return for territory. At this time Charles was clearly not in a position to cede any territory at all, but may well have expressed support for such an agreement. This episode, in any case, seems to prefigure the treaty of Saint-Clair-sur-Epte. Two years later, in 898, King Odo died and Charles the Simple reclaimed the throne. Now he was able to pursue his own policy with regard to the Vikings, and there was no reason why this should not be a policy of negotiation, something to which his predecessor had been strongly opposed.[98]

Dudo of Saint-Quentin describes in great detail the agreement concluded by Rollo when he first arrived in the lower Seine area. According to Dudo, he met the archbishop's emissaries at the port of Saint-Vaast de Jumièges and agreed to spare the city of Rouen.[99] Dudo of course situates this episode in 876, but according to Jacques Le Maho, the 'pact of Jumièges' could not have been concluded before 898.[100] One of the clauses of the agreement allowed for Scandinavian settlement in the region. From this point on, the new Scandinavian inhabitants and the native population lived side by side along the river. Clearly, such close proximity was unacceptable to the clerics who had taken shelter in Rouen and its surroundings, and a good many of them went into exile. The monks who had settled in Saint-Paul with the body of Saint Clair moved to a town in Vexin, which became known by the name of their saint, Saint-Clair-sur-Epte. The monks of Saint-Marcouf withdrew to Senlis, then to Corbény.[101] Only the clerics from Coutances remained in the city of Rouen, which demonstrates that it was considered a safe place, its security presumably guaranteed by the Scandinavian chief who controlled the region – probably Rollo. This agreement with the Archbishop of Rouen prefigures others with the king, but also with the aristocrats of the kingdom. Rollo was no longer isolated within the Frankish world. He had established relations of various kinds with the major figures of Neustria and become part of their networks of alliance, often based on ties of kinship. It is in this context that we should view the famous marriage of Rollo and Popa.

The question of Rollo's relations with the aristocracy of the Kingdom of West Francia has been revived thanks to the recent anthropologically based work of Pierre Bauduin.[102] As always, we must first go back to Dudo of Saint-Quentin. According to Dudo, after capturing and destroying Bayeux, Rollo took many prisoners away with him. Among them was Popa, the daughter of Béranger, *praevalens princes* ('the dominant prince of the region').[103] Subsequently, Rollo married Popa and they had a son named William, who became his successor and was known as William Longsword. Historical tradition has seen Béranger as Count of Bessin, which is not improbable, since he may well have exercised this function concurrently with others. In that case, his authority might have extended over a much larger territory. René Merlet and Hubert Guillotel have both established a connection between this Béranger of Bayeux and the Marquis Béranger who signed a charter in Saint-Martin de Tours in 892, which would make him the friend – and therefore the equal – of Robert, brother of King Odo.[104] Just like his predecessor, Count Henry, Béranger may have belonged to the powerful Hunrochide family, which had established itself in many regions of the former Carolingian Empire, including Flanders, Lotharingia, Alamannia and Frioul.[105] Béranger may have shared with his friend Robert the former Neustrian command of Count Henry. He extended his authority over Maine, Hiémois and Bessin, that is, the whole western part of that 'march'.[106]

Pierre Bauduin has pointed out, however, that there is another tradition concerning Popa's origins, derived from the *Annals of Jumièges*.[107] In this version, she was the daughter of Guy, Count of Senlis, and therefore the sister of Bernard of Senlis, who was to play an important role in Normandy when William Longsword was duke. Paradoxically, Dudo of Saint Quentin himself provides support for this second tradition by presenting Bernard of Senlis as William's maternal uncle (*avunculus*).[108] It is difficult to be sure of Popa's true origin, and some have joked about 'Popa's two fathers'.[109] Katherine Keats-Rohan has suggested a solution that would make it possible to reconcile the two traditions. Popa's mother may have belonged to the family of the counts of Vermandois (the Herbertides). Her first husband was Béranger of Bayeux, her second Guy of Senlis. Popa was a child of the first marriage, Bernard of Senlis of the second. This would make Popa Guy's stepdaughter, not his daughter, and Bernard Popa's step-brother, and indeed the maternal uncle of William Longsword.[110] Whatever Popa's real origins, it is certain that she belonged to the high Frankish aristocracy. In marrying her, whether willingly or unwillingly, Rollo was entering a powerful network of kinship, which would facilitate his integration into the political life of the kingdom, even though he did not take advantage of it immediately.

After the events of the years 886–90 (and his marriage to Popa), Rollo seems to have left Neustria for many years, probably for England – which reverses the chronological order suggested by Dudo. William was probably born overseas, while his father was still a pagan.[111] Rollo did not return to the estuary of the Seine until towards the end of the reign of Odo or the beginning of that of Charles the Simple, in 898. This would place the 'pact of Jumièges' with the Archbishop of Rouen somewhere between 898 and 906.[112] After this agreement, Rollo settled permanently in the lower Seine area, with many Scandinavian or Anglo-Scandinavian colonists. Playing his role as a Viking chief, Rollo resumed his operations against the neighbouring regions. During the summer of 911, he launched an attack on Paris, which ended in failure. Then he travelled to Chartres, to which he laid siege. This action provoked a sharp response from the leading figures of the kingdom and led to the battle of Chartres.

Besieged by Rollo's forces, Bishop Joseaume of Chartres appealed to the barons of the kingdom. Some responded, but not all. The army that fought against the Normans was led by Robert, Marquis of Neustria, Richard the Justiciar, Duke of Burgundy, and his loyal follower, Manasses, Count of Dijon. The Count of Poitiers, Ebles Mancer, may have arrived too late to take part in the fighting. On 20 July 911[113] this coalition inflicted a severe defeat on the Normans beneath the walls of Chartres. It is difficult to interpret this episode.[114] What is particularly interesting is that there were many absentees from the coalition. Herbert II of Vermandois had ignored the appeal, as had all the northern barons. Even Ebles-Mancer's delay may not have been fortuitous. But the most conspicuous absentee was King Charles the Simple. There were clearly two opposing views within the ruling elite. Some were hostile on principle to any agreement with the Vikings. This was the policy championed by King Odo during his reign and pursued by his brother Robert. In the other camp we find Herbert of Vermandois and the king himself. It is worth recalling that Charles the Simple had been associated, willingly or unwillingly, with a first attempt at agreement in 896–7.[115] He may have been inspired by the example of Alfred the Great, who had agreed to the establishment of Viking kingdoms in the Danelaw, in return for the conversion of the Scandinavian kings to Christianity. Lucien Musset has shown the extent to which the founders of Normandy were inspired by this precedent.[116] In addition, the king was supported by the new Archbishop of Rheims, Herive, who proved as favourably disposed to the conversion of the Scandinavians as his predecessor, Fulk, had been violently opposed to it.[117]

Saint-Clair-sur-Epte (911)

Paradoxically, the Norman defeat at Chartres allowed those who favoured negotiation to gain the upper hand, by pointing the way to a necessary compromise. Defeated they may have been, but Rollo's Normans were still firmly entrenched in the heart of the kingdom. The best solution therefore was to begin negotiations, which would lead to the famous 'treaty' of Saint-Clair-sur-Epte. The period following the battle of Chartres was filled with lengthy negotiations, which are described in great detail by Dudo of Saint Quentin.[118] Dudo begins with an account of a royal council, at which it was agreed that, since the Franks were unable to resist the Normans militarily, they would have to negotiate with them. Given the sorry state of the kingdom, the solution was to cede to Rollo the territory between the Andelle and the sea.[119] The ambassador sent to Rollo was Archbishop Franco of Rouen. Dudo's critics have of course pointed out that the archbishop at the time was not Franco, but possibly Witto, although that is by no means certain either. The chronology of the archbishops at this period is somewhat vague, and clearly Dudo did not know any better than we do.[120] Be that as it may, the archbishop conveyed the

Frankish proposals to Rollo, but added his own demanded that Rollo convert to Christianity. Next, Dudo describes Rollo's council. His Danish councillors carefully considered the offer and suggested a number of measures designed to hasten the peace process, such as a three-month truce and a personal interview between the king and Rollo, who would commit himself 'to his service'. On his return, the Archbishop of Rouen presented his mission as a great success and aroused the enthusiasm of the aristocracy – an enthusiasm not shared by King Charles. At this point, Marquis Robert, who does not seem to have been present at the royal council, spoke up. He approved the terms of the proposed treaty and even offered to be Rollo's godfather when he was baptized, as well as his friend.[121]

The planned encounter finally took place in Saint-Clair-sur-Epte,[122] and the final negotiations got under way. Rollo obtained some extra concessions: the land yielded would no longer extend from the Andelle to the sea, but from the Epte to the sea.[123] As the two rivers were some 50 kilometres apart, this change represented a substantial enlargement. Rollo also pointed out that the territory in question had been laid waste and demanded a 'land to plunder'. He was offered Flanders. He refused and finally accepted Brittany.[124] This really meant the territory that would become lower Normandy, which had largely been under Breton control since the concession of 867. At last, the investiture ceremony took place, described by Dudo in the minutest detail. Rollo put his hands in those of Charles the Simple, the *immixtio manuum* by which he subordinated himself to the king. In return, the king gave him the hand of his daughter Gisela, and above all the land situated between Epte and the sea, for him to keep *in alodo et in fundo* (as a hereditary estate, not as a fiefdom). He also received 'all of Britanny, so that he may draw enough from it to live'.[125]

Then this solemn session took a farcical turn. The bishops present suggested that, as a sign of his submission, Rollo should kiss the king's foot. This was an unusual request, which seemed designed to humiliate to Rollo. After some discussion, he delegated the gesture to one of his men. The designated person seized the royal foot and raised it to his lips, but without stooping, so that the king fell backwards! For a moment, it looked as if things would turn nasty, but then all ended well, with general laughter. Finally, at Rollo's request, a solemn oath was taken by the Franks present, including the king and Marquis Robert. It was an oath of 'Catholic faith', by which they committed themselves to respect the concession granted to Rollo and his descendants forever.[126]

The exact date of this ceremony is unknown. It is most likely to have taken place in the autumn of the year 911, between the battle of Chartres (July 911) and Rollo's baptism (912).[127] The time for Rollo to undergo instruction before baptism had to be reduced to a minimum. According to Dudo, Archbishop Franco baptized Rollo, Marquis Robert agreed to become his godfather, in accordance with his offer, and Rollo took the Christian name of Robert. Like Clovis before him, he was not baptized alone, but with 'his companions, his warriors and his whole army'. After the ceremony, he asked the archbishop which were the most venerated churches 'on his land' (in other words, in his ecclesiastical province). Franco mentioned the principal cathedrals, Rouen, Bayeux and Évreux, and the great monasteries, Mont-Saint-Michel, Saint-Ouen and Jumièges, and even Saint-Denis ('at the limits of our power'). The text says nothing about the state of these monasteries, of which several had been completely abandoned by 911. Rollo responded by committing himself to giving to these churches part of the land that had been conceded to him.[128] This last episode, as reconstructed by Dudo, is not purely imaginary. We have the traces of actual gifts of land by Rollo to the abbeys of Saint-Ouen de Rouen (the estate of Longpaon)[129] and Saint Denis (the estate of Berneval).[130] On the other hand, there is no evidence that any gifts were made in Bessin and Avranchin, which were not acquired by the Normans until 924 and 933. The passage, however, is not without interest. The archbishop and his successors were clearly keen for the dukes to expand westwards, an expansion that was to lead within twenty years to the reunification of their ecclesiastical province. The fact remains that it is very difficult to be sure of the exact extent of the territory conceded in 911. Dudo mentions only the valley of the Seine, 'from the Epte to the sea'. We therefore need to refer to other texts, which are not very precise but which have the advantage of having been written closer to the events.

Dudo was writing nearly a century later, and no trace has been found of the text of any 'treaty' of Saint-Clair-sur-Epte. It is by no means certain that it was even written down. On the other hand, some almost contemporary documents throw an interesting light on the extent and terms of the concession of 911.[131] The closest documents to the event are two charters signed by Charles the Simple. On 14 March 918, the king conceded to the abbey of Saint-Germain-des-Prés the old abbey of La Croix-Saint-Ouen in the *pagus* of Madrie, with all its property.[132] The concession was made at the request of Marquis Robert, Count Herbert II of Vermandois and Bishop Abbo of Soissons. There was, however, an important qualification, which deserves to be quoted in its entirety: this gift did not include 'the part of the abbey which we conceded to the Normans of the Seine, that is, to Rollo and his companions, for the protection of the kingdom [*pro tutela regni*]'.[133] This passage explains the essential reason for the concession, from the king's point of view. The intention was to yield territory to a Scandinavian leader who would henceforth be capable of protecting the heart of the kingdom from further Viking incursions. The evidence suggests that Rollo carried out this task to the letter, even though it was not officially included in the clauses of the treaty. This commitment did not, however, prevent him from launching further pirate raids on areas not controlled by the king, such as Brittany and Flanders.

From the point of view of the barons of Francia, the concession of 918 had important consequences. Robert was the lay Abbot of Saint-Germain-des-Prés and it is highly likely that he also performed the same function at the abbey of La

Croix-Saint-Ouen. By adding the property of the latter abbey
to Saint-Germain-des-Prés, he recovered what he could and
kept land close to the territory of the Normans. Herbert of
Vermandois also had an interest in this transaction, since he
probably controlled the counties of Vexin and Madrie. This all
becomes clear when we examine the second charter granted by
Charles the Simple in the same year, on 14 May.[134] This time,
the king conceded to Saint-Germain-des-Prés, again at
Robert's request, several estates close to Paris (Suresnes[135] and
Bouafle[136]), another in Beauvaisis (Thiverny[137]) and that of
Sérifontaine[138] in Vexin, on the Epte, which adjoined the
borders of the new Normandy. These gifts clearly concerned
those who controlled the territories in which the estates in
question were situated[139] – none other than Marquis Robert
and Count Herbert. It becomes obvious that the concession to
the Normans referred to a series of possessions, whose fron-
tiers were respected. The new boundary did not follow the
administrative borders, but those of these possessions. After
the 'treaty' of 911, it was important for the Frankish aristocrats
to consolidate their property located outside Normandy.
Where these were close to the border, and therefore particularly exposed, it may well have seemed advisable to entrust
them to a religious institution, which, being under the
protection of the king, would be better able to defend them
against any possible encroachment by the Normans.[140]

As we have seen, the boundaries of the territory conceded
were somewhat vague. The *Annals* of Flodoard, written close
to the events, supply us with some important details. In 923,
King Raoul crossed the Epte and 'introduced himself with
force on the land which had recently been conceded to the
Normans'.[141] By this date, the Epte was clearly seen as the
eastern boundary of Normandy. Talking about the year 925,
Flodoard mentions that the fortress of Eu was occupied by the
Normans.[142] In his *History of the Church of Rheims*, he
mentions 'the *pagi* bordering the sea, with the city of Rouen'.[143]
These maritime *pagi* could well be Pays de Caux and Talou.

The whole north and east of the diocese of Rouen seems to have been in the hands of the Normans. In the west, the borders were less clear-cut. Flodoard refers to the claims of the newcomers to the lands situated beyond the Seine, that is, on the left bank of the river. The Normans occupied part of the County of Madrie as far as the Eure, where the abbey of La-Croix-Saint-Ouen was situated. But we cannot be certain that the town of Évreux, or Évrecin in general, was part of the original concession. The Risle has often been seen as the boundary, which is pure hypothesis. It was not until 924, according to Flodoard, that the Normans received Le Mans and Bayeux, in other words the regions of Maine and Bessin.[144]

The founding of Normandy was the end result of a long process which stretched over almost a century (820–911). Rollo received royal authority, while enjoying a *de facto* independence. His situation was virtually the same as that of Robert, Marquis of Neustria, or Henri II, Count of Vermandois, whose equal he now was. He also agreed to convert to Christianity, a sine qua non of integration into the Frankish world. From now on, the king only had to deal with a single Scandinavian, who would protect him against any new incursions on the part of his fellow countrymen. This agreement was to everyone's advantage, and on the whole it was respected by both parties. The 'treaty' of Saint-Clair-sur-Epte gave birth to a new principality, which soon grew to include almost the whole of the ecclesiastical province of Rouen, the former second Provincia Lugudensis. It would preserve its relative independence (within the Kingdom of France) for nearly three centuries.

4

A NEW PRINCIPALITY

The Vikings had founded states in various regions of Western Europe, but the only one that lasted was Normandy. This durability can partly be explained by the personality of its founder, Rollo, as well as the personalities of his successors during the tenth and eleventh centuries. Of course this is not the only explanation. The new state was often threatened during the first century of its existence, especially in the periods of minority (942–6 and 996–1001). The first dukes managed, although not without difficulty, to unite the different elements of the population, Scandinavians, Bretons and Franks. They were able to integrate with the ruling classes of the time and establish the foundations of a remarkably well-administered state.

It has become common for historians to call the rulers of Normandy after 911 'dukes', though in reality their title was not fixed until the middle of the eleventh century. The texts most often use the titles 'count' or 'marquis'. The new Normandy was in fact considered a border 'march'. The border in this case was the sea, but it was a border constantly under threat from Viking raids. The title of marquis had already been applied to Robert, 'Marquis of Neustria', and sometimes to the Count of Vermandois,[1] Herbert I being responsible for the 'march of the Oise'. The new territory had been carved out of the possessions of these two men, who were the most powerful figures in the kingdom at that time. The Norman rulers seem to have taken over the titles that were abandoned by their Robertian lords: they were called 'marquis' when Hugh Capet was a duke (after 960) and 'duke' when he became king in 987.[2] For practical purposes, the traditional usage will be followed here. The first duke, then, was Rollo, who ruled Normandy for more than fifteen years after the treaty of Saint-Clair-sur-Epte.

After 911, Rollo continued to behave like a Viking chief, conducting expeditions to Flanders and expanding his principality westwards by seizing Bessin in 924.[3] Nevertheless, he respected the contract he had made in 911 with the Carolingian king. He kept an effective watch on the lower Seine, which ceased to be the route by which the Vikings penetrated the heart of the kingdom. That said, he also behaved as a territorial ruler and played a role in various power struggles between barons. As far as the internal situation of the duchy is concerned, we have to rely on Dudo's account, which is difficult to verify. Dudo presents us with an idyllic vision of the early years of Normandy. The old aristocracy had left the region, as had most of the bishops and abbots. The conceded territory was regarded as deserted. The duke was the sole landowner and was able to share it out among his companions. According to Dudo, 'he divided the land among his followers *à la corde*', which may be a reference to a new register. Dudo adds that Rollo decreed laws.[4] This may well be the origin of Norman law, which combined many elements of Frankish law with significant contributions from Scandinavia.[5] It was a common law, purely oral, which became codified only later, after it was written down between the end of the twelfth century and the beginning of the thirteenth. Dudo depicts Normandy as a land of peace and security. Rollo, he says, banned the keeping of domestic animals, and demanded that at the time of tilling the ploughshares be left in the fields. This is an allusion to the 'peace of the plough' which is mentioned in the Norman customary. Dudo even tells an anecdote to illustrate the application of these measures. Wanting to test the effectiveness of the duke's protection, the wife of a peasant from the *villa* of Longpaon stole her husband's ploughshares from the fields.[6] Her husband obtained the substantial sum of five sous from the duke as compensation. But the culprit was unmasked through a trial by ordeal. The duke sentenced her to be hanged, along with her husband, explaining to the latter, 'You will die in accordance with two just sentences, because you are your wife's master and should have punished her, and because you were her accomplice in the theft and did not denounce her.'[7]

Again according to Dudo, Rollo prepared his succession. He left the government of the duchy to his son William in about 927, that is, five years before his death in 932 or 933. William Longsword, who ruled until 942, continued and completed the expansion of Normandy westwards, receiving Contentin and Avranchin from the king.[8] Scandinavian through his father and Frankish through his mother, he had no need to convert, having been brought up as a Christian. He should have been accepted without difficulty by both communities; he nevertheless faced a rebellion, hard to situate chronologically, which can be related to this westward expansion.

The rebels included both Bretons and Normans.[9] The Bretons involved lived in Contentin and Avranchin, and also in Bessin, which may also have just been subjugated. The Normans were Scandinavians who also refused to submit to the authority of the Counts of Rouen. We know that many Vikings had been long established in the region, and that they had managed to preserve their independence until then. This was no longer possible with William Longsword, who wanted to integrate them into his duchy. The leader of the rebellion, Riouf, seems to have been from Évrecin. Orderic Vitalis in fact calls him 'Riouf of Évreux'.[10] This region seems to have long remained 'a poorly supervised fringe area', as Pierre Bauduin has written.[11] The extension of the principality westwards obliged William Longsword to take control of the diocese of Évreux, which now occupied a central position between his possessions in upper and lower Normandy. William managed to defeat the rebels and became, to quote Lucien Musset, 'the principal architect of the success of the Normans: it is with him that the Scandinavian graft onto the Romano-Frankish trunk finally bore fruit'.[12]

Even more than his father, William was totally integrated into the high aristocracy of the kingdom. His mother belonged to an aristocratic family and he in turn married Luitgarde, the daughter of Herbert II of Vermandois, in 935.[13] The lands in her dower were all situated in the newly controlled regions, at the limits of the Évrecin. These were the estates of Longueville, Coudres and Illiers l'Évêque,[14] on the border formed by the river Avre.[15] William continued his father's policy of expansion, in this case northwards, the main prize being the fortress of Montreuil.[16] This brought him into direct competition with Arnulf, Count of Flanders, which led to an ambush at Picquigny on the Somme, where he was killed on 17 December 942.[17]

Despite difficult beginnings, William's son Richard I would rule Normandy for more than fifty years, from 942 to 996. He was not the offspring of Luitgarde, but of a Breton concubine named Sprota. He had been sent by his father to Bessin to learn the language of his Scandinavian ancestors, which had already fallen out of use in Rouen[18] – an unmistakable sign of how well integrated the dukes and their entourage were in the world of the Franks. However, the new duke was only about ten and his authority was strongly disputed, especially by the Carolingian king, Louis IV d'Outremer. Louis settled in Rouen as if on conquered land and exiled young Richard to Laon. He reserved upper Normandy for himself and left lower

Normandy to his ally, the powerful 'Duke of the Franks', Hugh the Great. The Normans did not accept this seizure and appealed to two 'kings of the sea', first Sigtrygg then Harald. Duke Richard himself managed to escape from Laon and was able to regain power, in spite of the intervention of Louis' brother-in-law, Otto the Great, King of Germany.

By 947, at the age of fifteen, Richard had been recognized as the legitimate duke. There now began a long period of tranquillity, which would only be disturbed by a conflict with Theobald 'the Trickster', Count of Blois.[19] On the whole, peace and security again reigned in Normandy, which distinguished it from the other principalities of the kingdom. Richard relied on the Church for support, and restored much Church land, which had been without its rightful owners since the period of the invasions. The great monasteries were re-established, and the duke created a dynastic shrine at Fécamp.[20]

Richard I reversed the previous alliances. His predecessors had remained loyal to the Carolingians, but having been attacked by a Carolingian king himself, he turned rather to the Robertian Hugh the Great, forging a strong alliance cemented by his marriage to Hugh's daughter Emma. After Hugh's death in 956, Richard explicitly proclaimed himself a vassal of his son Hugh Capet, as is shown in a text of 968.[21] In a way, the 'Duke of the Franks' had replaced the Carolingian king, since neither Louis IV nor his successor Lothair proved capable of assuming his traditional role. The accession of Hugh Capet to the royal throne in 987 restored the situation to normal. From now on, Richard was again the direct vassal of the king, as his predecessors had been. Begun in about 945, these special ties between the Dukes of Normandy and the Robertians (and later the Capetians) would last for more than a century. The marriage of Richard and Emma produced no offspring. Instead, the duke had many children with a woman of Danish origin named Gonnor, who belonged to a family that had settled in Pays de Caux. She was the mother of the Crown Prince, who was also called Richard.

On Richard's death in 996, a new crisis of minority began, the first sign of which was a major peasant uprising in that same year. It was not in fact directed at the duke, but at the lords, who were trying to appropriate new powers to themselves, especially over the forests and the waterways.[22] It was put down harshly by Count Ralph of Ivry, a relative of the ducal family. It was he who held the reins of power during the whole period of minority, which ended in 1001.[23] In this first year of the eleventh century, Richard II appealed to an Italian abbot, William of Volpiano, to settle with a group of monks in the family monastery of Fécamp. It was a decisive stage in the monastic restoration, which would continue throughout his reign and those of his successors.

Drawn to religion, Ricard II had a great deal in common with his exact contemporary, the Capetian king Robert the Pious, and would strengthen the traditional alliance between the two dynasties. Richard helped Robert militarily in campaigns that led to the conquest of Burgundy. He also formed a new alliance with Brittany, expressed though an exchange of marriages. Richard's sister Hawise married Duke Geoffrey of Brittany, and Geoffrey's sister Judith married Richard. Richard II's two successors came from this legitimate union, Richard III and Robert the Magnificent. During the rule of Richard II, Normandy's borders became more or less fixed, with only a few minor enlargements under William the Bastard.[24] Although these borders may seem artificial, they were distantly based on the old Roman boundaries.[25] The initial task of the first four dukes had been to define and protect these borders, which in the beginning were constantly under threat. In doing so, they created and strengthened a durable principality.

The question of the borders of Normandy under the four dukes is a problematic one for historians.[26] There are few documentary sources concerning the tenth century in Normandy, particularly as regards diplomatic moves. Is it simply that documents have disappeared, as has often been thought, or was there a real 'retreat from writing' and a return to oral communication?[27] Neither the Franks nor the Scandinavians had any problem recognizing verbal commitments, sanctioned by solemn oaths. The clerics and monks, who were the only users of writing, had fled the region and did not return until the middle of the tenth century. Of course this creates a difficult situation for historians, who have to be content with archaeological finds, including coins, as well as accounts by annalists and chroniclers from outside the region. As before, our main sources are Flodoard and Dudo of Saint-Quentin.

Flodoard mentions a whole series of expeditions, mainly in two directions. To the north, the Normans clashed with another principality in the process of formation, Flanders. Between the two was Picardy, which was coveted by both these rival powers. To the west, they had to deal with the Bretons, who now occupied Cotentin and Avranchin. According to Dudo, both Flanders and Brittany had been mentioned in 911 as possible 'lands for plunder'. Rollo had refused Flanders, but accepted Brittany.[28] In his reconstruction of the story, Dudo may have been influenced, consciously or not, by what in fact happened in the course of the eleventh century: the Normans failed when it came to Flanders, but succeeded in Brittany.

This was not a predictable development. It seems likely that in the years following the treaty of Saint-Clair-sur-Epte, Rollo had respected the commitments he had made to the Carolingian king and was content with the territory conceded to him. The situation had changed with the coup led by Robert, Duke of the Franks. In 922, he succeeded in getting himself chosen as king by the aristocracy, and Charles the Simple was deposed. Robert I only had a short time in power. He was killed in 923 at the battle of Soissons. His son-in-law Rudolph, Duke of Burgundy, was chosen as king by the barons. As for Charles the Simple, he was being held prisoner in Péronne by Herbert of Vermandois. After Charles' deposition, Rollo considered himself to be released from his duties to the king. The personal ties had been broken, but nor did he feel any obligation towards the Robertian usurpers. It was at this time that the Normans of Rouen resumed their expansion beyond the territories granted them in 911.

In 924, according to Flodoard, Rollo negotiated with some of the barons, but in the absence of the new king, Rudolph. The talks were conducted by Archbishop Seulf of Rheims, Herbert of Vermandois and Hugh the Great, son of the dead king Robert. As a result of these negotiations, Rollo obtained 'Le Mans and Bayeux' (*Cinomannis et Baiocae*).[29] This laconic wording is distinctly problematic for historians. What exactly was the territory conceded? Was it really the whole of Bessin and Maine? What seems certain is that the Normans now had control of the country of Bayeux and the whole of central Normandy. Whether it also included Maine remains an open question. Lucien Musset was of the opinion that the agreement only involved Hiémois, which for a time had been within the dependency of Le Mans.[30] In fact, the whole of this region, including Bessin, had been part of the vast Duchy of Maine, which had been ruled by Marquis Béranger.[31] It seems unlikely that the Normans took possession of Maine at this time, but the agreement of 924 certainly allowed for a later claim on this territory – as was indeed to happen under William the Bastard. Be that as it may, it was a significant enlargement of Norman territory in the west. In making this major concession, King Ralph might have been trying to buy Rollo's loyalty and stop him from attacking Picardy. For the king, it was a fool's bargain, since the Normans attacked Picardy anyway.

At this time when the territorial principalities were being formed, Picardy was distinguished from the other regions of the kingdom by the fact that the Carolingian system remained in place there much longer than elsewhere. For much of the reign of Charles the Simple, the king's authority was still strong there, even though it gradually weakened.[32] In addition, Picardy was the kingdom's outlet to the sea, especially since the lower Seine had been yielded to the Normans. Since the days of Charlemagne, the estuary of the Canche had been a very active area, including as it did the port of Quentovic. Admittedly, it had been subjected to many attacks from the Vikings, but maritime activity had not disappeared, merely retreated upriver. The *castrum* of Montreuil, which overlooked the Canche, had assumed increasing importance, making Picardy a much coveted territory. The fall of the Caroligian king in 922 whetted the appetites of the barons. At least three of them had a direct interest in the territory: Rollo; Arnulf, Count of Flanders since 918; and Herbert II of Vermandois.[33]

In 923, the Normans of the Seine attacked the *pagi* located beyond the Oise.[34] On this occasion, they were joined by other Normans who were in the process of settling on the Loire. In a way, both groups were reviving the practices of the Vikings. In 925 we again find the Normans in the regions of Amiens and Beauvais, right in the heart of Picardy,[35] in a campaign concentrated around two emblematic fortresses, Eu, which was occupied by the Normans, and Montreuil, which was in the hands of Helgaud.[36] Count Arnulf of Flanders had already seized Boulonnais and intended to continue his expansion southwards. He attacked the castle of Eu, with other 'maritime Franks' and managed to seize it. The occupants were slaughtered or thrown in the sea.[37] Robert I's son Hugh the Great unexpectedly came to the aid of the Normans. At the end of 925, Robert and the Normans concluded a 'security pact'; this was the beginning of a new alliance that would last for much of the tenth century and beyond. The Normans soon regained Eu. Over the following years, various campaigns took place in this area, and Count Helgaud of Montreuil died in 926 while fighting the Normans.[38]

The western borders of Normandy were equally disputed. The Bretons still posed a serious threat to the new Norman possessions in Bessin and Maine. At the beginning of his rule, William Longsword faced a rebellion from those Bretons who had already been absorbed into the new principality. Dudo gives no date for this, but Flodoard mentions such an event taking place in the year 931.[39] William retaliated harshly, ravaging the territory of the Bretons. His attacks took place at the same time as those by the pagan Vikings of the Loire, making him, at least objectively, their ally. Breton resistance was led by two men, Alan Wrybeard and Béranger, who might have been the grandson of Béranger, Count of Bayeux and Le Mans, with whom we are already familiar.[40] Béranger was the ancestor of the counts of Rennes and Alan Wrybeard the ancestor of the counts of Nantes. In about 931, Alan fled to England, but Béranger came to a reconciliation with William Longsword. William's aim may have been to seize the whole of Brittany or at least to share it with the Normans of the Loire. That much is suggested by the discovery at Mont-Saint-Michel of a coin bearing the inscription 'William, Duke of the Bretons'.[41] Eventually, William would make do with a more realistic objective.

To obtain the Breton territories in a way that could not be disputed, William appealed to the king. In 927, at the very beginning of his rule, he had commended himself to Charles the Simple, whom Herbert of Vermandois had briefly released from prison.[42] After Charles' death, the situation was much clearer. With the Carolingians now apparently out of the picture, William could turn to the Robertian king without denying his old bonds of loyalty. So, in 933, he commended himself to Rudolph. In return, Rudolph granted him 'the land of the Bretons situated on the shore of the sea',[43] that is, according to most commentators, Cotentin and Avranchin.

By the time of William Longsword, then, the territory of Normandy had been established in almost definitive form. To the west, the border was now defined by the Couesnon, which marked the boundary of the diocese of Avranches. To the north-east, it was bordered by the Bresle and well protected by the fortress of Eu.[44] True, William Longsword would still intervene in the north to thwart the ambitions of Count Arnulf of Flanders. In 939, Arnulf seized the castle of Montreuil through cunning. Helgaud's son and successor, Herluin, turned to William for support.[45] With William's help, he managed to recapture the castle. This was a serious blow to

Arnulf's ambitions, but it made him William's impacable enemy. The Montreuil affair was certainly one of the reasons, if not the main reason, for the ambush at Picquigny in 942.

The southern borders were less clearly delineated. Although the concession of 924 may have included the whole of Maine, the territory that was in fact acquired corresponded only to the Hiémois. It was not until the end of the rule of Richard I, some time between 990 and 996, that the duke intervened in the region. The south of the diocese of Sées remained a 'march' that largely escaped the control of the Dukes of Normandy until the eleventh century and beyond,[46] and one part of this diocese would never become part of territory of Normandy, the future archdeaconates of Bellême and Corbonnais, which were added to the County of Perche. In the south-east, the river Avre was reached in the 930s,[47] but this was another fringe area, claimed by the Count of Blois, Theobald the Trickster. He seized the County of Chartres and even took possession of Évrecin for a few years (c.960–5). It was only after 965 that Duke Richard I was really able to assert his authority in Évrecin.[48] Similarly, the *pagus* of Lisieux seems to have escaped ducal authority until the end of the tenth century.[49]

As we have seen, the establishing and strengthening of the borders was the cause of many conflicts during the tenth century. The more or less avowed aim seems to have been to extend the authority of the duke over the whole territory which, on the spiritual plane, was dependent on the Archbishop of Rouen. This aim was almost completely realized. The only areas not to be absorbed into Normandy were the French Vexin, which belonged to the diocese of Rouen, and Perche, most of which belonged to the diocese of Sées. The case of Normandy is unique in the whole of the Kingdom of France. No other principality coincided almost exactly with an ecclesiastical province.[50] This suggests the extent to which the first dukes were able to form special links with the Church, and especially with the Archbishop of Rouen.

From paganism to Christianity

Relations between the Scandinavian rulers and the Church were not easy at first. Rollo was seen as a pagan chief, and could only be accepted if he agreed to be baptized. But this baptism, not only of Rollo but also of his companion, was not enough to make the Normans good Christians. Conversion was an eminently political act, as many Viking leaders had realized.[51] Was Rollo's conversion sincere? This is a very difficult question to answer. Dudo presents him as a committed Christian, who made gifts (even of regions he had not yet conquered) to the principal churches of the province of Rouen.[52] We know that there is a great deal of reconstruction in this version of events, written nearly a century later. In reality, we do not know how Rollo behaved towards the Church after 911. He had realized that the Church was a force to be reckoned with, but made no attempt to restore the ecclesiastical structures destroyed during the second half of the ninth century: during his rule, the only remaining episcopal seats were those of Rouen and of Bayeux, the latter of which seems to have been re-established quite rapidly.[53] Nor did he try to bring the monks back. Admittedly, he would then have had to restore the property which he had appropriated from the bishoprics and the monasteries and partly shared out among his followers. This crucial question of control of the land was the main reason for the considerable delay in normalization.

In addition, it may well be that Rollo had to mollify those Scandinavians who had remained attached to paganism or who had converted only superficially to Christianity. Did he himself remain a crypto-pagan? One source suggests this, but from an author, Adémar of Chabannes, who wrote some time after the events and was very unfavourably disposed to the Normans. According to Adémar, just before his death in 932 or 933 Rollo practised human sacrifices to appease the pagan gods, and at the same time made gifts to the churches in his principality.[54]

In this respect, the situation changed drastically under Rollo's son William Longsword, whose mother was a Christian princess and who seems to have been a sincere Christian himself. He was considered as an equal by the other territorial rulers of the kingdom, with whom he formed strong alliances, given concrete expression in marriage. In 935, William married Luitgarde, the daughter of Herbert II of Vermandois, who was related to the Carolingians. At the same time, his sister Gerloc was given in marriage to William Towhead, Count of Poitiers, at which time she abandoned her Norwegian name and adopted a Christian one, Adela, the name of the daughter of Rollo's godfather, Marquis Robert.[55] William Longsword was the first duke to take an interest in the restoration of the monasteries. By extending his border as far as the Couesnon, he brought the monastery of Mont-Saint-Michel within his sphere of influence. It was the only ecclesiastical establishment in the province of Rouen to have survived during the Viking period. The duke gave the canons of the Mont several estates in Avranchin. In addition he re-established an old abandoned monastery in the Seine valley, the Abbey of Jumièges. To achieve this, he turned to his sister Gerloc/Adela, who sent him twelve monks from the abbey of Saint-Cyprien de Poitiers, under the direction of Abbot Martin. If Dudo is to be believed, William himself was drawn to the monastic life, and told Martin of his desire to become a monk. Martin vigorously dissuaded him, pointing out that he would be more useful to the Church by staying in the place he occupied in society.[56] Once again, Dudo is probably exaggerating, but there may well be some factual basis for the words he attributes to his hero.

Riouf's rebellion was in large part motivated by William's attitude towards religion. The rebel Normans of whom he was the leader seem to have been old Vikings who wanted to preserve their cultural identity. According to Dudo, they accused the duke of being a Frank – which indeed he was through his father – and of conducting a policy that was too favourable to the Franks.[57] Dudo does not mention the religious question, but it is possible that these rebels considered William an over-zealous, even militant Christian. They may have feared that the duke would force them to renounce their pagan practices, whether performed openly or in secret.

This idea is confirmed by another author, who was closer to events. Flodoard recounts that after William's death in 943, King Louis IV d'Outremer and Hugh the Great combined their forces to fight the pagans. This campaign took place in Évrecin, in other words, the very region where Riouf's rebellion had originated. Hugh recaptured the *castrum* of Évreux, thanks to the help of the Christians who had received it from the Normans.[58]

This affair raises the question of the persistence of the old Scandinavian religion. It may even be wondered if there was a certain return to paganism within the indigenous populations due to the inadequacy of ecclesiastical supervision. In the absence of bishops in the Norman dioceses, were there still priests in rural parishes? Did the faithful still worship? There is nothing in the texts to help us answer these questions. Archaeology might throw some light on the matter, but no Scandinavian tombs have been found in Normandy. The only likely ones are two tombs in the shape of boats which were discovered by chance on the beach at Réville during the spring tides of 1962, and which have since disappeared again.[59] The only unquestionably Viking tomb on French soil was found on the island of Groix, in Brittany.[60]

The efforts of William Longsword, continued by his successors, at last bore fruit. The former Vikings became Christians, leaving no tangible trace of their old religion. As for William, he met a violent death at the hands of a Christian prince, although Dudo of Saint-Quentin presents events in such a way as to make his death seem like martyrdom.[61]

It was William's successor, Richard I, who would restore a regularly functioning Church, although he did so only at the end of his rule, once his power was firmly established. During most of his reign, only the bishoprics of Rouen and Bayeux were filled. The seat of Coutances also had titular bishops, but they lived in Rouen, where the church of Saint-Lô had been granted to them.[62] This makes Coutances the diocese which was abandoned by its ministers for the longest time, a century and a half, from 890 to the middle of the eleventh century. The situation of the other episcopal seats was hardly more enviable. Évreux was without a bishop for forty years (c.892–c.933), Bayeux for fifty years (c.876–c.927) and Sées for more than a century (c.881–c.986), like Lisieux (c.876-c.985) and Avranches (c.862–c.990).

Richard's personal role was critical. Three long vacant bishoprics were endowed with bishops almost simultaneously, between 985 and 990. Roger was appointed to Lisieux, in about 985, Azon to Sées, in about 986, and Norgod to Avranches in about 990. During the same years, the other bishoprics also received new bishops: Bayeux in 986 (Ralph of Avranches), Rouen in 987–9 (Robert), Évreux in about 988 (Gerald) and Coutances in about 989 (Hugh). In a few years, the duke had completely renewed the Norman episcopate.[63]

Before the new bishops were appointed, the possessions of the bishoprics had had to be restored. The duke had set an example by ceding a certain number of estates, and had been able to persuade many aristocrats to imitate him. Their reward mostly consisted of having members of their own families appointed as bishops. In this way, the restored properties remained under their control. We do not know for certain that this was the case in the tenth century, since the sources are virtually silent about the origins of the bishops, but the practice is well attested in the first half of the eleventh century. We need only look at the examples of Sigefroi and Yves of Sées. Sigefroi seems to have been related to the Bellêmes and Yves was actually the son of Wiliam I Talvas, Lord of Bellême. The powerful Bellême family was to exert a direct influence over the bishopric for much of the eleventh century.[64]

In the tenth century, there is only one well-known example, that of Robert, Archbishop of Rouen. Duke Richard I was determined to keep control over the bishopric of Rouen, and so entrusted it to his own son, Robert, who must have been quite young when he acceded to the episcopate. Robert did not, however, renounce the lay life, since he also received the County of Évreux, and as such was married and had three sons. Robert may not have been a very religious prelate, but he was a cultured man who was able to attract men of letters, such as the satirist Granier and the Irish poet Moriuht,[65] to the episcopal court. He had no hesitation in bringing intellectuals long distances to form what has been called his 'literary coterie'. It was in this context that Dudo of Saint-Quentin arrived in Rouen. Robert came to play a vital role in the duchy, especially during the periods of minority of the dukes, such as that of Richard II from 996 to 1001, and especially that of William the Bastard from 1035 to 1037.[66]

Robert was the first of a whole series of bishops who belonged to the ducal family, for example his successor, Richard II's illegitimate son Malger, who was Archbishop of Rouen from 1037 to 1054, or the two sons of Richard I's half-brother Count Ralph of Ivry: Hugh, Bishop of Bayeux from c.1011 to c.1049,[67] and John, Bishop of Avranches from 1060 to 1067, then Archbishop of Rouen from 1067 to 1079. Last but not least, there was William the Bastard's half-brother Odo of Conteville, Bishop of Bayeux from 1049 to 1097, who also acceded to the episcopate at a very young age and became, after 1066, William the Conqueror's virtual second-in-command.[68]

Before anything else, these bishops were great lords. They continued to practise a lifestyle befitting their social rank. They were more at home on the field of battle than in their cathedrals, and their favourite leisure pursuit was hunting. On the other hand, most would prove to be good administrators, showing great skill at enlarging the propery of their bishoprics. Far more concerned with temporal than with spiritual matters, they were sometimes drawn into power struggles which could lead to military confrontations. A case in point was Yves of Bêlleme, who fulfilled the functions of both Lord of Bêlleme and Bishop of Sées. In about 1048, in circumstances that remain mysterious, he found himself in the position of fighting enemies of his family who had entrenched themselves in his cathedral. To dislodge them, the hot-headed bishop saw no other solution than to set fire to the building, casuing a great scandal, which came to the attention of Leo IX, one of the first reforming popes. During the Council of Rheims in 1049, Leo addressed him with these words: 'What did you do, you perfidious man? You should be condemned by the law for daring to consign your mother to the flames.'[69] The pope was of course referring to the cathedral, which was the mother church of the diocese.

Another Norman bishop also had a brush with the pope at the same council, Geoffrey of Montbray, Bishop of Coutances. He was accused of simony, that is, of having bought his bishopric. The bishoprics, whose possessions had been won back and enlarged, were considered major sources of revenue, and were therefore highly coveted. Accused before the Council of Rheims, Geoffrey defended himself skilfully by claiming that his brother had bought the bishopric without his knowledge. He got away with having to make an oath, supposedly proving his good faith.[70]

Such men were not at all the the kind of bishop the popes of the Gregorian reform, from Leo IX to Gregory VII, were trying to promote. Naturally, the conduct of the bishops reflected that of the rest of the clergy. Most priests were openly married, not only in cathedral chapters but also in rural parishes, where the living was passed from father to son. The principal ills of the Church, in Normandy as elsewhere, were simony (the purchase of ecclesiastical offices) and Nicolaism (marriage or concubinage of priests).[71] To this must be added the grip of the temporal power over the clergy. In Normandy, it was the duke who appointed the bishops and, before long, the abbots of the principal monasteries.

From the beginning of the eleventh century, the dukes supported the efforts of the papacy to bring about reform.

Richard II authorized a famous monk, Richard, Abbot of Saint-Vanne, to come to Normandy to preach reform.[72] He even helped him to organize a pilgrimage to the Holy Land, granting him his patronage and making a financial contribution.[73] William the Bastard went further in the direction of reform by deposing Malger, the notoriously unworthy Archbishop of Rouen, during the Council of Lisieux in 1054 or 1055.[74] In his place, he installed Maurilius, a former monk from the ducal shrine of Fécamp, who was the prototype of the reforming prelate. The Norman dukes could be said to have led the way in Church reform. They supported the popes in their struggle against simony and Nicolaism. On the other hand, they refused absolutely to give up their right to make appointments, which would have meant renouncing their power over bishops and abbots – this despite the fact that the independence of the Church from the temporal authorities was one of the main planks of the reform movement, and was the main cause of the long drawn-out conflict between the popes and the Germanic emperors, the so-called Investiture Controversy. During the eleventh century, the reforming popes were too preoccupied with this major conflict to deal with the Dukes of Normandy, who also practised 'lay investitures'. But the conflict eventually broke out in the twelfth century, between the popes and the kings of England.

Finally, the dukes of the tenth and eleventh centuries played a major role in the rebirth of the monasteries. As we have seen, there were very few surviving abbeys in the province. Saint-Ouen de Rouen seems to have come under the direct control of the bishop. A new abbot was not appointed until the rule of Richard I, in about 960.[75] The other abbey was Mont-Saint-Michel, which housed a community of canons and monks following the Celtic rite.[76] It seems to have been on Richard I's initiative, once again, that a group of Benedictine monks led by Maynard I settled there in 965.[77] Subsequently his nephew and successor, Maynard II, also became Abbot of Redon and the Mont moved back within the Breton orbit. Ricard II took the situation in hand again in 1023, by sending Abbot Theodoric there from Fécamp.[78]

The monastery of Fécamp was the emblematic shrine of the dukes and the true point of departure of the monastic renewal in Normandy. Richard I was born in Fécamp and remained attached to the place all his life. He built a palace there, the remains of which have been excavated by Annie Renoux.[79] Next to it, the duke restored a former convent which had disappeared during the invasions, established a community of twelve canons, and in 990 rebuilt a magnificent church, of which Dudo of Saint-Quentin has left us a detailed description.[80] He would have liked to establish a monastery there, but Abbot Maiolus of Cluny, who was asked, made excessive demands.[81] Richard II, though, was able to realize his father's dream. In 1001, he managed to persuade William of Volpiano to settle in Fécamp. This Italian from Piedmont was influenced by Cluny: indeed, it was Maiolus himself who had brought him to France. Like many reforming abbots, he held several posts concurrently. He had been the Abbot of Sainte-Benigne de Dijon since 989 and was also the abbot of four other monasteries in Burgundy. William fulfilled his mission in Fécamp, founding a community of reformed Benedictines.[82] This abbey applied the rule of Saint Benedict, which was then the only one in use in the West, using methods similar to those of Cluny.

The Fécamp community was to have a great deal of influence throughout Normandy.[83] William of Volpiano, with a number of his Italian and Burgundian disciples, were the agents of monastic reform in the province. In 1017, Theodoric, who had been a monk in Dijon, became Abbot of Jumièges and fulfilled this function concurrently with that of warden of Bernay, a monastery founded by Duchess Judith. Shortly afterwards, the duke tried to regain control of Mont-Saint-Michel, which was no easy matter, as the monks guarded their independence jealously, and were probably not very favourably disposed towards reform. A first attempt was made in 1024, with a Roman named Suppo, another disciple of William of Volpiano, but he was chased away by the monks. A further attempt was made in 1024, with Theodoric, Abbot of Jumièges, with no greater success. Theodoric was soon forced to go back to Jumièges, where he died in 1027. After another abbot named Almod, Suppo finally managed to assume the post. He was to stay from 1033 to 1042.[84]

In 1028, William of Volpiano resigned the office of Abbot of Fécamp, ceding it to another of his disciples, John of Ravenna, who would occupy it for fifty years, until 1078.[85] The monastic restoration movement which he had initiated was continued, first by dukes Robert the Magnificent and William the Bastard, then by a number of lay barons, who all wished to build family abbeys. A few examples may be mentioned here. In Rouen, the Count of Arques and his wife restored the convent of Saint-Amand and founded the abbey of La Trinité-du-Mont in 1030.[86] In the valley of the Risle, Humphrey of Vieilles and his son, Roger of Beaumont, also founded both a convent and a monastery in Préaux: Saint-Pierre in 1034 and Saint-Léger in 1050.[87] In 1046, the Count of Eu's widow, Lesceline, founded the convent of Saint-Pierre-sur-Dives, which almost immediately was forced to move to Lisieux.[88] William fitz Osbern, a companion of William the Bastard, was responsible for two abbeys, in Lyre (1046) and Cormeilles (1060).[89] Last but not least, there is the special case of the abbey of Le Bec, founded not by an aristocratic family, but by a mere knight, Herluin, who became its first abbot. Founded in 1034, it would soon become a great intellectual centre thanks to the renown of its school, made famous by its Italian masters, Lanfranc of Pavia and Anselm of Aosta.[90] These Benedictine institutions were great breeding grounds for the future bishops and abbots of Normandy and – very soon – England.

From Rollo to Richard II and William the Bastard, the dukes became convinced Christians and increasingly strong supporters of the Church and the reform movement. However, the matrimonial practices of the first dukes were a long way from those laid down by the Church. This may have been one of the reasons for the slowness of the 're-Christianization' of the province, which only really took shape in the 990s. The question of ducal marriages is worth examining, since it shows the persistence of the customs the dukes had inherited from their Scandinavian ancestors.

Wives and concubines

The first dukes of Normandy contracted marriages with women from the Frankish aristocracy: Rollo with Gisela, daughter of King Charles the Simple, William Longsword with Luitgarde, daughter of Herbert II of Vermandois, in 935, and Richard I with Emma, the sister of Hugh Capet, in about 960, when the duke was about thirty.[91] These marriages were obviously highly political unions, which made it possible for the Norman dukes to become part of the network of alliances within the Frankish world. At a time when the kings, whether Carolingian or Robertian, were weak and their authority often disputed, it was the territorial rulers who wielded effective power. They made an effort to restore a balance that was constantly under threat. From this effort a dominant figure sometimes emerged: Herbert II of Vermandois until his death in 943,[92] then Hugh the Great, son of Robert I, until his death in 956.[93] His son Hugh Capet was able to recover only part of his lands and influence, after a difficult period of minority; the rest was disputed between the Dukes of Normandy and the Counts of Blois.[94]

In the second half of the tenth century and at the beginning of the eleventh century, the Duke of Normandy's chief adversary was the Count of Blois and Chartres, the principal heir of the old house of Vermandois. The counts of Blois contemporary with Richard I were Theobald the Trickster and his son Odo. Here, too, matrimonial politics played a vital role. When Theobald the Trickster became the second husband of William Longsword's widow Luitgarde, a conflict broke out over the border region of the Avre, where Luitgarde had kept property which was part of her dower.[95] The confrontation between the two houses were revived a generation later, between Richard II and the then Count of Blois, Odo II. Once again, the conflict had its origins in a matrimonial affair. In an attempt to establish peaceful relations with Odo, Richard had given him his sister Matilda in marriage (before 1005). Part of her dowry was half the manor of Dreux,[96] but Matilda died prematurely, and Richard, following the custom, claimed this territory. When Odo refused him, war ensued in 1013.[97]

Most marriages contracted by the dukes of Normandy proved childless. Neither Gisela, nor Luitgarde, nor Emma gave children to Rollo, William and Richard I. We may well wonder why. These princesses might have been very young when they married, which would not be unusual. Some no doubt died before reaching childbearing age. One of them did, however, give birth to children: Luitgarde had at least three with her second husband, Theobald the Trickster.[98]

Apart from these 'official' spouses, the first dukes had many concubines. There was nothing exceptional about this: the same could be said about most rulers at this time. There was nevertheless an important difference. The other territorial rulers only considered children born from official marriages as heirs, whereas the Norman rulers also recognized their illegitimate children. Rollo's three successors were all illegitimate: William Longsword, the son of Popa, Ricard I, the son of Sprota, and Ricard II, the son of Gonnor. Popa was a Frankish princess and Sprota a Breton concubine. As for Gonnor, she belonged to a family of Scandinavian origin which had settled in Pays de Caux. When they mention these unofficial unions, the Norman authors of the eleventh centuries, starting with William of Jumièges, describe them as being marriages *more danico*, 'in the Danish manner'.[99] This kind of union may be related to the Germanic tradition, sanctioned in Scandinavian law, in which cohabitation was recognized as a legal marriage. The concubines of the first dukes were considered legitimate wives, like the *frilla* in the Nordic world.

The case of Gonnor is particularly interesting. Her union with Richard I began in the 960s, and many children issued from it: Richard the Crown Prince, Robert, the future Archbishop of Rouen, Malger, who became Count of Corbeil, Robert the Dane and three daughters who made prestigious marriages, Emma, Hawise and Matilda. The union of Richard I and Gonnor seems to have been regularized in about 980, making Gonnor a true 'duchess of Normandy', the first we know. Gonnor's children were considered legitimate not only by the Normans, but also by other territorial rulers, who had no hesitation in marrying their own children to them. Richard I also had other concubines, who gave birth to Geoffrey, William, Robert (?), Papia and Beatrice. All were recognized by the duke as the equals of Gonnor's children.[100]

Overall, these descendants of dukes Richard I and Richard II were known as the 'Richardides', a term we already find in Dudo of Saint-Quentin. They formed the hard core of the Norman aristocracy, and the dukes relied on them to govern the duchy. When they reached adulthood, the male children had the right to the title of 'count', although still subject to the authority of the Count of Rouen, that is, the duke himself. The first to bear this title was not strictly speaking a Richardide nor even a son of the duke. This was Count Ralph of Ivry, the son of Sprota and her second husband, Eperlenc. His principal estates were situated in upper Normandy, around Rouen and the valley of the Eure, including the border castle of Ivry. He also had substantial lands in lower Normandy, in the diocese of Bayeux.[101] Ralph played a major role during the minority of Richard II and seems to have been the principal sponsor of the work of Dudo of Saint-Quentin.[102]

At first, the title of count was not linked to a specific territory. Subsequently, from the beginning of the eleventh century, the counts would each be given the task of defending a particular area of the border. Ralph's successors continued as counts of Ivry, but each of the Richardides had to be granted territory. We already know Robert, son of Gonnor, Count of

Évreux and Archbishop of Rouen. The sons of the other concubines also received counties: Geoffrey was given Brionne (on the Risle), William was granted first Exmes, then Eu (on the Bresle), and Robert received Avranches.[103] Later, two other border counties were established (or re-established) for new offspring of the ducal families, Hiémois and Mortainais.[104] The intention here was to take control of the southern border, which was not yet strongly established.

The first generation of Richardides was joined by a second generation, the children of Richard II. The situation, though, had completely changed. For Richard II, marriage *more danico* was now out of the question. This change can be explained by this duke's personal convinctions, but also by the evolution of the Church, in which the forerunners of the Gregorian reform were becoming active. Whatever the reason, Richard II married Judith of Brittany quite legally. This marriage, blessed by the Church, was celebrated in symbolic fashion in the abbey of Mont-Saint-Michel (before 1008).[105] From now on, it would be much more difficult to have an illegitimate son, born outside a princely marriage, accepted as an heir. This explains the difficulties encountered by young William the Bastard during his minority. This initial handicap did not stop him becoming a remarkable statesman and the conqueror of England. His predecessors, the dukes of the tenth and eleventh centuries, had maintained continuous, and sometimes conflictual, relations with their great island neighbour. To understand the events of 1066, which was to change the course of history, we need to go back and examine the first contacts between Normandy and England.

From Normandy to England

The Channel was never an insurmountable barrier. Contacts of all kinds existed during the Middle Ages between Great Britain and the northern coasts of the Kingdom of France. Alliances were forged between the Anglo-Saxon kings, especially those of Wessex, and the kings of the Franks or the territorial rulers within the kingdom. Baldwin I, Count of Flanders, married Judith, daughter of Charles the Bald, who had peviously been married to two kings of Wessex, Ethelwulf and Ethelbald. In 884, Baldwin's heir, Baldwin II, married Elfrida (Aelfthryth), the daughter of Alfred the Great. In 919, the Carolingian king Charles the Simple married Edgiva (Eadgifu), the daughter of Edward the Elder. At the time of Robert I's coup, in 922, Edgiva took refuge in England with her son, which is why he was called Louis *d'Outremer* ('from beyond the sea'). It was in England, too, that Mathuedoi, the Breton Count of Poher, and his son Alan Wrybeard sought refuge when their territory was attacked by a large force of Vikings in 920.[106]

Edward the Elder's successor on the throne of Wessex was Athelstan, a dynamic king who in 927 won great prestige by subjugating the Scandinavian Kingdom of York. He forged matrimonial ties with the main powers of the time. One of his sisters, Eadhild, married Hugh the Great in 926, and his other sister married Otto I, King of Germany,[107] making the Robertian Hugh the brother-in-law of his Carolingian rival, Charles the Simple. These two dynasties who fought over the kingdom actively sought the protection of the Anglo-Saxon king. Athelstan is mentioned by Dudo under the name Alstemus.[108] According to Dudo, a close relationship formed between Athelstan, who had the title 'Basileus of the English and of all Britain',[109] and the Duke of Normandy. This is hardly surprising, given that Rollo had spent a great deal of time in England and that William Longsword was also born 'beyond the sea'.[110] William played a vital role in the two major events of the year 936: the restoration of the Carolingian dynasty with the seizure of power by Louis IV d'Outremer, and the reconquest of Brittany by Alan Wrybeard, who was able to put an end to the state established by the Normans of the Loire.[111]

Subsequently, relations deteriorated between Duke Richard I and King Ethelred of England. Ethelred was subjected to constant Viking attacks and accused his Norman neighbour of supporting the aggressors. Pope John XV had to intervene to reconcile the two rulers. His legate managed to negotiate a peace treaty, which was concluded on 18 March 991. The two parties promised not to aid their respective enemies. This agreement had fortunate consequences. Trade developed on both sides of the Channel and the Normans were able, among other things, to export French wine to the port of London.[112]

It can be seen that in the tenth century and at the beginning of the eleventh century the Duke of Normandy pursued an independent foreign policy, which owed nothing to his suzerain lord, the King of France. He was not the only one in this position. Other territorial rulers acted in the same way: William V, Duke of Aquitaine (towards Italy), Odo II, Count of Blois then of Champagne (towards the Kingdom of Burgundy), and Baldwin IV, Count of Flanders (towards the empire, but also towards England, where he was in competition with the Normans).

At the time of Richard II, the situation of England deteriorated further. The kingdom faced a second wave of Scandinavian invasions, which began in the 980s, according to the chronology established by Lucien Musset.[113] This wave, in fact, more or less affected only England, which was subjected to repeated attacks by the Danish army of King Sven Forkbeard. Relations between England and Normandy were again bad. Ethelred believed that the Normans had failed to respect the terms of the treaty of 991 and that they were favouring a hostile enterprise, by allowing the Danes to take shelter along the coast of the duchy.[114] In 1000 or 1001, the King of England even launched a reprisal attack on the Cotentin coast, but the English who landed were almost completely wiped out by Viscount Nigel.[115]

The young Duke Richard and Count Ralph, who held the reins of power, realized the danger: they started new negotiations with Ethelred. These quickly led to an agreement, sealed by a marriage. The duke's sister Emma was given in marriage to Ethelred in 1002. Two half-Norman sons would emerge from this union, Edward and Alfred.[116] In the short term, the King of

England tried to take advantage of this new alliance. Many Scandinavians were still living in England after the fall of the Danelaw kingdoms. Ethelred now saw them as the enemy within, and planned a massacre of all the Scandinavians in his kingdom, which was supposed to take place on Saint Brice's day, 13 November 2002. But the plan backfired. There were many survivors and King Sven used the attack as a pretext to launch an outright war. He attacked with increasingly large armies, in 1003, 1006 and 1009. In 1013, Ethelred was forced out of his kingdom: he found refuge in Normandy with his queen, Emma, and their two sons. But then Sven died unexpectedly on 3 February 1014, and Ethelred set off with Emma to regain his kingdom. His two sons were left in safekeeping in Normandy.[117]

The war was not over. Sven's son, Cnut, took up the torch. On the Anglo-Saxon side the troops were led by Edmond Ironside, the son of Ethelred and an English concubine named Aelfgifu. Two Scandinavian 'kings of the sea', Lacman and Olaf, the future King of Norway,[118] took part in the fighting, perhaps on the English side. This last stand by the Anglo-Saxons proved to be in vain. Ethelred and Edmund Ironside both died in 1016.[119] Cnut became King of England and in 1017 forced Queen Emma to marry him, which was a clever way to legitimize his conquest. The kingdom was to remain under Danish domination for a quarter of a century, until 1042. Richard II was obliged to recognize the *fait accompli*, especially as his sister remained queen of England. Strong ties would be forged between the English and Norman princes, who were cousins. This goes some way to explaining the unusual evolution of Anglo-Norman relations under Robert the Magnificent and William the Conqueror.

5

ROBERT THE MAGNIFICENT

The legitimate son of Duke Richard I and Duchess Judith, Robert was a remarkable figure who stands out among the other Dukes of Normandy. He died young, at the age of about twenty-five, having been duke for only eight years. His story is known to us through the work of William of Jumièges, writing some twenty-five years – a whole generation – after his death[1]. The few pages that William of Jumièges devotes to him leave many questions unanswered. Some of these blanks were filled in, more than a century later, by Wace[2] and Benedict.[3] Unlike William of Jumièges, these authors were not writing books of history in Latin, but epic poems in French, intended to be recited, or even sung, although they certainly had a historical element. Wace and Benedict were not addressing the same public as the ecclesiastical authors of the eleventh century: they were writing for the brilliant court of Henry II and Eleanor of Aquitaine, whose favourite authors they were.

Duke Robert was the first of the dynasty to be given this title, usually reserved for younger sons.[4] In the family, the eldest traditionally bore the name Richard, as the three dukes Richard I, II and III who succeeded one another between 942 and 1027, that is, over eighty-five years (three generations). Richard II's youngest son, Robert, had the same name as his uncle, Robert, Archbishop of Rouen, who played a vital role during his period of rule and survived him, dying only in 1037. Duke Robert has been given several nicknames by historians. He is sometimes called Robert the Liberal, recalling his undoubted generosity towards the Church in his later years. The nickname Robert the Devil can immediately be dismissed, deriving as it does from an unfortunate confusion between the duke and a legendary character.[5] The nickname Robert the Magnificent is far preferable, and conveys well his colourful, adventurous side. Before and just after the beginning of his rule, he seems to have been an unruly young man. Subsequently, he changed drastically, becoming a responsible statesman who took to heart his role as leader of the rich Duchy of Normandy, restored ducal authority, and intervened in the royal domain and in the neighbouring principalities, Brittany and Flanders. Last but not least, he embarked on an independent foreign policy, becoming closely involved in the affairs of England, and displaying a real spirit of adventure. This final element led him to undertake a dangerous pilgrimage to Jerusalem. Rebellious by nature, he refused to submit to any authority, especially that of his brother Richard III.

Brothers and enemies

Richard III was far from being an insignificant ruler. He had been well prepared by his father to take over the duchy. At the end of his rule, Richard II had entrusted him with the command of a military expedition to the country of Burgundy,[6] some 400 kilometres from Normandy,[7] in order to help the duke's son-in-law, Count Renaud of Burgundy, who had been imprisoned by his enemy Hugh, Bishop of Auxerre and Count of Chalon-sur-Saône.[8] Richard III managed to seize the castle of Mimande[9] and was on his way to Chalon when Hugh surrendered and freed

Renaud. Richard III seems to have continued and strengthened the traditional alliance between the Dukes of Normandy and the Capetian kings of France. This alliance was to be strengthened by his intended marriage to Adela, the very young daughter of King Robert the Pious. This marriage had been the object of intense negotiation between the two parties. We know the result thanks to an extremely important document, the dower granted to Adela.[10] As was the custom, the young princess received a large amount of land and property in Normandy, taken from the ducal estate. The intention was to protect her interests in case of her husband's premature death. She would be entitled to keep these possessions for herself, which would allow her to live as befitted her rank. The negotiations had probably begun while Richard II was still alive, but were not finalized until the accession of Richard III. The document is dated January, probably in the year 1027. Adele was to receive a large part of Cotentin, including the town of Coutances, Valogne and the castle of Cherbourg, and the estate of Caen, which was still semi-rural.[11] These arrangements were never put into practice.[12]

On the death of his father, Richard III had no difficulty in asserting his authority over the barons of the duchy: he apparently succeeded Richard II without any problems. The only person to question his accession was his young brother, Robert, who had received a territory to administer, far from the capital of the duchy, the County of Hiémois. This county was situated in central Normandy, between the sea and the southern border.[13] Its capital was the fortified town of Exmes,[14] which during the unrest of the High Middle Ages had served as a refuge for the monks of Sées. The choice of this 'privilege'[15] was perhaps not very well judged. It was in a region that had not really submitted to the authority of the duke in Rouen.[16] Besides its capital, the county included a new fortess at Falaise,[17] which would become Robert's favourite residence: it was here that he met his lover Herleva. The fact remains that Robert rebelled against his brother Richard III. It was the classic rebellion of the younger against the elder brother, of which there were many in the history of these principalities, and even in the history of the Capetian kings. The problem was quickly resolved.[18] Richard III besieged Robert in Falaise, and Robert surrendered. He had to pay his brother a vassal's homage, and everything went back to normal. He was not, apparently, deprived of the County of Hiémois.[19]

Richard died in August 1027, having been duke for only a year. His death remains shrouded in mystery. He was still very young, not much more than twenty. William of Jumièges claims that he died of poisoning,[20] but says nothing about who might have been responsible. Later historians studied the question, and wondered who stood to benefit from the crime. The twelfth-century English monk William of Malmesbury was the first person to name Robert the Magnificent as the culprit.[21] It was a serious accusation, much repeated subsequently, which greatly damaged his reputation. It was in this perspective that Robert's pilgrimage to the Holy Land was interpreted as a penance, an attempt to obtain forgiveness for his 'crime'.

Did Robert the Magnificent really murder his brother to become duke? In reality, we have no idea. In the absence of convincing documentation, we ought perhaps to give him the benefit of the doubt. It is by no means even certain that Richard III was murdered. Of course, the death of this young ruler in the prime of life caught everyone's imagination. But we know how fragile human life was in the Middle Ages. A serious intestinal condition could well have presented the same symptoms as poisoning and, in the absence of effective medication, led to a similar death. Whatever the cause, Richard's premature death would allow Robert to accede to the ducal throne at the age of about seventeen.

The difficult beginnings of a rebel prince
Robert came to power in difficult conditions. Even apart from possible suspicions of murder, the new duke seemed to be an unruly and inexperienced adolescent. His close relations, the

Richardides, had hoped to seize power. The most powerful of them were two churchmen, Robert, Archbishop of Rouen and Count of Évreux, and Hugh of Ivry, Bishop of Bayeux. Archbishop Robert must have assumed that he was in a perfect position to exercise some kind of regency. For his part, Hugh remembered that his father, Ralph of Ivry, had held the reins of power during the minority of Ricard II, from 996 to 1001, and may have envisaged playing the same role for Duke Robert.

There is every reason to believe that these two men of the Church, who were also great lords, disputed the authority of the new duke. What we know for certain is that Robert the Magnificent besieged them in their respective strongolds of Évreux and Ivry. Based on the border of the duchy, Hugh appealed to Frenchmen from the royal domain to reinforce his garrison. He could not have done this without at least the tacit support of King Robert the Pious and Queen Constance, who probably considered that the traditional alliance between the king and the Duke of Normandy had been broken by the death of their son-in-law Richard III. Whatever the case, Hugh of Bayeux's attempt failed lamentably. The French reinforcements did not arrive in time, and the duke managed to seize the castle of Ivry. The outcome was a long exile for the bishop.[22] The struggle with Archbishop Robert was more difficult. The archbishop could not long withstand the duke's onslaught against Évreux, any more than Hugh had been able to resist at Ivry. He therefore went into exile in France, where he consulted his colleagues in the episcopate, primarily Fulbert of Chartres.[23] Fulbert advised him to use spiritual weapons against a duke who was considered a rebel against the Church. The archbishop promptly excommunicated the duke and may even have placed an interdict on the duchy.[24] This was an extremely severe punishment, which banned clerics from saying mass and distributing the sacraments. Affecting the Christian population of the province like this was a way of putting pressure on the duke.

It was during this troubled period that the duke began confiscating Church property. He may well have personally seized a number of possessions of the abbey of Fécamp, including Argences,[25] Heudbouville[26] and Maromne.[27] In fact, we only know of these early seizures from the charters that later restored these properties.[28] According to the terms of one of these charters, the duke gave 'pernicious advice' to certain great lords. For example, Roger I of Montgommery, based in the south of Pays d'Auge,[29] destroyed Vimoutiers market, which had been created by the monks of Jumièges.[30] Much more confiscation of Church property must have taken place at the beginning of Robert's rule, especially from the bishoprics of Rouen and Bayeux, whose bishops were considered rebels.[31]

The unruly young man called attention to himself on another matter: he refused to marry officially. He was involved in a relationship with a young woman from Falaise named Herleva, whom he had certainly known before his accession. The story of this young woman is as much part of legend as of history. The known facts are few. What we do know derives from the work of Orderic Vitalis,[32] written in about 1110. When he was Count of Hiémois, during the rule of Richard III, Robert liked to reside in the new fortress of Falaise. It was there that he met Herleva, whom the authors of the eleventh century call Arlot – in modern French Arlette. She was the daughter of a *polinctor*, that is, an artisan in leather, a tanner or embalmer.[33] In any case, Herleva was of much lower social rank than Robert. In the previous century she would have been considered a *frilla*, a legal concubine, and her children would have been legitimized without any problem, but this was a period in which the Church was increasing its control over marriage, especially the marriages of kings and other rulers.[34] It should be remembered that Robert himself was the son of a perfectly legal marriage between his father and Judith, daughter of the Duke of Brittany. In matters such as this, it was out of the question to put the clock back.

What happened is the stuff of legend, a legend that first appeared in the work of the twelfth-century authors Wace[35] and Benedict[36] and then was developed by later writers and has come all the way down to the present day. At one time, guides to the castle of Falaise used to tell visitors how the Count of Hiémois had noticed Arlette from one of the windows of the keep as she was washing clothes in the river Ante.[37] Unafraid of anachronism, they had no hesitation in pointing out the window in question, overlooking 'Arlette's fountain' – despite the fact that this keep was built by Henri I Beauclerc, nearly a century later. Be that as it may, Herleva gave birth to William, and the duke made him his heir, despite the conditions of his birth.[38] The enemies of the young William would later have no hesitation in branding him a bastard. Robert clearly cared about his son's mother and took the trouble to regularize her situation a few years after his accession,[39] at a time when his attitudes, especially with regard to the Church, were undergoing a radical change after his early, erring ways. This change can be seen as the turning point of his rule.

Back to the straight and narrow

The archbishop and the duke, representing the two powers, had finally understood that they had to find common ground. They therefore began negotiations. To obtain the lifting of the excommunication and the interdict, the duke was forced to recall the archbishop, reinstate him in all his offices, spiritual and temporal, and restore all his property. For his part, the archbishop had drawn the lesson from these events that his nephew would never let anyone control him. For the rest of his rule, he would remain loyal to him.[40]

Robert's change of attitude towards the Church can be seen in his charters.[41] These documents rarely have dates attached, so that it is difficult to know when exactly these new arrangements were made. According to Lucien Musset, the reconciliation between the two Roberts took place in 1028,[42] certainly before 1030. The first thing to be done was to restore the heritage of the archbishopric of Rouen. Many nobles had taken advantage of the circumstances to seize Church property.[43] In two practically similar documents,[44] the duke and the archbishop noted the deplorable state of the possessions of the cathedral of Rouen.[45] They first listed those which were still held by the archbishop: Pierreval, near Rouen, several estates in the Talou and 'Vy' in French Vexin.[46] They next restored many properties in the counties of Rouen, Talou and Hiémois, in Pays de Caux and Évrechin, in Norman Vexin and in Beauvaisis. This joint restitution suggests that the archbishop had also seized property from his own church. This is far from impossible: the archbishop was also a secular ruler, as Count of Évreux.[47]

During the following years, Duke Robert was to go further. In about 1030, when he was about twenty, he seems to have manifested a sincere desire for reconciliation with the Church. He may well have been influenced by a number of great lords who wished to redeem their sins by making large gifts and even founding new institutions. The most convincing example is that of Viscount Gisselin of Arques, and his wife Emmeline. In 1030, when they founded the abbey of La Trinité-du-Mont,[48] the duke confirmed their gifts and exempted the monastery from any obligation to him.[49] Robert gave property or rights to many Norman abbeys, such as Saint-Ouen de Rouen, Saint-Wandrille, Jumièges, Mont-Saint-Michel – in other words, the main institutions in Normandy at the time.[50] He of course had a particular interest in Fécamp.

The abbey of Fécamp was the principal ducal monastery, founded by Robert's father and grandfather, Richard I and Richard II, who were buried there. By 1034, Robert had restored its main estates, Heudebouville, Maromne and Argences,[51] which had been confiscated in his youth. It is unlikely that the monks really wanted to keep an estate as far-flung as Argences, in the diocese of Bayeux. On the other hand, Bishop Hugh of Ivry certainly was interested in the estate, which must explain the curious arrangement concluded in Fécamp on 11 April 1034, at the instigation of the Bishop of Bayeux.[52] Hugh proposed to the monks that they give him the land at Argences for the duration of his life in return for a hundred 'guests', that is, peasants not attached to a particular estate.[53] In addition, he gave the abbey three churches, two estates and twenty 'free men', in other words, freemen depending on the bishop. It was about this time, in fact, that serfdom disappeared in Normandy, which distinguished it from other regions of the kingdom. On the bishop's death, Argences would revert to Fécamp, which could still keep his gifts. This agreement was clearly very attractive to the abbey. The fact that it was ratified by the duke suggests that it may have been the price paid by the bishop, a former rebel, for his return to favour. He was also to be involved with another abbey founded by Robert in his diocese.

The deed of foundation of Cerisy is dated 12 November 1032 and explicitly mentions the presence of the bishop.[54] The duke granted the Benedictine monks a site on the ducal estate,[55] as well as the wood of Molay,[56] the tithes of the Bois-d'Elle[57] and the wood of Maupertuis,[58] and those of the forests of Cerisy and Lyons.[59] He also gave them property in Bayeux, Rouen, Caen, Épinay-sur-Odon[60] and Vienne-en-Bessin.[61] It is worth noting in passing the importance given to forests and vines. The monks received the vineyards of the duke's estate in Rouen and three acres in Argences on which to plant a new vineyard.[62] The new abbey was to be built on the site of an old monastery from the High Middle Ages, which had been destroyed at the time of the Scandinavian invasions. But the foundation had political as well as religious objectives. It was no coincidence that the ducal foundation came within the diocese of the unruly Bishop of Bayeux, who had just made peace with the duke. The principal intention was clearly to keep an eye on him. The first abbot of the new monastery, Durand, came from Rouen, more specifically from the great abbey of Saint-Ouen. Cerisy was the first Benedictine monastery in the western part of Normandy, at the far end of the diocese of Bayeux, very close to Cotentin, in a vast, heavily wooded area. The duke seems to have realized at this time that the Church could help him to extend his authority over the outlying regions of his duchy. Cerisy was a pioneering institution: it would be many more years before any layman followed the duke's example in this region.[63] The founding of the abbey was also, and primarily, the result of Robert's personal choice. If he wanted to repent for the sins of his youth, this was the best way to do it, according to the criteria of the time. The founding of Cerisy was followed by that of Montivilliers.

The restoration of Montivilliers dates from the very end of Robert's rule. The official certificate is precisely dated, 13 January 1035, at Fécamp,[64] which means that it was drawn up during the assembly Robert had called just before he left on his pilgrimage. Once again, this was in the nature of a restitution: in his youth, Robert had seized two dependencies of Montivilliers, the churches of Saint-Aubin de Harfleur and Saint-Martin-du-Manoir.[65] The process that led to the founding of the new abbey had begun some years earlier, at the instigation of a certain Beatrice, apparently the duke's aunt.[66] This pious woman had urged the duke to found the first convent in Normandy.[67] There had once been a convent on the site, founded in 684, but it had disappeared during the Scandinavian invasions. A previous attempt at restoration had taken place under Richard II, who had given the convent to the abbey of Fécamp, but they had made it a simple dependency occupied by monks. Now, in taking back the convent, Robert compensated Fécamp by giving it the abbey of Saint-Taurin d'Évreux.[68] In its founding charter, the duke ceded to the restored convent a number of properties located nearby, in Pays de Caux, including the churches of Montivilliers and Harfleur, the *suburbium* of Montivilliers and the port of Harfleur. Unusually, all these properties were close together. There were only a few outlying donations, like Chiffreville[69] and La Haye-du-Theil.[70] The most remarkable thing is that the duke, with the agreement of Archbishop Robert, granted the abbey exemption from having to pay any episcopal tribute. He was clearly protecting the institution from the authority and interference of the bishop. Montivilliers was to remain an autonomous enclave within the diocese of Rouen until the French Revolution.

The duke's example was followed by a certain number of barons. It is at this period that we see the first abbeys founded by the aristocracy: apart from La Trinité-du-Mont, there were Le Bec[71] and Saint-Pierre de Préaux. We have more information about the last of these, which was founded at this time by Humphrey of Vieilles.[72] In 1035, Robert added his own touch to the new abbey, by giving it the estate of Toutainville[73] – in return, admittedly, for a few gifts: twelve gold *livres*, two coats and two horses. This was Humphrey's payment for the duke's participation, and it bought him protection against any possible confiscation. Following a custom of the time, he slapped his three sons, Roger (of Beaumont), Robert and William, in order for them to keep a vivid memory of the event. Finally, the duke asked his young son William to go there and place the symbol of the donation on the altar of the church of Préaux.[74]

Before leaving for the East, Duke Robert regularized the situation of William's mother, Herleva, by arranging her marriage with a lord from the valley of the Risle named Herluin[75]. Two sons were to be born from this union: Odo, the future Bishop of Bayeux, and Robert, the future Count of Mortain.

From 1028–30, Duke Robert had shown increasing respect for the rights of the Church. In doing so, he had re-established his authority within the duchy, which had been undermined by his youthful actions. He was now in a position to pursue a true external policy, within the Kingdom of France, and even abroad.

A daring external policy

For a long time, the Dukes of Normandy had been close allies of the kings of France. Under Robert the Magnificent, this traditional alliance was to grow weaker. Robert's accession coincided with a serious crisis within the royal family. The king naturally wanted his elder son Henry to succeed him and even had him crowned in 1027, while he himself was still alive. But the queen, Constance of Provence, intrigued for her second son, Robert, to gain the crown. On the death of Robert the Pious in 1031, Henry was forced to flee. He was given refuge in Fécamp by Robert the Magnificent, who pledged him his own support and that of his uncle, Malger, Count of Corbeil[76]. With this help, Henry defeated his brother at the battle of Villeneuve-Saint-Georges,[77] and regained the throne as Henry I. He showed his gratitude to Duke Robert by granting him sovereignty over French Vexin, which had been part of the diocese of Rouen but not of the Duchy of Normandy. Norman influence now extended as far as Pontoise. In fact, this gift would turn out to be a poisoned chalice, which for nearly two centuries would be a bone of contention between the Dukes of Normandy and the kings of France.

Taking advantage of the king's weakness, Robert had no hesitation in intervening militarily in several large fiefdoms in the kingdom, beginning with Flanders. Count Baldwin IV had been in power for more than forty years. No doubt weary of waiting to succeed, his son Baldwin rebelled againt him. He had been boosted in his ambitions by his marriage in 1028 to Princess Adela, the daughter of Robert the Pious, who had previously been betrothed to Ricard III. Baldwin IV was forced to flee and went into exile in Normandy.[78] Robert agreed to lead an expedition to Flanders. He captured the fortress of Chocques[79] and restored Baldwin IV to power.[80] The old count and the young duke were to die almost at the same time, in 1035–6.

All these external interventions were within the Kingdom of France,[81] but Robert also had an interest in the Kingdom of England. For a long time, the Dukes of Normandy had been watching the situation across the Channel, and had formed a close alliance with the Anglo-Saxon royal family.[82] Richard II's policy towards his great northern neighbour had always been cautious. He had been able to contain the revanchist passions of the young English princes, Edward and Alfred, who had taken refuge in Normandy. Robert was closer to them in age and may well have let them persuade him to intervene. What happened next we know from the account by William of Jumièges.[83] Robert assembled a great fleet at Fécamp, but it was blown off course by a storm and did not reach England, instead ending up near Jersey.[84] This failure seems quite curious, and we may wonder if Robert really intended to land in England. Could it be that he had simply made a gesture to satisfy his cousins, the English princes, while harbouring other intentions? Whatever the case, he used the fleet not against the English, but against the Bretons, with whom he was then in conflict.

The Duke of Brittany, Alan III, was also a cousin of Robert the Magnificent, his mother, Hawise, being the sister of Richard II. During his minority, Brittany had been placed under the guardianship of the Duke of Normandy. Alan III tried to take advantage of the unrest that followed the death of Richard II to break free. But Robert retaliated vigorously as soon as his power was consolidated. He first built a powerful fortress on the border.[85] Then he launched a land attack on Brittany. Finally, he took advantage of the presence of his fleet in the area to ravage the coast. Alan III was forced to submit. He asked Archbishop Robert, their mutual uncle, to mediate. A meeting took place at Mont-Saint-Michel, and Alan acknowledged himself Robert's vassal. Through his actions, the Duke of Normandy had re-established, and even strengthened, his hold over the neighbouring duchy.[86]

By the time he was twenty-five, Robert the Magnificent was clearly one of the most powerful rulers in the Kingdom of France, capable of asserting his authority over his neighbours and even having an independent external policy. Obviously, his mysterious expedition to England is mainly of interest because it prefigures that led by his son William thirty years later. But now, at the point where Robert was firmly established in the duchy and the kingdom, he would call everything into question by deciding to leave for Jerusalem.

The journey to Jerusalem

Robert the Magnificent did not leave on a whim. He had clearly thought long and hard about the journey, as William of Jumièges states.[87] We may find such a decision surprising, especially as it led to a tragic conclusion. But pilgrimages were very common in the Middle Ages, to Santiago of Compostella, Rome or Jerusalem. Obviously, a pilgrimage to the Holy Land was the most hazardous. In the first third of the eleventh century, the holy places were still under the control of the Fatimid caliphs of Egypt, who did not put too many obstacles in the way of Christian pilgrims.[88] In 1035, Robert was in the full flower of his youth. His pilgrimage may have been motivated as much by curiosity and a desire for adventure as by religious considerations. Many of his contemporaries made this journey, among them the unruly Count Fulk Nerra of Anjou, who went to Jerusalem four times and always came back.

Whatever the reasons for his departure, the duke made his preparations for the long journey. The main problem to be resolved was the succession. Robert had no legitimate heir and his bastard son was still very young, only seven or eight. For some time, Robert had been doing his best to involve him in the exercise of power. William had put his signature to several documents of his father's and had sometimes added his own donations.[89] Now the duke decided to go further and involve his vassals in the process of succession, using the means given him by feudal law. On 13 January 1035, he held a great assembly in Fécamp, at which the Archbishop of Rouen and the other bishops of the province, as well as the great secular lords, were all present. It was in the course of this meeting that the founding of the abbey of Montivilliers was made official.[90] Then the duke announced his imminent departure and named his son William as his heir. The barons apparently raised no objection. They all agreed to the duke's demand that they pledge an oath of loyalty to William.[91] This bound them to him very firmly. By rebelling against him, as many of them would later do, they would be betraying their oath.

We have few details of the route taken by Robert. Those we do have come from Wace, writing in the following century.[92] According to Wace, the duke travelled to Burgundy, crossed the Alps through the Great St Bernard Pass, and went on to Rome. The reigning pope was Benedict IX, who was then about fifteen.[93] It is not known whether Robert went through southern Italy, where many Normans had already settled. He then travelled across the Byzantine Empire, choosing the land route. Although ill, Robert completed his pilgrimage and reached Jerusalem. He died on the return journey, at Nicaea, not far from the Bosphorus.[94]

Duke Robert had ruled for only eight years. Despite the brevity of his career, he remains an exceptional figure. Considering his youth, he managed to assert his authority to a remarkable extent, both within his duchy and outside. But he was clearly a man with a taste for adventure. Two episodes from his life are particularly deserving of attention, the expedition to England and the pilgrimage to the Holy Land. The first of these remains a mystery, and is of particular interest when we think of what came later. The pilgrimage might only have been an interlude in his rule if Robert had not died during the journey. By dying prematurely, he left his duchy in a disastrous state. Young William was only eight years old when he succeeded his father, and this led to a long period of unrest. He would, however, overcome these difficulties, assert his authority, and embark on the greatest adventure in the history of Normandy, the only one which had truly lasting consequences: the conquest of England.

6

WILLIAM THE CONQUEROR

With William, we come to the climax of the Norman adventure. During the period of his minority, the young bastard's authority was disputed and his life threatened. But he would surmount all these obstacles and become accepted as the true leader of his duchy. He would go further than his father, having more time at his disposal. Early on in his rule, he asserted himself over the King of France and the neighbouring feudal lords, becoming the most powerful territorial ruler in the kingdom. In 1066, he proved himself capable of seizing a favourable opportunity and conquering the Kingdom of England, thus becoming the equal of his suzerain lord, the King of France – a fact which the latter found almost intolerable. In order to achieve this surprising result, William demonstrated unquestionable political and military genius. He was the greatest figure in the history of Normandy, the man who best symbolized the extraordinary collective triumph of the Normans. The expedition he led did not take him far, only to the other side of a narrow arm of the sea. But it was his most successful adventure, one that had been long meditated, and one that led to a lasting political entity, the results of which can still be felt to this day.

A troubled minority

In 1035, William the Bastard was eight years old. His father's death whetted many appetites, and so the young duke was caught between the various factions jockeying for power. At first, Richard I's son, Archbishop Robert, held the reins of power. He was well placed to do so, as the senior member of the Richardides and head of the Church in Normandy. But he was already elderly, and died in 1037. It was at this date that unrest spread throughout the province. The rebels first aimed at the members of William's immediate entourage. Of these, three were particularly important: his tutor, Turold, his guardian, Gilbert of Brionne, and his steward, Osbern of Crépon. They did the best they could to protect the young duke, Osbern even sleeping beside him; but all three were assassinated, Osbern actually in William's bed! It is interesting to note that the assassins did not dare touch the young duke himself. The people who had sent them had not forgotten that they had sworn an oath of loyalty to him at Fécamp a few years earlier.[1] We know the names of at least two of these people, Rudolph of Gacé and William of Montgommery. Rudolph of Gacé, one of Archbishop Robert's sons, seized power and took the title of 'guardian', but clashed with other nobles who wanted to take advantage of the climate of anarchy to advance their own interests.

Prominent among these rebels was the Montgommery family. Roger I had been one of Robert the Magnificent's closest companions.[2] Branded a rebel, he was forced to flee, finding refuge at the court of King Henry I of France, but he had many sons who remained in the duchy. Among them was William, who was killed soon after assassinating the steward Osbern. Roger II forged ties with another rebel family by marrying Mable, the daughter of William II Talvas, the Lord of Bellême.[3]

William of Bellême hoped to take advantage of circumstances to create his own principality – since his possessions were situated on the borders of Normandy, Maine and Perche, he was largely exempt from the duke's authority. Nor were the other territorial rulers in the region able to restrain him. The Lord of Bellême was renowned for his cruelty. He had murdered his first wife in order to marry the daughter of Rudolph of Beaumont, Viscount of Maine, thus forming an alliance with one of the most powerful lords in the region. During the wedding festivities, he had no hesitation in launching a savage attack on one of his guests, his vassal William Giroie, blinding, castrating and mutilating him. William Giroie somehow survived this ordeal, but was left with no other option than to become a monk, at the abbey of Le Bec. His close family naturally wanted to avenge him, which led to a long-standing feud between the Giroies and the Bellêmes.

The events of this period of anarchy are not covered by the contemporary authors William of Jumièges[4] and William of Poitiers, the biographer of William the Conqueror.[5] Both writers had to be tactful, since the chief troublemakers had subsequently become close associates of Duke William. This was particularly true of Roger II of Montgommery and Mable of Bellême. All the preceding information comes from a much later writer, Orderic Vitalis, a monk from the abbey of Saint-Évroult,[6] who wrote after all the protagonists were dead.[7] This abbey had suffered at the hands of the Bellêmes, so Orderic Vitalis was well placed to describe their misdemeanours. For historians, his work is a valuable source for the period 1040 to the 1140s.[8]

During William's minority, many Norman lords built private fortifications without the duke's authorization, all in motte-and-bailey form. In the following century, such fortifications were described by Suger,[9] Abbot of Saint-Denis as 'being born of adultery' – an image that reminds us how unusual the situation of Normandy was within the Kingdom of France.

Ever since Richard I, the Dukes of Normandy had been almost the only territorial rulers to impose their authority over the whole of their territory. They had forbidden private fortifications and taken control of the existing castles, placing ducal garrisons in them, under the command of a castellan. This system of ducal fortresses allowed them to defend the border. The south-east of the duchy, for example, was protected by the castle of Tillières, on the Avre.[10] Its castellan was Gilbert Crespin, who was to find himself involved in the events of these years of anarchy, when the system itself would be put to the test.

The King of France, Henry I, was not at all happy about this fortress, regarding it as having been built to defend Norman territory againt him. During the minority of William, the King Henry could hardly be said to have behaved as a suzerain lord should have behaved towards his vassal in difficulty. According to the feudal rules, he should have protected him; what he did instead was to take advantages of the circumstances, by demanding that the castle of Tillières be surrendered. Rudolph of Gacé and the young duke therefore ordered Gilbert Crespin to hand over the castle to the king, who set about dismantling it.[11] Then he rode through the duchy with much sabre-rattling, getting as far as Argentan,[12] before restoring the castle of Tillières for himself![13] Encouraged perhaps by this royal example, other neighbours of the duchy tried to turn the situation to their advantage. The Duke of Brittany, Alan III, claimed that Robert the Magnificent had entrusted him with the guardianship of his young cousin, William the Bastard. Not being able to prove this, he too now invaded the duchy, but met his death near Vimoutiers.[14] These external interventions also encouraged some of the duke's representatives to become rebels. Such was the case with Thurstan Goz, Viscount of Hiémois, who seized the castle of Falaise in about 1042. This rebellion failed because of the determined stand of Rudolph of Gacé, who laid siege to the castle, in the presence of the young duke. Thurstan Goz surrendered and was forced into exile.[15]

In 1042, William the Bastard was fourteen or fifteen years old, almost an adult. The rebels sensed that it was time for them to risk their all. Thurstan Goz's rebellion had been an individual act of sedition, but can be seen as a foretaste of what was to come. Thurstan was one of the viscounts in the west of the duchy, a region where the duke's authority was not well established. It was here that a much more serious rebellion broke out a few years later, in 1046. This time, the aim was to eliminate William, who was now nearly nineteen. The main rebels were Nigel of Saint-Sauveur, Viscount of Cotentin, Renouf of Briquessart, Viscount of Bayeux, and a number of lords from the region, including Hamon the Toothy, Lord of Creully,[16] Ralph Taisson, Lord of Thury,[17] and Grimoult, who possessed the vast estate of Plessis, in Cinglais.[18] Once again, the eleventh-century authors say little about these events, since most of the rebels subsequently returned to favour.[19] It is Wace who provides most of the details, which are all the more convincing in that he knew the region well.[20] To mount a rebellion on such a grand scale, a leader was needed, if possible one related to the duke's family. The man chosen was Guy of Burgundy, the son of Count Renaud of Burgundy and Richard II's daughter Alice. Guy was also known as Guy of Brionne, having received the castle of Brionne from William the Bastard, his cousin, after the death of Gilbert.

This rebellion was a true conspiracy. According to Wace,[21] the rebels made a vow to 'strike William' – which could mean to strike him dead. They decided to take advantage of a hunting party in the game-rich forests of Cotentin,[22] where, in the castle of Valonges,[23] the duke was due to reside. According to Wace, William was warned by a jester named Goles. He fled at top speed, avoiding the main roads and towns such as Bayeux. He crossed the bay of the Veys at the Saint-Clément[24] ford and headed for Ryes,[25] where he came to a halt. Lord Hubert of Ryes gave him a horse, as well as his three sons as an escort.[26] Crossing the Orne at the Foupendant ford, William at last reached Falaise, his birthplace, and took refuge in the castle.[27]

The victory of Val-ès-Dunes (1047)

Given the seriousness of the rebellion, which involved half his duchy, William, following the rules of feudal law, appealed to his suzerain lord, the King of France. It may seem surprising that he should turn to the man who had invaded Normandy a few years earlier, but he had little choice. Nor could the king shirk his obligation. By acting in this way, William demonstrated his political skill. Royal support was highly symbolic, and might even stop some of the rebels in their tracks. William gathered an army of contingents that had stayed loyal to him, mostly from upper Normandy, and met up with the king's army on the plains to the east of Caen. It was there, between Bellengreville[28] and the Orne, that the battle of Val-ès-Dunes took place, in the spring or summer of 1047.[29]

A detailed account of the battle can be found in Wace's *Roman de Rou*.[30] The duke and the king both approached from the east. William had left from Argences, and met up with Henri at Valmeray.[31] The rebels approached from the west and had their backs to the Orne. The forces seem to have been more or less equal at the point when battle was about to be joined. Then another force arrived from the south. These were the men of Cinglais, led by Ralph Taisson, consisting of some 400 soldiers, including about 140 cavalry. These are the only figures we have regarding the battle. Obviously this force would be a significant asset for whichever side it fought on. Ralph was part of the conspiracy and, like the others, had vowed to 'strike' the duke. But at the crucial moment, he hesitated. He approached William and hit him with his glove, thus fulfilling his vow. Then he offered him his support. This change of sides significantly strengthened William's forces and seemed likely to decide the outcome of the battle – and the duke and the king did indeed win the day. The rebels were driven back towards the Orne where, weighed down by their armour, many drowned.

The leaders either fled or, like Nigel of Saint-Sauveur and Grimoult of Plessis, were taken prisoner. Guy took refuge in his castle at Brionne, to which William laid siege, with the result that Guy was soon forced into exile in Burgundy. The other leaders, too, were deprived of their fiefdoms and condemned to exile, including Nigel and probably Renouf of Briquessart. It should be said that William did not apply the same treatment to all the rebels. He was obliged to treat his great vassals with consideration. Viscounts Nigel and Renouf were soon pardoned, were able to reclaim their property and return to court. On the other hand, the duke was implacable towards the rebels of lower rank, like Grimoult of Plessis, who was confined in the tower of Rouen where he was soon killed, without any form of trial.[32] His estate was confiscated and later given to the church of Bayeux.[33]

After the battle, William set about restoring order to the duchy. In Normandy, the duke was traditionally the guarantor of the 'duke's peace'. Since the end of the tenth century, the Church had been trying to promote 'God's peace'. Monks such as Richard, Abbot of Saint-Vanne de Verdun, had come to the region to preach peace. The objective was to protect clerics and unarmed laymen, and to avoid wars between Christians, especially private wars between feudal lords. For a long time, this kind of confrontation had remained very infrequent in Normandy, thanks to the effectiveness of ducal authority, but this had ceased to be the case since 1035. William wanted to turn his victory to good account. With the Church's support, he organized a peace council in the new town of Caen.[34]

This assembly seems to have taken place in the open air, on the right bank of the Orne, and was attended by bishops, clerics and monks. The monks from the abbey of Saint-Ouen de Rouen brought with them the relics of their patron saint.[35] It should be noted, however, that the bishop of the diocese, Hugh of Bayeux, was not present. It is very likely that he had had connections with the rebels, since the conspiracy had been hatched in Bayeux,[36] but he was ostentatiously absent from both the battle and the council. In 1047, he was busy leading an army of invasion into lands belonging to the abbey of Préaux.

He was acting not as a bishop, but as the heir to the Count of Ivry, determined to protect his family's lands in the Risle valley by every means possible.[37] He seems, in fact, to have been the archetype of the bad bishop, who respected neither the duke's peace nor God's. Many secular rulers also attended the council – 'counts ... barons and vavasours', according to Wace. They all swore on the relics of Saint-Ouen to respect 'God's truce'. This is the first documented evidence of this practice, which consisted of limiting private wars by forbidding any fighting from Wednesday evening to Monday morning. In addition, those who attacked people or property woud be excommunicated and would have to pay the bishop a fine of nine *livres*.[38] To commemorate this event, a chapel was subsequently built, dedicated to Sainte-Paix, which still survives today.[39]

Thus, by the age of twenty, William the Bastard had reasserted ducal authority and established a new peace, guaranteed by the Church. He now had to think about marriage, in order to ensure the future of his dynasty. William and his chosen princess, Matilda of Flanders, were to form a remarkable couple.

A queen for life

In the upper echelons of the aristocracy, marriage was a way of cementing political alliances between great families. Feelings hardly entered into the equation. A young man's father and mother generally took care of marrying their son, or, failing them, his close relatives, on either his father's or mother's side. William's marriage was an exception. His father was dead and his mother was not in a position to exert any influence in the matter.[40] William was therefore one of the few rulers of his time to choose his future wife for himself. Unlike his father, he was determined to make a princely marriage, blessed by the Church. He had probably been advised to do so by his entourage. William of Poitiers suggests as much,[41] as does Wace, who writes: 'On the advice of his barons, William took a wife of high rank, in Flanders, the daughter of Baldwin, granddaughter of Robert King of France, daughter of his daughter who was born of Constance.'[42]

William, then, chose to contract an alliance with the other great principality of northern France. In so doing, he was re-establishing an old alliance,[43] and the planned union set a seal on the reconciliation between Baldwin V and the Normans. In addition, Matilda was an excellent match: as the daughter of Adela of France, she was of royal blood. We do not know excactly how old she was at the time of her marriage, but everything suggests that she was of child-rearing age. William did not marry a child, as was often the case. It seems likely that he chose a wife he genuinely liked, or indeed that he was 'in love'. He was certainly to remain faithful to her: he is not known to have had any concubines or any illegitimate children, which was extremely rare for a ruler at this time. In all probability, William's marriage was as much a love match as a political union.

Despite these favourable auspices, the marriage plans ran into serious difficulties. Once again, contemporary authors are very discreet on the matter, and we must wait until Orderic Vitalis before we get any kind of explanation.[44] It seems that the plans were vetoed by the ecclesiastical authorities, and even by the pope himself. The Church strictly prohibited marriage between blood relations, and between cousins, marriages were forbidden to the seventh degree of kinship. But William and Matilda were fifth cousins,[45] and there was an even closer tie of kinship: as a child, Matilda's mother Adela had been 'married', that is, betrothed to William's uncle, Richard III, before marrying Baldwin V of Flanders. Of course, the first 'marriage' of Adela of France had never actually taken place and could be considered void. The ecclesiastical authorities, however, being ill disposed to both the Duke of Normandy and the Count of Flanders, refused to accept this.

At other times, the kinship between William and Matilda would not have been considered problematic. The great royal and aristocratic families were in the habit of marrying their children to each other. Even taking into account the very strict rules imposed by the Church, a certain kinship was inevitable, and the local ecclesiastical authorities usually turned a blind eye and granted the necessary dispensations. The pope very rarely became involved in such matters. But this particular marriage plan coincided with the beginnings of Church reform, of which one of the most important elements was the reform of morals, not only of clerics but also of laymen. Christian marriage, blessed by the Church, was being imposed, especially on rulers, who were expected to set an example to the mass of the faithful. The first great reforming pope was in fact the pope reigning at this time, the Alsatian Leo IX, who had not forgotten that he had been appointed by Emperor Henry III, of whom the Count of Flanders was then the enemy.[46] But the pope had other grievances against Duke William. The pope was then in conflict with the Normans of southern Italy, who were in the process of conquering the country, making inroads into the papal territories in particular. A few years later, the pope would head a vast coalition intended to chase the Normans out of Italy. In his mind, the Normans of Normandy were no different from the Normans of Italy – and in any case, he felt no sympathy towards them.

In 1049, Leo set out on a long journey across Western Europe to promote reform. He called a council in Mainz, in the presence of the emperor, and another in Rheims, in the Kingdom of France, on 2 and 3 October 1049. Five of the seven Norman bishops attended. With the aim of the council being to promote peace and Church reform, one of the main topics of debate was simony, that is, the purchase of ecclesiastical charges. King Henry I of France considered himself the main target and did all he could to prevent the council being held, but to no avail. The Norman bishops also found themselves in the dock. Malger was well known as a simonist, and also to have concubines, which explains his absence. Geoffrey of Montbray, Bishop of Coutances, had to defend himself against the charge of having bought his bishopric. As for Yves, Bishop of Sées and Lord of Bellême, he had to explain why he had burnt down his own cathedral in an assault on his enemies who had taken refuge there.[47] The marriage of William and Matilda was also discussed, and the council explicity forbade the union.

Nevertheless, the marriage went ahead in about 1050, at Eu, on the northern border of the duchy. Baldwin V came from Flanders with his daughter Matilda.[48] It seems to have been a private wedding. William's mother, Herleva, was present, but none of the Norman barons attended, not even the Count of Eu, Robert, who belonged to the Richardides. William had disregarded the papal ban. Were there any ecclesiastical sanctions against the duke and duchess, such as excommunication and even interdict, as Lanfranc's biographer Milo Cespin,[49] and subsequently Wace, both state?[50] It is far from certain. What is possible is that several ecclesiastical dignitaries – Lanfranc, prior and master of Le Bec, Robert of Jumièges, Archbishop of Canterbury, and John of Ravenna, Abbot of Fécamp – attempted to intercede with the pope. But Leo IX refused to be swayed. He was just then preparing his military expedition against the Normans of Italy (his army was to be defeated in 1053).

Relations between the papacy and the Normans were not normalized until several years later, under another pope, Nicholas II, who both recognized the authority of the principal Norman leaders in Italy and confirmed the validity of William's marriage. In return for this recognition, according to Orderic Vitalis and Wace (our only sources of information on the matter), the pope imposed a penance on the duke and duchess. William committed himself to establishing charitable institutions in the principal towns of Normandy and to founding two abbeys (with Matilda) in Caen.[51] This latter was clearly William's own choice, since he was trying to make this new town the second capital of his duchy.

The founding of Caen

Caen is situated at the point where the old Roman road leading from Bayeux to Lisieux crosses the Orne. Recent archaeological excavations have revealed a Gallo-Roman settlement on the hill beside the valley to the north.[52] During the High Middle Ages, a whole series of villages was established on the banks of the Orne: Saint-Martin, corresponding to the old Gallo-Roman site, Saint-Ouen-de-Villers, to the west, Darnetal and Calix, to the east, and Saint-Michel-de-Vaucelles, to the south, on the other side of the river. In the eleventh century, all these villages would merge to form a new town.

Duke William was not, strictly speaking, the founder of Caen. The town is mentioned for the first time during the rule of Richard II, in two documents dating from 1025,[53] then under Richard III, in the dower granted to Adela in 1026–7.[54] William's predecessors had thus probably hoped to create an urban centre in this area of western Normandy, where their authority remained weak.[55] It was William, though, who gave the final impetus which transformed the town into one of the major cities of the duchy. The rebellion of the western lords had shown him how vital it was to have an outpost of ducal power in lower Normandy. Throughout the eleventh century, however, the new town had to cohabit with its close rival, Bayeux. At the beginning of the twelfth century, Bayeux was destroyed during the civil war between William's sons,[56] and from that point on, Caen would gain the upper hand and become the unquestioned second capital of the duchy.

In the ecclesiastical domain, however, Caen did not supplant Bayeux, which remained the seat of the bishopric. Consequently, Caen was not entitled to be called a *cité*, which supposed the presence of a bishop, but only a *bourg*. Though only one of many new towns created at that time in the whole of western France, Caen was one of the most obvious manifestations of the demographic growth and urban development that was particularly strong in Normandy. William gave Caen the characteristic elements of a large medieval town. Taking advantage of the presence of a rocky spur overlooking the valley, he began in about 1060 the construction of a vast stone castle, covering five hectares – an exceptional size for the time.

The town itself was surrounded by a wall, of more symbolic than military importance.[57] This building work coincided with the founding of the abbeys. In the absence of a bishopric, the presence of two great abbeys – a monastery and a convent – would give Caen the eccelesiastical stamp necessary to any medieval town worthy of the name.

The convent, devoted to the Trinity, was founded first, in about 1059, by Duchess Matilda.[58] The first abbess, who came from Saint-Léger de Préaux, was also named Matilda. The monastery, dedicated to Saint Stephen, followed a few years later, in about 1063. Lanfranc, Prior of Le Bec, became its first abbot. The building of the abbey churches began immediately, but the work would drag on for a long time. The abbey church of La Trinité was dedicated first, on 18 June 1066,[59] but the building was not finished until the twelfth century. Although begun later, the abbey church of Saint-Étienne was built more quickly. The work was already well advanced by the time of its dedication, on 13 September 1077.[60] These two churches are among the masterpieces of Norman Romanesque art, which was flourishing at this period,[61] and are a striking manifestation of the resurgent power of the Duke of Normandy.

After 1047, William still had to face various rebellions, most from members of the ducal family. The Richardides were obviously unable to accept the triumph of this bastard duke. Apart from Guy of Burgundy, though, they had not taken part in the great western rebellion. Three of these rebels are particularly noteworthy. The first is Richard I's great-grandson William Werlenc, Count of Mortain. He was forced into exile in Italy. The second is Richard I's grandson, William Busac, Count of Eu: the duke laid siege to the castle of Eu in about 1050.[62] Exiled to the court of King Henry I, William Busac had to yield the county to his brother Robert.[63] The third is Count William of Arques, the son of Richard II and his concubine Papia. It took the duke two years, from 1052 to 1054, to deal with him: William of Arques was finally exiled too, to the court of Eustace, Count of Boulogne.[64]

William of Arques was the brother of Archbishop Malger of Rouen.[65] We have already seen what a bad archbishop Malger was considered to be. Now Church appointments also became part of the power struggle. In 1049–50, Duke William replaced Bishop Hugh of Bayeux, a Richardide, with his half-brother, Odo of Conteville, who was barely twenty. This appointment must have seemed like a provocation to the other Richardides, and was one of the causes of their rebellion. Admittedly, William had given them some satifaction in 1050 by appointing as Bishop of Lisieux Hugh of Eu, brother of the rebellious count.[66] Anxious to promote reform in the province, the duke wanted to get rid of his great-uncle the archbishop. In 1054 or 1055, he called a council in Lisieux, which deposed Malger. His replacement was a monk from Fécamp named Maurilius. The new archbishop, of course, fully supported Church reform.

During these years (1047–54) William felt strong enough to turn his gaze outwards and pursue an active external policy. The growing power at the time was that of the Count of Anjou, Geoffrey Martel. He had seized Touraine, and his progress worried King Henry I. Where his principal vassals were concerned, the king, master only of a small royal domain around Paris, had no other choice but to run with the hare and hunt with the hounds. For the moment, he decided to act against Anjou. In 1049, he laid siege to the fotress of Mouliherne.[67] Duke William, as the king's vassal and debtor,[68] agreed to take part in the siege and distinguished himself by his skill as well as his courage.[69]

The siege of Mouliherne did not bring down Geoffrey Martel, who took possesson of the County of Maine, between Anjou and Normandy. William may have felt directly threatened. In addition, Geoffrey was able to take advantage of the civil war then raging in the estate of Bellême. William II Talvas was defeated by his son Arnulf, but the latter did not enjoy his victory for long, since he was soon assassinated. The estate then fell to Yves of Bellême, brother of William Talvas and Bishop of Sées.[70] Seizing his opportunity, Geoffrey Martel took control of Domfront and Alençon, two border strong-holds belonging to the Bellêmes.

By entering the fray, Duke William was attacking both the Count of Anjou and the Lords of Bellême, who were refusing to obey the duke's authority. We do not know the exact chronology of events between 1049 and 1051. It seems likely that after taking Mouliherne, William laid siege to the castle of Domfront, captured it and annexed Passais.[71] This was the last new territory to be added to the duchy, more than a century after the conquests of Rollo and William Longsword. Passais, however, was not absorbed into the ecclesiastical province of Rouen, but continued to be a dependency of the bishopric of Le Mans and the archbishopric of Tours.

After Domfront, William besieged Alençon, which had been built by the Lords of Bellême but had come out on the side of the Count of Anjou. The town was extremely important from a strategic point of view, being situated on the very borders of Normandy.[72] According to William of Poitiers, the Duke of Normandy, on capturing the castle and the town, showed great magnanimity towards the defenders.[73] Writing in the twelfth century, Wace tells a very different story.[74] During the siege a group of defenders had mocked William by beating the animal hides protecting the top of the tower, crying:

La pel, la pel al parmentier
ço apartient a son mestier[75]
(The skin, the skin of the tanner
 That belongs to his trade)

The cry was an unmistakable allusion to William's lowly origins, and to his maternal grandfather's trade. This was a sensitive subject for William, and he had dealt severely with those barons who had disputed his authority for the same reason. He had, however, shown them some consideration, only punishing them with exile. With mere commoners, he had no such scruples. When the town was taken, he ordered those who had insulted him to have their hands and feet cut off.[76] This act of cruelty is known to us only through texts written long after the event, but it is no less probable for all that. It points to one particular facet of William's character, a character formed during a very difficult youth. When he thought he was within his rights, he could be pitiless to those who stood in his way. This is the first example we have of this attitude, which would resurface later during the conquest of England. For now, William had re-established his authority over the southern fringes of the duchy. Not that the rivalry between the Duke of Normandy and the Count of Anjou was over. Over the next few years, it would degenerate into open war, with the duchy itself as the theatre of operations.

The invasion of Normandy

From the beginning, Normandy had often been subject to internal uprisings and rebellions, but it had never been attacked from the outside. This was to happen for the first time in 1054. The explanation can be found in King Henry I's change of attitude towards the duke. Still practising his policy of running with the hare and hunting with the hounds, Henry now considered that his most dangerous vassal was no longer Geoffrey Martel but William the Bastard. He therefore concluded an alliance with the Count of Anjou, which was formalized in a treaty on 15 October 1052.

Hostilities began in a limited way. Henry sent an army to support William of Arques, and was given the castle of Moulins-la-Marche, in the south of the duchy.[77] His anti-Norman ardour was certainly borne out by the many exiles who had found refuge in his court. He now prepared to mount a large-scale joint operation with the Count of Anjou.

The first campaign took place at the beginning of the year 1054. The king divided his forces in two. The first army was placed under the command of his brother Odo, and crossed into Normandy across the Bresle. The second army, comprising the king's forces and those of Geoffrey Martel, entered

Normandy across the Avre. The two armies were to meet outside Rouen. For his part, William did not react in the usual way: he avoided all direct confrontation. His army was also divided into two. He himself advanced from lower Normandy to the Seine, towards the king's forces. Two great vassals, Robert of Eu and Walter Giffard, were given the task of following Odo's army to upper Normandy, where they were able to take advantage of their adversaries' negligence. One evening in February or March, Odo's force was bivouacking in the village of Mortemer, on the Eaulne, near Bray,[78] without having taken the most elementary precautions. The French soldiers had drunk too much and the camp was unguarded, with the result that they were attacked in their sleep and were either killed or taken prisoner. Only Odo and a few others managed to escape. The news was promptly announced to Henry I, who decided to leave Normandy and conclude a truce with the duke.[79] He had not given up, however, and soon prepared a new invasion.

The second campaign took place three years later, in 1057. Drawing a lesson from the previous failure, the king and the Count of Anjou decided to form a single army. They entered Normandy from the south and advanced deep into the interior, going along the valley of the Orne. Once again, William did not respond immediately, but waited for the right moment. The opportunity presented itself when the invading army tried to cross Dives marsh eastwards from the village of Varaville.[80] One of the few possible routes was a road that went along the sea wall separating the marsh from the sea and leading to the 'Dives ford'.[81] To move along this narrow passge, the Franco-Angevin army was forced to stretch out. The king and the count were at the head of the column and were already on the hill overlooking the site when William attacked. He had waited for high tide to pounce on the rearguard. The French and the Angevins were easily routed, and many drowned in the sea or the marshes.[82] The king could do nothing: he was reduced to contemplating the disaster from the top of Bassebourg hill.[83]

The two battles of Mortemer and Varaville have one thing in common. They were not the usual cavalry confrontation, which was the kind of battle preferred at the time. William had no hesitation in using guile, waiting for the right moment to pounce on the enemy, launching his men against soldiers who were either resting or in a difficult position. He proved himself a clever tactician, a real military strategist. In addition, by acting in this way, he saved his strength while sparing the lives of his men. In this particular case, his cause was just, since he was defending his territory against an invasion. In other circumstances, he had no hesitation in attacking outside territories like Maine or Brittany.

In the years following the battle of Varaville, the political situation changed completely. William's enemies, King Henry I and Count Geoffrey Martel, both died in the same year, 1060. Their successors were not in a position to pursue the same anti-Norman policies. The new king, Philip I, was only eight and his guardian was William's father-in-law, Baldwin V of Flanders. Geoffrey Martel had no children and the inheritance was disputed between his two nephews, Geoffrey the Bearded and Fulk Rechin, the latter finally gaining the upper hand in 1068.

In the meantime, William was free to act as he wished in Maine, of which he undertook the conquest in 1063. The last Count of Maine, Herbert II, had died without children in 1062, bequeathing the county to the Duke of Normandy. He did, however, leave a potential heir, his sister Margaret. William quickly married her to his eldest son, Robert Curthose, who was then about twelve.[84] His principal adversary in the county was Geoffrey, Lord of Mayenne. To seize his castle, the duke is said to have employed unorthodox methods: he asked two children to slip into the castle and set fire to it from inside.[85]

Now master of Maine, he turned his attention to Brittany, where Duke Conan II was trying to shake off the Norman yoke and directly challenging William. William launched an expedition in 1064. His aims were limited, being to support one of Conran's rebellious vassals, Ruallon, Lord of Dol. This episode is recounted by William of Poitiers,[86] but is best known for being depicted in the Bayeux Tapestry.[87] William took with him Harold, Earl of Wessex, who at the time was an envoy at the duke's court. The principal result of the expedition was the lifting of the siege of Dol. The powerful Norman army forced Conan to flee, and then continued its advance as far as Dinan,[88] perhaps even as far as Rennes.[89] Conan was not defeated for good, but was sufficiently weakened not to worry William. The Duke of Normandy had his own allies in Brittany – especially Conan's uncle, Odo of Penthièvre – who were to supply him with large contingents for the conquest of England. As for Conan, he met his death, opportunely for William, on 11 December 1066, while laying siege to Château-Gontier.[90]

These two expeditions, to Maine and Brittany, had allowed the Duke of Normandy to ensure the tranquillity of his southern and south-western borders at a time when he was planning the invasion of England. He believed himself King Edward the Confessor's designated heir. Edward was over sixty, and in poor health, and a successor would soon need to be found. William had considered every eventuality. He had certainly not ruled out the possibility of a military expedition to conquer the kingdom. This was to be the greatest adventure of his life.

The circumstances of the conquest

Edward the Confessor, son of the Anglo-Saxon king Ethelred and Queen Emma, had been King of England since 1042. Cnut the Great had died in 1035, his son Harold Harefoot in 1040 and his other son Harthacnut in 1042. Edward had lived in exile in Normandy for a long time. He had strong links with the ducal family and had brought many Normans to England, including Ralph the Timid, appointed Earl of Hereford and given the task of defending the Welsh border, and three bishops. The best known of these is Robert Champart, the former Abbot of Jumièges who was first appointed Bishop of London in 1044, then Archbishop of Canterbury in 1051. These Normans were not well liked by the English, especially by the great aristocratic families. At the head of this 'anti-Norman' movement was Godwin, Earl of Wessex and leader of the anglo-Danish 'party'.[91] Godwin had many sons, of whom several would play a major role in the years to come, Sven, Harold and Tostig. He also had a daughter, Edith, whom he had been able to marry off to King Edward in 1045. This marriage had produced no children.

Edward seems to have been a weak king, torn between contradictory influences. In 1051, urged by the 'Norman party', he decided to attack the other faction. Godwin and his sons were forced into exile. They almost all found refuge in Flanders, Tostig having married Baldwin V's half-sister, Judith.[92] Only Harold settled in Ireland. Judith was placed under house arrest at the abbey of Wherwell in Hampshire. As Edward had no children, the problem of the succession arose. It was at this time that Edward named as his successor his cousin, Duke William the Bastard. The question was far from settled, however, as Godwin and his family returned to England in 1052. Restored to favour by the ever-fickle king, they again seized positions of power. An assembly summoned by Godwin ordered the expulsion of all Normans, including the Archbishop of Canterbury. Robert Champart was replaced as archbishop by Stigant, who was already Bishop of Winchester; this appointment was not accepted by Pope Leo, or by his successors. In the eyes of the ecclesiastical authorities, Stigant remained an 'intruder' archbishop.[93]

Godwin died in 1053. Most of his possessions went to his son Harold, who received the huge earldom of Wessex and became the strong man of the kingdom. Harold could not accept William of Normandy as heir to the throne, even though he had no idea as yet of seizing it himself. In 1057, the *aetheling* Edward, son of Edmund Ironside and nephew of Edward the Confessor, was brought back from exile in

Hungary, but he died shortly afterwards, leaving only a young son, Edgar, still a minor.

For his part, King Edward was still determined to bequeath his kingdom to William. To confirm his promise he sent Harold as his envoy to the duke in 1064. It was a clever move, since Harold would find himself in a very difficult situation while in Normandy, having to defend positions that were contrary to his own ambitions. This journey is described in detail by William of Poitiers[94] and depicted in the Bayeux Tapestry,[95] the whole first part of which is devoted to this episode. William took Harold with him on his military expedition to Brittany. According to the tapestry, Harold distinguished himself during the crossing of the border, rescuing soldiers from the quicksands around Mont-Saint-Michel.[96] William made him take 'many oaths', according to William of Jumièges.[97] The tapestry shows the oath taken over the relics of Bayeux.[98] William of Poitiers only mentions the one at Bonneville-sur-Touque,[99] but informs us as to the contents of these oaths. He distinguishes two kinds. The first is a classic loyalty oath: Harold declares himself a vassal of William, who gives him back his own lands as a fiefdom. The second relates to the succession. Harold promises William 'to ensure him possession of the Kingdom of England on the death of Edward'.[100] In the meantime, he would be William's representative at the king's court.

King Edward died a year after Harold's return, on 5 January 1066. Harold did not respect his oaths and had himself crowned King of England, with the agreement of the *Witangemot*,[101] the governing assembly, which wanted to avoid the kingdom being placed in the hands of a foreigner. Harold seemed to be the only man capable of preserving English independence and providing a military response to the attacks that would be sure to ensue. The new king was crowned by Stigant, the illegitimate Archbishop of Canterbury.[102]

Harold had no legitimate claim on the crown. He belonged neither to the English nor to the Danish royal family, which had long ruled England. His sister had been queen of England, but this was not a sufficient qualification. Harold became king through circumstance alone. William, being the great-nephew of Edward's mother Emma, was a closer relative of the dead king. Above all, he had unquestionably been made a promise by Edward, which had been confirmed by Harold himself. Two other candidates to the throne also had legitimate claims. No one seriously thought of offering the throne to the young *aetheling* Edgar. Instead, an outsider, Harald Hardrada,[103] King of Norway, stepped forward, presenting an old agreement between his predecessor, Magnus the Good, and King Harthacnut. This was obviously a pretext, but Hardrada had the military means to support his claim. Harold would have to take account of Harald Hardrada as well as William the Bastard.

The two pretenders to the English throne made active preparations for invasion. We know more William's efforts. First, he entered into an intense round of diplomatic activity. He had to make sure that he would get as much cooperation as possible within the Kingdom of France. He could count on the support of his father-in-law, Baldwin V, who was the guardian of Philip I, which guaranteed him contingents from Flanders and the Île-de-France. His alliance with the family of the counts of Penthièvre would bring him Breton contingents. Naturally, he could rely on the Norman feudal army, which had often demonstrated its effectiveness, but it could only be mobilized for forty days – manifestly insufficient for an expedition like this. Beyond that time, William would have to pay the Norman cavalrymen and infantrymen, just as he paid the other contingents. The Duchy of Normandy was one of the most prosperous regions in the kingdom, and the duke was rich enough to finance the campaign. The army would not be 'Norman', but 'Frankish', as the Bayeux Tapestry clearly indicates.[104] The whole northern part of the Kingdom of France had been pressed into service.

To cross the Channel, William needed a fleet. New boats were built, including the flagship, the *Mora*, a gift from Matilda to her husband.[105] Many other vessels were requisitioned, all ships of Viking style, beautifully depicted on the Bayeux Tapestry.[106] Wace quotes the figure of 696 vessels in all, which is not at all improbable.[107] William was obviously relying on his barons, both secular and ecclesiatical, to bring him not only men – their own vassals – but also boats. A contemporary list provides us with the names of the largest contributors: Count Robert of Mortain (120 ships), Bishop Odo of Bayeux (100), Count Richard of Evreux (80), William fitz Osbern, steward, Count Robert of Eu, Viscount Hugh of Avranches, Roger of Montgommery and Roger of Beaumont (60 ships each), Hugh of Montfort (50 ships and 60 horsemen), Walter Giffard (30 ships and 100 horsemen), the Abbot of Saint-Ouen de Rouen (15 ships and 100 horsemen) and the Abbot of Fécamp (one ship and 20 horsemen).[108] This list shows us the extent to which William's great vassals had been pressed into use. They were all his councillors, and he knew he could count on them.[109] They would become the principal barons of the new Kingdom of England. The conquest was to be a collective enterprise, although William was the unquestioned leader. His most important supporters were his two half-brothers, Robert of Mortain and Odo of Conteville, who contributed the largest number of ships. They would be constantly at William's side during the expedition, as is clearly shown in the Bayeux Tapestry.[110]

The boats transported both men and horses for the cavalry.[111] Viking-style ships did not need ports: they were excellent 'landing craft', which could draw directly alongside the beaches. But it would still be necessary to find a sheltered place to accommodate so large a number of ships, and natural harbours of this sort were not very common. The bay at the estuary of the river Dives was one, its proximity to Caen making it particularly suitable. William seized the opportunity presented by the circumstances to honour his promise to found two abbeys (with Matilda). The abbey church of La Trinité was dedicated on 18 June, although the work had hardly advanced. It was a way of preparing spiritually for the fight to come, while at the same time satisfying Pope Alexander II.[112] The pope had in fact blessed the expedition – targeting as it did a usurper king crowned by an intruder arch-bishop – and had sent a standard and a relic of Saint Peter.[113] The fleet began to assemble in the spring, and the departure was fixed for the first of August.

But the crossing was delayed. William of Poitiers puts this down to unfavourable winds.[114] Even though the weather does, of course, play a vital role in such circumstances,[115] this is not a very satisfactory explanation. The wait continued for more than a month and a half. On 12 September, the fleet at last set off, but not for England. It moved to another auspicious anchorage, Saint-Valéry, where the estuary of the Seine forms a bay similar to that of the Dives.[116] Here William waited for another two weeks before finally launching his fleet across the Channel.[117]

This wait was not in fact due to chance, and a very satis-factory explanation has been provided recently by Pierre Bouet.[118] William demonstrated a keen sense of strategy, and even a certain Machiavellian cunning. He was not unaware that Harold's army was waiting for him on the beaches. An imme-diate landing would have led to a bloodbath. But Harold could not keep his troops conscripted indefinitely, especially not the *fyrd*, which was composed of local peasants. William had calculated correctly: on 8 September, Harold discharged his fleet and part of his army and withdrew to London, leaving the coast undefended. He was presumably convinced that William had delayed the invasion until the following spring. But William was still waiting, because he knew that another invasion of England was just then under way.[119]

We have no knowledge of the relations between William and the King of Norway. Had they negotiated a division of the Kingdom of England? It is not impossible. What is quite likely is that the two pretenders to the throne had made contact. The intermediary may have been Tostig, who had broken with his brother Harold and was now cooperating with his worst enemies, including the King of Norway. We know that Tostig travelled between Norway and Flanders several times during this period, and may also have visited Normandy.[120] Such journeys by sea could have been quite rapid, and information circulated freely between the English Channel and the North Sea. Harald and William were both sly old foxes. Although united against Harold, they were rivals for the kingdom. A joint attack was in both their interests, as it would force Harold to divide his forces. They also knew that whoever attacked first would be at a disadvantage, because Harold's troops would still be fresh. In this game, William had a significant trump card: the climate of Normandy allowed him to wait longer than his partner and rival. In fact, Harald Hardrada did attack first.[121]

The Norwegian army landed on the banks of the Humber, not far from York, on 18 September.[122] Immediately, King Harold rushed north. The two armies joined battle on 25 September, at Stamford Bridge.[123] The outcome was an overwhelming victory for Harold: his own brother Tostig and the King of Norway both perished in the battle. William's waiting game had paid off. His principal rival had been eliminated and his adversary had been weakened by a testing battle. This crucial episode is completely underestimated in contemporary Norman sources; it is mentioned only by William of Poitiers, William of Jumièges and the Bayeux Tapestry remaining completely silent.[124] This Norman cunning did not sit well with the flattering image of William that the ecclesiastical authors wanted to transmit to posterity.

William waited to hear the outcome of the battle before finally making his decision. Three days later, he gave the order for departure, and the crossing took place on the night of 28/29 September. The fleet landed without difficulty at Pevensey.[125] William had time to settle in near Hastings and make his arrangements before the return of Harold, who was returning south at top speed. The invading army prepared calmly for the decisive confrontation: the Battle of Hastings.

Hastings, 14 October 1066

The Battle of Hastings was one of the great battles of history. It is known to us only from Norman sources. William of Jumièges gives almost no details. Our information comes primarily from William of Poitiers, taken up and amplified by Wace, who adds a few original elements.[126] To these classic sources, we must add a poem contemporary with the events, the *Carmen de Hastingae Proelio* (*Song of the Battle of Hastings*), probably written by Guy of Amiens.[127] English sources, on the other hand, are practically silent about the battle.[128] Many English-speaking historians have since studied the subject.[129] In France, Pierre Bouet has thrown fresh light on the battle by reinterpreting the Latin and French texts.[130]

William had the advantage of being the first on the scene. He nevertheless allowed the English troops to take up positions on the ridge of Senlac Hill (a site since called Battle).[131] We do not know why he granted his enemies this 'favour'. It was in the English army's interest to take up a fixed position: if the battle involved movement, its infantrymen would not last long against the Norman cavalry.

We have no precise figures of the numbers of troops involved. It is generally believed that the two armies were of equal size, each having between 7,000 and 8,000 men.

The English army was composed of two different forces: on the one hand, the *housecarls*, elite soldiers, often of Scandinavian origin, who moved about on horseback, but fought on foot, and on the other, the *fyrd*, consisting of peasants mobilized for the occasion. The Bayeux Tapestry clearly illustrates the difference in weaponry between the two categories of fighters. The *housecarls* were equipped, like the Normans, with coats of mail, shields and helmets with nasal guards.[132] Their offensive arms were the spear, the sword and the dreaded battle-axe.[133] The members of the *fyrd* were poorly armed, generally possessing only one offensive weapon (a spear or an axe) and a shield.[134]

(above) Detail of a ninth-century picture stone depicting a Viking ship from the Isle of Gotland. *(Historiska Museet, Stockholm/Bridgeman)*

(right) Gonnor, widow of Richard I, Duke of Normandy, makes a donation to the abbey of Mont-Saint-Michel. On her right is her younger son, Robert, Archbishop of Rouen and Count d'Évreux, together with representatives of the nobility. This picture demonstrates the new ducal power in Normandy, enforced on the Church and on the lay aristocracy. *(Bibliothèque Municipale, France/Bridgeman)*

A scene from the Bayeux Tapestry showing the death of King Harold (on the left) at the end of the Battle of Hastings.

Geoffrey Plantagenet, Count of Anjou (1131–1151) and Duke of Normandy. Husband of the Empress Matilda (widow of the Holy Roman Emperor, Henry I) and father of Henry II of England, he was the first of the Plantagenet dynasty. (*Musée de Tessé, France/Bridgeman*)

The columns in the crypt of the Abbaye-aux-Dames in Caen (now L'Église de la Saint Trinité), founded in the late eleventh century by William the Conqueror and his wife Matilda. Matilda was buried in the church under a slab of black marble on her death in 1083. *(Peter Willi/Bridgeman)*

(above) The Siege of Antioch during the First Crusade (1097–1098). Bohemond, son of Robert Guiscard, took the principality of Antioch after a lengthy siege and in doing so founded one of the eastern-most outposts of the Norman empire.
(Bibliothèque Municipale de Lyon/Bridgeman)

(left) A mosaic depicting the coronation of Roger II, King of Sicily, by Christ himself. A papal bull invested Roger, previously Count of Sicily and Duke of Apulia and Calabria, with the royal crown in 1130.
(La Martorana, Sicily/Bridgeman)

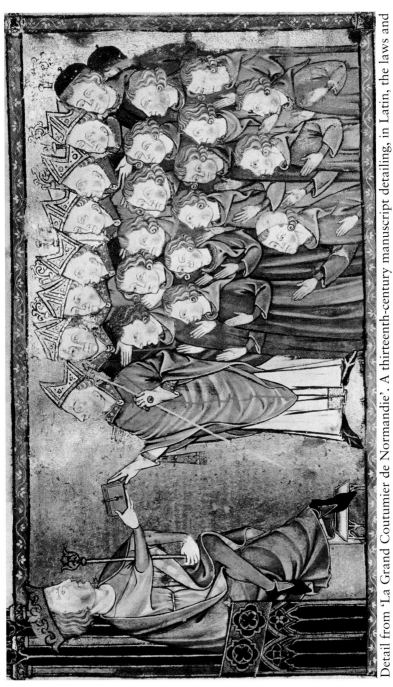

Detail from 'La Grand Coutumier de Normandie'. A thirteenth-century manuscript detailing, in Latin, the laws and customs of Normandy. Norman law remained in continuous use until the Revolution in 1789.

(Musée de la Ville de Paris, France/Bridgeman)

The cathedral in Palermo, built on the order of William II, King of Sicily, in 1174. There is a marked Norman influence in the exterior architecture, particularly in the intersecting arches.
(Duomo Monreale, Sicily/Bridgeman)

William's army included contingents of various origins, but there were three distinct elements: well-armed cavalry, who constituted the main force, infantry and archers. The presence of a large number of archers on the Norman side is extremely important: they were to play a vital role in the battle. The English, by contrast, had few archers.[135]

On the night of 13 / 14 September, then, Harold had drawn up his troops on the ridge of the hill, with the *housecarls* in the centre, protecting the king, and the *fyrd* on either side. Faced with this plan of attack, William divided his army into three bodies, corresponding to its different contingents. The centre was occupied by the Normans, directly facing the *housecarls*. The two wings were held by the allies, French and Flemish on the right, Bretons on the left, both facing the *fyrd*.

The battle took place over the course of the day, as was standard in the Middle Ages. It began at about nine o'clock in the morning, and was over by nightfall, which comes early during October. As we have seen, William often avoided direct confrontations. The only true battle he had been involved in had been that of Val-ès-Dunes, in 1047. Now, nearly twenty years later, when he was close to forty, the cautious Duke of Normandy would again risk his all on a bloody, head-on clash of two armies. Such battles were believed to depend on 'God's judgement', since only God could grant victory. But, during the action, William would do all he could to increase his chances of winning.

Hostilities began with the Normans shooting arrows towards the English, who had formed a joined wall of raised shields.[136] As the Bayeux Tapestry clearly shows, the arrows came down and hit the English shields, the English having had plenty of time to protect themselves.[137] The damage inflicted was minimal. Then began a classic assault, first by the infantry, then by the heavy cavalry. These assaults proved totally ineffectual, as they met with the *housecarls'* 'wall of shields'. The Norman attackers were in fact in a disadvantageous position, having to climb the hill to reach the English, who were well entrenched on the ridge. The frontal attack having failed, William decided to use trickery. The Bretons on the left wing pretended to flee. The men of the *fyrd* could not resist the temptation to pursue them, even though they had received orders from Harold to keep to their positions. As they ran down the hill, they were slaughtered by the Norman cavalry. This manoeuvre was repeated several times with great success. Each time, Harold's troops were decimated. By the end of the day, however, the housecarls were still resisting, successfully defending Harold's command post.

William knew that 'God's judgement' had to end with the death of one of the two pretenders to the throne. He decided to try a new approach in order to reach Harold. It was at this moment in the battle that the archers played a decisive role. William ordered them to get as close as possible to the enemy ranks and to shoot higher so that the arrows would go over the wall of shields.[138] Many English, poorly protected by the helmets of the time, were hit in the face. Harold himself received an arrow in the eye.[139] The English ranks began to scatter. William seized the opportunity and led a command of four men, with the specific aim of finishing off the king. The little group managed to slip through the enemy ranks to the command post. The *Carmen de Hastingae Proelio* gives a detailed description of this final action: one of the horsemen struck the king on the head, the others in the chest, the stomach, and the thigh.[140] Harold was killed: 'God's judgement' had favoured William. The vanquished English fled, pursued by the Normans and their allies.

William was the undisputed winner. Much of the English aristocracy lay dead on the battlefield. The advance of the victorious army was now unstoppable. William headed for London, and on Christmas Day 1066 was crowned King of England in Westminster Abbey.[141] It would not, of course, have been proper for Stigant, the Archbishop of Canterbury, to conduct the ceremony, and his place was taken by the Archbishop of York, Ealdred.[142] Now that he was King of

England, William still had to pacify and persuade the English to recognize his authority. This was to be no easy task.

Political skills

Winning a decisive battle takes an excellent military leader, which William unquestionably was. To take over a territory effectively and keep it over a long period requires great political skills. William had proved in the past that he had these, too. But much more was at stake now.

At first, the new king hoped that he could win round his former adversaries. He considered that he had been quite within his rights to conquer the country, since he had been promised the throne by the previous king, Edward. 'God's judgement' having favoured him, he assumed that the English would all rally to him without any problem. We know of one English reaction from the *Anglo-Saxon Chronicle* (version D). The anonymous author, who seems to be resigned to the inevitable,[143] asserts that the English were punished for their sins. At first, William presented himself as the successor of the Anglo-Saxon kings, not only Edward, but Harold too. He drafted a number of documents in Old English, and made an effort to learn the language of his new people.[144] Some of this attitude may be glimpsed in the Bayeux Tapestry, which is one of the first testimonies we possess on these events. In it, Harold is referred to as 'king', just as he is in a number of charters.[145] He is even singled out and praised for his bravery.[146] The Latin commentary is very neutral, and may be read in both a pro-English and a pro-Norman light.[147] This early line only lasted a few years, until it came up against the harsh reality of Anglo-Saxon rebellions.

The first rebellion broke out in Exeter, in the south-west of the kingdom, in 1067–8:[148] it was easily quelled. The most serious rebellion took place in the north, in several stages, during 1069–70.[149] It was harshly put down by the king, who systematically ravaged the region. The Fens, around the Isle of Ely,[150] were the scene of a final rebellion, in 1070–1.

Considering how well disposed William had been initially, it is worth investigating the true reasons for these resistance movements.[151]

One of the causes was certainly the military occupation of the country by foreigners. The Normans and their Breton and French allies were only a tiny minority of the population. To ensure their authority, they built motte-and-bailey castles everywhere, as they had learned to do on the continent. Easy to build, these improvised fortresses withstood all attacks, as was the case with the castle of York in 1069. The rebellions led to an increase in the number of Norman castles, which was obviously not the outcome intended by the rebels. London had three, including the famous Tower, which was an example of the huge stone castles that gradually replaced the old motte-and-baileys and which can still be admired today.[152]

In addition, the country's aristocracy changed completely. Many English nobles had died in battle. Those who remained were often guilty of rebellions and eliminated, like the last earls Edwin and Morcar (in 1071) and Waltheof (in 1075).[153] The new aristocracy was largely Norman, but also partly Breton, Flemish and French. The new lords immediately seized the English manors,[154] wielding power over the Anglo-Saxon peasantry with a rod of iron. Some took local wives, but most had wives on the continent. Obviously, they retained their Norman estates and had to divide their time between the two sides of the Channel, which was not an easy thing to do, as William himself was to discover.

One of William's biggest problems, in fact, was how to rule simultaneously two territories divided by sea. In the Middle Ages, a leader needed to be physically present in order to maintain authority. This was particularly true in England, where the new king's authority had not yet been firmly established.[155] Rebellions generally broke out when the king was in Normandy. On the continent, conversely, William had no difficulty within the duchy itself, which was well governed in his absence, mainly by Queen Matilda. The same could not be said of the external dependencies. The new Count of Anjou, Fulk Rechin, seized the opportunity to regain possession of Maine. To win it back, William had to organize an expedition in the middle of the winter in 1073. Some years later, in 1086, a final rebellion broke out, led by Hubert, the Lord of Sainte-Suzanne. This time, William was unable to seize his mighty fortress, despite laying siege to it in the normal way. It was one of his bitterest failures.[156]

In England, William had given up the idea of relying on the support of the Anglo-Saxons. In this respect, the year 1070 was the turning point of his reign. The king's first move was to regain control of the Church. He could not of course deal with the clerics as he had with the lay powers: the eccelesiastical authorities had to be handled with kid gloves. He summoned a council of the English Church in Winchester.[157] At his prompting, the council agreed to depose some notoriously unworthy prelates, primarily Stigant, the intruder Archbishop of Canterbury. Then he appointed his own men, Norman or continental clerics, to the vacant seats. His friend Lanfranc, Abbot of Saint-Étienne de Caen, became Archbishop of Canterbury and head of the English Church. The Normans Walkelin and Herfast, two clerics from the royal chapel, were given the seats of Winchester and Elmham respectively. Another Norman, Thomas of Bayeux, became Archbishop of York, a seat made vacant by the death of Ealdred.[158] Few bishoprics remained in the hands of Anglo-Saxon prelates. Similarly, in the monasteries, William gradually replaced the abbots. The great Norman institutions supplied many abbots and at the same time were given property in England. William also had no hesitation in altering the ecclesiastical map of the kingdom, transferring many episcopal seats to larger towns.[159] He had never dared to do anything similar in Normandy.

In his twenty-one-year reign, William managed to establish his authority firmly over the country he had conquered. His power was absolute, although he had failed to achive the consensus he had hoped for at the beginning. The kingdom had become a virtual Norman colony. Lords from across the Channel now owned most of the land. They also had at their disposal the only military force allowed in England.

At the end of his reign, William decided to discover the precise state of his kingdom. Holding his Christmas court in Gloucester, he launched a great survey which was to be carried out during the following year, 1086. The intention was to find out the number of inhabitants, the size of properties and the income they brought in. The survey was undertaken from a historical viewpoint, since the value of each property was to be recorded three times: as it had been before 1066 (at the time of King Edward), then after 1066 (when it had been taken over by its new masters), and finally in 1086. Commissions presided over by bishops or nobles were given the task of gathering and checking the information collected locally.[160] Then everything was summarized and written down in a great register, called the *Domesday Book*.[161] Like Christ on the Day of Judgment examining the actions of all men, the King of England would know all the inhabitants and all the properties in his kingdom. Naturally, there were a few gaps. London and Winchester, the two capitals, did not appear in the text.[162] The lands of the north, near the Scottish border, were not surveyed. The survey of East Anglia was not finished in time to be included: this became the *Little Domesday Book*.[163] But such a census was unique for its time. No other document of this kind has been preserved in Western Europe, nor was any ever made. It is an extraordinary mine of information for historians. William finished his reign by providing his contemporaries, and posterity, with striking proof of his good administration. From this point of view, the conquest was a real success.

William's last years were marked by a series of misfortunes. In 1082, William arrested and imprisoned his half-brother, Odo, Bishop of Bayeux and Count of Kent. Odo had been his most loyal supporter, and had often acted as viceroy when William was away in Normandy.[164] The reasons for his arrest remain a mystery. It seems that Odo had tried to organize a military expedition to Rome, without William's agreement. Whatever the reason, William considered him a traitor and kept him in prison until his death.[165] In 1083, the queen died and was buried in the choir of the abbey church of La Trinité in Caen, which she had founded.[166] William was deeply affected: Matilda had been a loving wife, an efficient collaborator and an attentive mother. She had nevertheless been torn between her duties as a wife and as a mother in the late 1070s, when her eldest son, Robert Curthose, had rebelled against his father. Matilda had maintained secret contacts with her son, a fact which William found hard to forgive.[167]

Philip I had become William's enemy, which was hardly suprising: the King of France found it hard to accept the extraordinary rise of one of his own vassals. As King of England, William was now his equal in rank, even though he remained his dependant in Normandy (and Maine). Philip lacked the means to fight this powerful adversary himself, and so he eagerly embraced Robert Curthose. In 1077–8, William and Robert confronted one another at the siege of Gerberoy.[168] After a brief reconciliation during the 1080s, the rebel son again found refuge with the King of France.

Given the balance of power, Philip I was confined to military operations on the borders of Normandy. The territory at stake was French Vexin, which the king had ruled directly since 1077.[169] William had no intention of seizing this territory.[170] But the local lords, vassals of the French king, were multiplying their incursions into Normandy, and William decided to launch a reprisal expedition at the beginning of September 1087. The Norman troops captured and burned down the town of Mantes, but William was seriously wounded.[171] He was brought back to Rouen, to the priory of Saint-Gervais. He took some days to die, and had time to pardon his son Robert, whom he confirmed as his successor to the Duchy of Normandy, as well as his half-brother Odo, whom he (reluctantly) freed. The Kingdom of England was to go to his youngest son, William Rufus.[172] He clearly did not see the combined duchy and kingdom surviving. William died on 9 September, and his body was taken to the abbey church of Saint-Étienne de Caen, where he was buried according to his wishes.[173]

William the Conqueror remains the greatest figure in Norman history. He created a kind of state that existed nowhere else in the Christian West, an authoritarian feudal monarchy. Needing the support of the Norman and continental lords who had helped him in the conquest, he amply rewarded them with fiefdoms. He introduced into England a feudal system hitherto unknown there, the 'Norman feudal system' which had proved its worth in the duchy. The king made sure that the lands of his principal vassals were dispersed throughout the kingdom, in order to avoid the formation of principalities that might threaten his authority. He retained a very large royal estate and built many fortified castles, which served to protect him against possible rebellions.

After the unrest of the early years, the English population had submitted to the new power structure, although they certainly had not accepted the new regime willingly. There were few upheavals for the peasants, who simply changed masters. The old aristocracy had virtually died out, either on the battlefield, or as a result of the rebellions of the years 1067–71. The population of the towns, especially the larger ones, was now quite cosmopolitan. Inhabitants of different origins lived on apparently good terms, and there was a great deal of intermarriage between the communities.[174] Good relations were furthered by undoubted economic growth and by many exchanges with the towns of Normandy and the continent. England had become a bilingual country. The conquerors had imposed their language, which would evolve into a dialect of French known as Anglo-Norman. This dialect would be spoken by the aristocracy of the kingdom for centuries, until the Hundred Years War. Not that the English language had died out: it remained the language of the people, but was profoundly influenced by French, in its vocabulary and in its structures. Modern English is another product of the Norman Conquest.

What is true of language is also true of many other fields. All things considered, England is the product of a fusion between two civilizations, Frankish and Anglo-Saxon, rather than Norman and English. Nor was the influence in one direction only. In many ways, the England of Edward the Confessor had been a more advanced country than the Normandy of William. This was particularly true in the field of administration. William retained the institution of the Chancellery, although he did not establish one in Normandy. He made use of the network of sheriffs, who effectively represented the king in the counties. As for the legal and financial institution of the Exchequer, it was born within the Anglo-Norman context and developed simultaneously on both sides of the Channel.[175]

And yet, although William the Conqueror is glorified in Normandy, he has left a bad reputation behind him in England. Of course, many English historians agree in recognizing the fundamental contribution of the Normans to English civilization. But most English people today identify more easily with the conquered Anglo-Saxons than with the Norman conquerors, even though the latter are also their ancestors.[176] A good example is the inscription carved on the pediment of the British military cemetery in Bayeux after the Allied landings of 1944:

Nos a Guillelmo victi, victoris patriam liberavimus
(We who were vanquished by William have liberated the country of the victor)

Historical myths do not always survive. The great hero of the Norman adventure is not recognized as such by the inhabitants of the land he conquered. The opposite could be said of southern Italy, another region of Western Europe subjugated at the same period by other Normans. In this area, which has known many different invaders, the Normans are the only ones who still find favour with modern Italians, especially Sicilians. The principal conqueror of southern Italy was a contemporary of William and another hero of the Norman adventure, Robert Guiscard.

7

THE STORY OF THE HAUTEVILLE BROTHERS

The eleventh century was the great century of the Norman adventure. At the same time as the Duke of Normandy was capturing the prestigious Kingdom of England in the north of Europe, so in the south other Normans, of much humbler extraction, were setting out to conquer, first southern Italy, then Sicily. In the eleventh century, their successors created, from scratch, the Kingdom of Sicily, which survived until Italian unification. This amazing exploit was entirely the work of a handful of bold and determined men from the Duchy of Normandy who were able to take advantage of favourable circumstances. The story of the Normans of southern Italy is known to us through contemporary authors, who chronicled the deeds of the most illustrious of these figures.

The first author chronologically is Amatus of Monte Cassino, a monk from the famous monastery founded by Saint Benedict, writing in about 1080, at the time of Abbot Desiderius, who was always favourably disposed to the newcomers. The work of Amatus was written in Latin, under the title *Historia*

Normannorum, but we only know it through a fourteenth-century French translation, *Ystoire de li Normant* (*History of the Normans*).[1] A few years later, at the end of the eleventh century, William of Apulia wrote a long poem to the glory of the most illustrious Norman of the period, Robert Guiscard,[2] and at almost the same time another Benedictine, Geoffrey Malaterra, wrote a history of the conquest of Sicily, and especially of the principal conqueror, Robert Guiscard's brother, Roger I.[3]

In the eleventh century, Italy was far from being a unified country. The north was the Kingdom of Italy, ruled by the Holy Roman Emperor. Every future emperor had to go at least once to Rome, to be crowned by the pope. Before his coronation, he was entitled to be called only 'King of the Romans'. As his authority was not greatly respected in the kingdom, especially in the towns and cities, he had to travel well-armed. The centre of Italy had belonged to the pope since the donation made by Pippin the Short in 756 and confirmed by Charlemagne in 774 when he destroyed the Kingdom of the Lombards.[4] The south was even more fragmented than the north and the centre. Much of it – the *themas* of Langobardia[5] and Calabria – was still under the domination of the Byzantine emperors. The rest was divided into entities mostly led by Lombard princes: the Principalities of Salerno, Capua and Benevento, the last of these claimed by the pope. Other territories were former Byzantine duchies, such as Gaeta and especially Naples. As for Amalfi, this was an autonomous town and a major maritime trading centre. Finally, there was Sicily. This had been under Muslim domination since the ninth century,[6] and much of the Greek population had been replaced by immigrants from North Africa. The coastal regions of southern Italy were constantly subjected to raids by Muslims from Sicily, and usually proved unable to deal with them. It was in these circumstances that the Normans came to intervene in the region.

The first arrivals
The circumstances surrounding the arrival of the first Normans remain obscure, and the stories told about it are

tinged with legend. What is certain is that southern Italy was on the route of the great Christian pilgrimages to the Holy Land, which long predated the Crusades. Palestine had been ruled by the Muslims since the seventh century, and from the end of the tenth century was part of the Fatimid Empire, whose capital was Cairo. The pilgrims passed through Rome and then through Monte Gargano, a famous shrine in Apulia dedicated to Saint Michael. It may be supposed that the Normans, who had their own shrine to the archangel at Mont-Saint-Michel, had a particular interest in this great shrine, the oldest in the West.[7] Then the pilgrims would often take to sea, which was quicker and safer than the land route, despite the dangers of Arab piracy.

According to Amatus of Monte Cassino, the founding event took place in 999. That year, Norman pilgrims passed Salerno on the way home from the Holy Land. They found the town under siege from the Saracens and liberated it, even though there were only forty of them. They set off again for Normandy, but subsequently returned, as they had promised the inhabitants they would. William of Apulia gives us another version of these beginnings. He says that the founding event took place some years later, in about 1015. This also involved pilgrims being asked for help, this time by a Lombard aristocrat named Melus, who wanted to liberate Apulia from Byzantine domination. A military expedition was organized, which led to the battle of Cannae in October 1018. Although it was a resounding defeat for the Normans, they remained in the region.

These two examples illustrate one of the essential reasons for the Normans' success. The newcomers were excellent fighters. In particular, they had mastered the new technique of fighting on horseback, which would become the standard cavalry technique throughout the West, but which was still unknown in these outlying regions. The Normans were experts in handling spears, could manoeuvre as a group and excelled at cavalry charges.[8] Subsequently, they also demonstrated their ability to build castles very rapidly. At first, these castles were simple motte-and-baileys, using the rudimentary technique tried out in Normandy during the periods when ducal power had been weakened. Such castles were an excellent way to keep control of a conquered region. The Normans used them in both southern Italy and in England. When the situation had been stabilized, the wooden palisades were replaced by stone walls, especially easy to build in Italy where stone was plentiful.[9]

The first Norman to settle in southern Italy was Rainulf (perhaps called Renouf in Normandy). He had fought as a mercenary in the service of the Duke of Naples, and as a reward was granted the County of Aversa in 1029. The time of mercenaries was not over, however. Although the Normans were often the adversaries of the Byzantines, they had no hesitation in joining their army if the fee was high enough. In 1038, for example, they took part in the expedition led by George Maniakes against Muslim Sicily. Maniakes' army was quite mixed, and included elements of the 'Varangian guard', such as Harald Hardrada, the future King of Norway.[10] Among the Normans, some soldiers stood out, including two members of the Hauteville family, William Ironarm and his brother Drogo. The Sicilian expedition ended in failure in 1040, but it had given these Normans the opportunity to prove themselves within a real army. Moreover, they had noted some of the weak points of Muslim Sicily and would remember them when they embarked on the conquest of the island twenty years later.[11]

The temporary alliance with the Byzantines would not long survive this campaign. In 1040, the towns of Apulia rebelled against the authority of the emperor, under a succession of leaders: Ardouin, Atenulf and finally Argyros. The Lombards again needed the Normans' help. Naturally, the Normans accepted, but must have decided not to let the spoils of victory escape them this time. They began the systematic conquest of Apulia. Theoretically, they were acting for the Prince of Salerno, Guiamar V. In reality, they created the first Norman state in Italy. They divided the region into twelve counties: Civitate, Siponto, Ascoli, Melfi, Lavello, Cannae, Trani,

Minervino, Venosa, Acerenza, Montepeloso and Monopoli. The Byzantines retained only a thin coastal strip around the capital, Bari, and the peninsula of Otranto, including the towns of Brindisi and Taranto: in other words, only the heel of the Italian boot.[12]

In creating these counties, the Normans reproduced a feudal model which was dominant in northern France but hitherto unknown in southern Italy. Nevertheless, they did not establish in Italy the 'Norman feudal system' then being established in the mother country. In order to work well, this system required a strong central authority, which existed in Normandy between 1001 and 1026, under Richard II, then again after 1047, under William the Bastard. But the various Norman leaders in Apulia thought of themselves as equals and found it hard to accept a superior authority, apart from the purely honorary one of the Prince of Salerno. They had to recognize, however, that they needed a leader, if only to command military operations. The man who emerged was William Ironarm, who took the title of count in 1042.[13] When he died in 1046, his brother Drogo succeeded him, taking the title of 'Count of the Normans in the whole of Apulia and the whole of Calabria'.[14] Theoretically, then, his power was not limited to the conquered territories: it extended over all the lands the Normans hoped to conquer, including Calabria. Drogo was the leader of a people, rather than the master of a specific territory. The title also established a form of hereditary succession. From now on, the leaders would preferably be chosen from among the Hauteville family.

Younger sons
The Normans of southern Italy were primarily soldiers, which meant that they belonged to the minor aristocracy. In Normandy, not all the sons of these families could become established. The eldest took the lion's share (two-thirds), according to Norman custom.[15] The younger sons had no other choice but to leave and seek their fortunes elsewhere.

That is what happened to the Hauteville family, about which we are a little better informed, although the origins of the family remain shrouded in legend. The first member of the family known to us was a minor aristocrat in the diocese of Coutances, Tancred, Lord of Hauteville. There are three Hautevilles in the modern-day department of La Manche,[16] but traditionally Hauteville-la-Guichard has been accepted as the birthplace of the family.[17] This lord had twelve sons, obviously a highly symbolic number. Only one remained in Normandy; the others left for Italy. They arrived in several waves, there being great differences in age between these children of two marriages. Five sons from the first marriage arrived in the 1030s: William Ironarm, Drogo, Humphrey, Geoffrey and Serlo. The sons of the second marriage do not seem to have arrived before about 1045. The oldest was Robert, nicknamed Guiscard (the Cunning), followed by Malger, William, Alfred, Hubert, Tancred, and the youngest, Roger, who was also to play a major role.[18]

Not all Normans came, like the Hautevilles, because of a hunger for land. Many emigrants were nobles who found it hard to tolerate the rise in ducal power. Richard II had regularized the administration, with viscounts as supervisors, and the local lords were left with few powers. Some were tempted to rebel, but they knew they risked banishment without trial from the duchy, because of a law of Scandinavian origin called *ullac*.[19] To avoid the duke's anger, some preferred to anticipate the punishment. Some Normans went to Spain, where they took part in the *Reconquista*; some even went as far afield as Anatolia.[20] Most, however, set off for Italy, where many of their fellow countrymen had already settled. Among these exiles, mention should be made of Osmond Dregot – he had killed a friend of the duke (*c.*1015), William Werlenc, Count of Mortain, who was related to the ducal family (*c.*1056) – and Robert of Grandmesnil, Abbot of Saint-Evroult, who would be in charge of several Italian monasteries (1061).[21]

The attractions of Italy itself should also be borne in mind. It was already a rich country, with magnificent landscapes and beautiful ancient monuments which greatly impressed the authors of the time. Those who had passed through Italy as pilgrims no doubt painted an idyllic picture and encouraged others to set out. So it was that the first Normans came, and came again. Thanks to the study of personal and place-names, we know that most of them came from lower Normandy, especially from the dioceses of Coutances and Bayeux.[22] These were relatively poor regions, where ducal authority was not well established until William the Conqueror. The Normans were joined by immigrants from other principalities, such as Brittany, Anjou and Maine. They all spoke Romanesque dialects (except for the Breton speakers) and understood each other without any difficulty.[23] In texts written in Italy, they were always referred to as *Galli* or *Franci*.[24]

After a few decades, there were enough of these Normans and similar immigrants to bring about a backlash. The pope and the Lombard princes were worried about their rise to prominence, which threatened the traditional balance of power. The local populations were less and less tolerant of being dominated by foreigners. It was in these difficult circumstances that a new leader would emerge, also from the Hauteville family.

The eldest son of the second marriage of Tancred of Hauteville, Robert Guiscard, arrived in southern Italy in about 1047 or 1048, when his brother Drogo was already recognized as the leader of the Normans. He must have hoped to receive land immediately, but his brother treated him harshly, sending off to 'earn his spurs' in Byzantine Calabria. Robert had to fight hard, using a mixture of force and cunning, to capture one fortress after another in the region. Employing the method which had served his countrymen so well, he built a motte-and-bailey castle at Scribla, which has been excavated by Anne-Marie Flambard,[25] and another at San Marco Argentano.[26] Operating in such a marginal region did not satisfy Robert, who was not lacking in ambition. In 1048, he also took part in fighting in the Principality of Benevento.

It was in this same year, 1048, that Leo IX was appointed pope by Emperor Henry III. He was the first reforming pope.[27] He would react strongly to the Norman threat to the papacy and its traditional allies. At the same time, the authority of the Normans was being undermined from within. The power of the Hautevilles was resented by several barons. Drogo was assassinated in 1051,[28] as was Guaimar V, the last remaining supporter of the Normans, in 1052. Leo IX now set about drawing together all the malcontents and organizing a vast anti-Norman coalition.

The pope managed to gather a large army composed of men of very different origins. Most were Italians, backed up by two contingents of hardened warriors: Greeks sent by Constantine IX, and German cavalrymen, recruited thanks to the support of Henry III. The pope decided to lead the campaign himself. Battle was joined at Civitate, in the north of Apulia, on 17 June 1053. The divided Normans all came together for this decisive encounter. The Italians and Greeks were quickly put to flight by the Normans. Only the Swabian cavalry remained, excellent fighters who resisted to the last man. The Normans emerged victorious from this terrible confrontation. Once again, they had demonstrated how brilliantly they had mastered combat on horseback with spears and swords: only the Germans were their equals.[29] Robert Guiscard had of course taken an active part in this great battle. It brought him great renown, which would subsequently prove highly useful to him.

Leo IX was severely affected by this defeat, which marked the failure of one of his greatest designs. Taken prisoner by the Normans, he was treated with dignity, but had no choice but to agree to their demands and accept the legitimacy of Norman power. In return, the Normans pledged their loyalty to him. The Normans' military victory was a great political and diplomatic success for them. Leo IX found it hard to recover from these events, and he died a few months later, on 19 April 1054, in Rome.[30] His successors were still appointed by the emperor, but they did not live long enough to assert their authority. Things would change with Nicholas II, who would deal directly with Robert Guiscard.

Humphrey had died in 1057, and his younger brother Robert had no difficulty in being recognized as his successor. In the years following Civitate, the Normans had free rein to embark on further conquests. Rainulf's son Richard of Aversa seized the Principality of Capua in 1058, then the Duchy of Gaeta in 1063. He became the accredited protector of the Benedictine monastery of Monte Cassino, whose abbot, Desiderius, was an invaluable supporter of the Normans.[31] Robert Guiscard himself completed the conquest of Calabria, with the help of his younger brother Roger, the last of the Hautevilles, who had recently arrived. The conquered areas were generally shared equally among the two brothers, who ruled them jointly.

The election of Nicolas II in 1058 was not like the preceding ones: Emperor Henry III had died in 1056 and his son, Henry IV, was still only a child. Elected 'by the clergy and people of Rome',[32] Nicolas II would prove to be a great reformer. His first concern was to remove papal elections from external influences, especially secular ones. The choice of pope was therefore reserved for the college of cardinals of the city and province of Rome. It was a measure dictated by circumstances, but proved surprisingly long-lived, being still in use today. In addition, the pope had it declared through the Roman synod[33] that no ecclesiastical office could be conferred by a lay person, 'either free or for gold'.[34] The struggle against simony was resuming in earnest. The power of the emperor was being directly challenged by these measures, and Nicolas needed support: naturally he turned to the Normans. This was a major reversal. The new pope was willingly accepting an alliance which had been imposed on Leo IX by force.

The new papal policy was formalized in 1059 at a synod held in Melfi, the capital of Norman Apulia. The pope attended personally. Richard of Capua and Robert Guiscard pledged their loyalty to him. The Norman rulers were now officially vassals of the pope. They would defend him against his enemies, especially the Germans. In return, they would benefit from his spiritual protection, the value of which was recognized by all Western Christians. In addition, the pope invested them in the territories they had gained. Richard was recognized as Prince of Calabria and Robert Guiscard as 'Duke of Apulia and Calabria, as well as Sicily yet to be conquered'.[35]

Robert had not succeeded in uniting all the Norman possessions and still had to reckon with Richard of Capua, but he had acquired the title of duke, conferred on him by none other than the pope. This son of a minor lord from Cotentin had raised himself by his own merits to the same rank as his contemporary, Duke William the Bastard, who came from a long line of dukes. In 1059 there were two Norman duchies, at the two ends of Western Europe, and their two leaders would distinguish themselves with major conquests, one in England, the other in southern Italy and Sicily. Robert was indeed to embark in the following years, with his brother Roger, on the conquest of that great island.

The conquest of Sicily

The conquest of Sicily took thirty years, from 1060 to 1091. It was led jointly by Robert and Roger, who divided the conquered territories between them, as they had done in Calabria. The two brothers once again took advantage of circumstances: their armies were often not large, and almost always smaller than those of their Muslim adversaries. It should not be forgotten that neither of them, especially not Robert, limited their activities to Sicily, where they made only sporadic appearances. They were often on the mainland, making new conquests, putting down frequent rebellions by their undisciplined vassals, or preparing military adventures against the Byzantine Empire.[36]

Sicily had first been subjugated by the Fatimids, who had seized Palermo in 917. Then for a long time power had been exercised by the Kalbid emirs, who recognized the distant authority of the Fatimid caliph. But the power of the Kalbids was strongly challenged in the eleventh century, both from outside and from within.[37] It had been seriously shaken by the attempted reconquest led by George Mainakes between 1038 and 1040. Since then, the island had been in the grip of centrifugal forces, torn between Muslim emirs, Arab and Berber, who were constantly warring with one another. Sicily is usually divided into three geographical sections, around three former capitals: the Val di Mazara (the west, with Palermo), the Val Demone (the north-east, with Messina) and the Val di Noto (the south-east, with Syracuse). These three areas each had different rulers. The Berber leader Ibn Mankut occupied the west and controlled the towns of Trapani and Mazara. Another Berber, Ibn al-Hawwas, possessed most of the Val di Noto, with Agrigento and Castrogiovanni, but not Catania, which belonged to the Emir Ibn al-Maqlati. The rest of the island, to the north and west, still obeyed the Emir of Palermo, the last son of Yusuf al-Hasan, who had been chased out of Palermo in 1052–3. Another emir, Ibn ath-Thumna, seized Syracuse and defeated the Emir of Catania. It was he who would turn to the Normans, whom he intended to employ as mercenaries in order to gain the upper hand over his adversaries. Ibn ath-Thumna is known to us through Geoffrey Malaterra, who calls him Betumen.[38]

In 1060, Robert and Roger had just completed the conquest of Calabria, seizing the capital Reggio, which was also the south-ernmost tip of the mainland, facing Messina. They responded favourably to the Muslim emir's appeal and landed in Sicily in the autumn of that year. The conquest of Sicily was, officially at least, completed by both brothers, who established joint rule – a *condominium* – over the subjugated regions. This curious system often caused problems, and Robert and Roger had to spend a great deal of time resolving their personal conflicts.

The stages of the conquest are known to us thanks to the work of Geoffrey Malaterra. They have been well summarized by Marie-Agnes Lucas-Avenel, the leading specialist on the author,[39] and I shall follow her account. The first stage consisted of three expeditions which all took place during the year 1061, in February, during the summer and at Christmas. The Norman troops seized Messina and penetrated deep into the interior of the island as far as Agrigento. The invaders were guided by their Arab ally, Emir Ibn ath-Thumna, who led them to the territory of his enemies, above all Ibn al-Hawwas, who held Enna and Agrigento. Roger set up his headquarters at Troina, a town situated at the top of a hill, which made it possible to keep watch on a vast area and avoid surprise attacks. By the end of this first year, the Normans controlled the whole of the Val Demone.

The second stage occurred during the years 1062 to 1063. The Normans now began to encounter major difficulties. First, the Muslims assassinated their ally, Ibn ath-Thumna, whom they considered a traitor. Then the Greeks of Troina rebelled against Norman domination, besieging Roger in the citadel during the winter. Forced to depart for Calabria to look for fresh supplies, he left his wife, Judith (who belonged to the family of the counts of Évreux) in charge.[40] The Muslims gathered their forces for a final offensive against the Normans. The encounter took place at Cerami, near Troina, in the spring of 1063. Although the odds were stacked against him, Roger again emerged victorious.

The third stage extended from 1064 to 1070, and was marked by the return of Robert Guiscard to the Sicilian scene. For the first time, the two brothers laid siege to Palermo, the Arab capital of the island, but without success. Once again alone, Roger won a further battle against the combined Muslim forces at Misilmeri, near Palermo, in 1068.

The final stage began in 1071. That year, Roger left Sicily to join his brother and take part in the final phase of the siege of Bari, the Byzantine capital of southern Italy and the last place to resist the Normans. Bari fell at last on 16 April 1071. Immediately, Robert and Roger returned to Sicily. Drawing a lesson from what had happened at Bari, they blockaded Palermo from both land and sea. Roger led the land siege, while Robert commanded the Norman fleet, which prevented any new supplies from reaching the town. Demoralized and starving, the inhabitants of Palermo capitulated on 10 January 1072. Immediately, the two brothers quarrelled bitterly over the fate of their new conquest. According to Amatus of Monte Cassino, they again established a *condominium*, whereas Geoffrey Malaterra states that they divided the towns between them, Robert keeping only Palermo. What we know for certain is that Robert would soon lose interest in Sicily and leave his brother to complete the conquest. The Val di Mazara would be entirely subjugated by 1078, the Val di Noto not until 1091.[41]

The conquest of Sicily was a series of skirmishes, ambushes and raids. The Norman army, comprising no more than a hundred cavalrymen, proved surprisingly mobile, moving from one part of the island to the other, many times over. But to take control of it, they had to seize a large number of fortified *castra,* and the sieges were always lengthy. The frequent disputes between the two brothers were in large part responsible for the slowness of the conquest. Roger may be considered the one true conqueror of the island, and that is how he is presented by his biographer, Geoffrey Malaterra, who never ceases singing his praises. To Geoffrey, Roger is the arm of God, given the task of defeating and subjugating those considered pagans. Of course, Geoffrey wrote his work after the First Crusade had begun, and clearly saw his hero as a precursor of the Crusaders.[42]

Roger became Count of Sicily. With the death of his brother Robert in 1085, the *condominium* was over, and Roger assumed authority over the whole territory. Modern Sicilians are proud of Roger, whom they call *il Gran Conte* ('the Great Count'). After the capture of Palermo, which he made his capital, Roger I would rule Sicily for the next thirty years.

The majority of the population of Norman Sicily were Muslims. There was a small minority of Greeks, composed of Christians who had not recognized the authority of the pope in Rome since 1054. They remained loyal to the Byzantine Emperor, and did not regard the Normans as liberators. From a religious point of view, they were in a very weak position, since there was only one Greek bishop left in Sicily, in Palermo. The Normans would respect the different religions on the island. The Muslims were not persecuted in any way. Robert and Roger merely contented themselves with a few symbolic acts. Soon after the capture of Palermo, for example, the city's great mosque was converted into a church and later became a cathedral. At first, the only Christians who followed the Latin rite were those who had taken part in the conquest with Roger; these were mostly from Normandy, of course, but also, according to Geoffrey Malaterra, from Anjou, Maine and the Île de France. They were joined by colonists from both southern and northern Italy. Gradually, the balance of the various groups within the population would change. For a long time, however, the Muslims remained a majority and Arabic persisted as the main language of communication, as well as the language of scholars, although Latin and Greek were also used in official documents and many French and Italian dialects were spoken. From the start, Norman Sicily was a multicultural and multilingual area.

Roger I's ambitions were limited to Sicily. Not so his brother Robert Guiscard, who, once the siege of Palermo was over, continued his conquests on the mainland. In 1076, with Richard of Capua, he seized the Principality of Salerno. The following year, 1077, the cities of Naples and Benevento also fell to his troops, and he continued to advance northwards, to the Abruzzi. The Normans were moving ever closer to Rome, and already encroaching on papal territory. The pope at the time was Gregory VII, who had been elected in 1073. He symbolized Church reform, and even lent his name to it ('the Gregorian reform'). Gregory briefly considered using force to prevent these encroachments, but gave up the idea, because he needed the military strength of the Normans to defend himself against Emperor Henry IV: the so-called Investiture Controversy was at its height in 1077, with the famous episode of the Walk to Canossa.[43] By 1078, the Normans had conquered the whole of southern Italy. Richard was still master of the Principality of Capua, but Robert had taken the lion's share for himself: he controlled the whole of Apulia and the Principalities of Salerno and Benevento, as well as Calabria and (with his brother Roger) Sicily. His ambitions did not end there. He had let Roger take care of what remained of Muslim Sicily, but he himself had his eyes set on a grander prize: the Byzantine Empire.

Robert was an old adversary of the Byzantines: it was against them that he had made his finest conquests, Apulia and Calabria. He had learned much from them, especially as far as war at sea was concerned. Like them, he had planned and led large-scale combined sea and land operations in order to capture both Bari and Palermo. To achieve this, he had assembled a fleet formed in large part by Greek sailors (especially Calabrians). He admired the luxury and wealth of the empire and dreamed of leading an expedition to Constantinople. He knew that the emperor's land armies could not withstand the Norman cavalry. In addition, he was well aware of the recurrent weakness of the empire, caused by the advance of the Turks in Anatolia,[44] palace disputes and succession crises. In 1078, in fact, the empire was plunged into one of these crises and Robert Guiscard decided to seize the opportunity.

Robert had married one of his daughters, Helen, to Prince Constantine, heir to Emperor Michael VII Doukas, and took a personal interest in the situation in Constantinople, in the hope that his daughter would become empress. In 1078, Michel VII was deposed and Robert started to make preparations for an expedition into Byzantine territory. These preparations lasted several years. Robert had the support of Pope Gregory VII, who hoped that the campaign would bring the Greeks back to the Church of Rome. Robert and his troops landed in Illyria in May 1081 and immediately laid siege to Durazzo (now the city of Durrës in Albania). The town fell, but Robert was unable to press home his advantage, since he was no longer dealing with the weak Michael VII, or even his successor, Nicephorus III, but with the best Greek general of his time, Alexius Comnenus, who had seized the throne. Alexius would re-establish imperial power, stabilize the borders and found the last great Byzantine dynasty, which would last for more than a century, from 1081 to 1185. Alexis was not only an excellent soldier, but also a skilful diplomat. He in his turn understood Robert's weaknesses. He encouraged the barons of Apulia to rebel and negotiated with the Holy Roman Emperor, Henry IV.

At the time, Henry IV was at the height of his conflict with the pope. The Investiture Controversy had taken a dramatic turn, and was now a major confrontation between the two higher powers of the Western world: spiritual power, embodied by the pope, and temporal power, embodied by the emperor. The pope released the German vassals from their oath of loyalty and urged them to choose a new king, Rudolph of Rheinfelden, who could be considered an 'anti-king'. For his part, Henry IV no longer recognized the authority of Gregory VII and in 1080 he appointed an 'anti-Pope', Clement III. The same year, Rudolph was killed on the battlefield. Henry IV now envisaged advancing on Rome, overthrowing Gregory VII, and installing his anti-Pope in St Peter's and the Lateran. The entreaties of Alexis Comnenus, accompanied by large financial contributions, could not have fallen on more fertile soil. Henry IV did in fact organize an expedition to Italy in 1081, followed by a second in 1082. In the course of the third, in 1083, he seized the Vatican.[45] He returned in March 1084, at Easter, and had Clement VII crowned in St Peter's. Each time, Gregory VII was forced to take refuge in the Castel Sant'Angelo.

The pope had his back to the wall. He had no another solution than to turn to the Normans. In 1081, he launched an appeal for help to Robert Guiscard. Robert waited until the capture of Durazzo, in 1082, before interrupting his campaign in Byzantine territory. His first task was to put down the revolt of the barons, which he managed without great difficulty. Robert then headed for Rome, which he reached in May 1084. He had no difficulty in entering the city, which was not very well protected by its immense wall dating back to the time of Emperor Aurelius. Henry IV had left the city again, leaving behind a large German garrison. The city itself took the brunt of the fighting and was partly burned, something for which the Romans could not forgive Robert Guiscard. Brutal their methods might have been, but the Normans succeeded in overcoming the German garrison and expelling it from the city. Pope Gregory was released from the Castel Sant'Angelo. However, owing his salvation to these burdensome allies as he did, he was forced to follow them to their territory. He ended his days in Salerno, dying on 25 May 1085. His tomb is still in the cathedral there.

Robert Guiscard had set off again in 1084 to continue his war against the Byzantine Empire. He was helped by his son Bohemond who, during his absence, had conducted several campaigns in Macedonia and Greece, and twice defeated Emperor Alexius. In 1085, Robert again led a joint operation with Bohemond. The Venetian fleet, allied with Alexius, was defeated and destroyed off Corfu. Robert was unable to take advantage of this success, however: he met his death on the island of Cephalonia on 17 July 1085.[46]

Robert's death put an end to his 'imperial dream', to use Pierre Bouet's expression.[47] His heir did not have the necessary stature to continue his adventurous projects. In this respect, his true successor was his nephew, Roger II, son of Roger I.

The heirs of Robert and Roger I

Although of very modest origin, the Hauteville brothers had carved out vast states at the point of the sword. But acquiring territory by conquest was not sufficient for them to be accepted by kings and other rulers belonging to old dynasties. To do this, they had to contract clever marriages. Rainulf of Aversa had set an example by marrying the sister of Duke Serge IV of Naples. The Hautevilles would do the same. William Ironarm married the niece of the Prince of Salerno, Guaimar V, and his brother Drogo married one of Guaimar's daughters. Robert Guiscard had previously married a Norman woman named Alberada,[48] and she had given him at least two children, Bohemond and Emma, who would be the mother of Tancred, the future Prince of Galilee. By the time Robert had become leader of the Normans in Apulia, in 1057, this wife was a burden to him, an obstacle to his ambitions. He therefore had the marriage annulled, on the pretext that they were too closely related. In 1058 he married a woman worthy of his rank: Sykelgaita, another of Guaimar's daughters. This marriage would prove highly useful politically. It made the Norman domination more acceptable to the native population. In addition, Sykelgaita was a strong-willed woman, conscious of her illustrious origins, and ready to fight tooth and nail to protect her children's interests. These children, of which there at least ten, were considered Robert's only 'legitimate' offspring. The seven daughters were all married off to the heirs of great families. The most prestigious of these marriages has already been mentioned: that of Helen and the son of the Byzantine Emperor. Another daughter, Matilda, married Ramon Berenguer II, Count of Barcelona. As for the three sons, they ensured the continuity of the dynasty. The eldest, Roger Borsa, was quickly accepted as heir by the 'Italians', because he was half Lombard. On the other hand, he had difficulty in being accepted by the barons because he was only half Norman! Fortunately for him, young Borsa found an effective protector in the person of his uncle, the 'Great Count' Roger I of Sicily, who managed to force his acceptance. Actively supported by his mother, Roger Borsa ruled the Duchy of Apulia up to his death in 1111; his son William succeeded him until 1124.[49]

Roger I had been married three times. His first two wives belonged to the high Norman aristocracy and were related to the ducal family. The first was Judith of Évreux, who had helped him greatly at the beginning of the conquest of Sicily. The second, Eremburga, was the daughter of William the Conqueror's nephew, Count William of Mortain. These two wives provided him with daughters, who all made good marriages. The most prestigious of these marriages were those of Judith's daughter Matilda with Raymond of Toulouse, who was one of the principal leaders of the Crusade, Constancia with Conrad, son of Emperor Henry IV, and Felicia with Coloman, King of Hungary. It was Roger's third marriage, to Adelaide Del Vasto, of the Piedmontese Aleramici family,[50] which produced male heirs. The eldest, Simon, succeeded his father as Count of Sicily, ruling from 1101 to his death in 1105, when he himself was succeeded by his brother, Roger II. Both Simon and Roger were very young when they acceded, and their mother Adelaide held the reins of power until she left Sicily in 1113 after her marriage to Baldwin I, King of Jerusalem.[51]

Roger II now found himself ruling both Sicily and Calabria. Belonging to the second generation of Normans in Italy, he had inherited all the good qualities of the Hautevilles. He was a fine soldier and an excellent politician. In a few years, he would succeed in uniting all the Norman possessions in southern Italy and be granted the title of king. So it was that, some decades after William the Conqueror, another Norman achieved the status of monarch.

Roger II settled in Palermo, the former Muslim capital, while his mother preferred to stay in Messina. He would rely particularly on Eastern Christians and converted former Muslims for support, trusting them more than he trusted the Norman and Frankish barons. In addition, he used many Muslims in his army. They were very useful when it came to fighting Christians, especially papal troops. From the first years of his rule, Roger pursued an active external policy towards the Muslim world. He launched several expeditions against towns in North Africa and seized the island of Malta. The same year, his cousin William, Duke of Apulia, died without an heir. As the last son of the Hauteville family, Roger II considered himself his rightful successor and would henceforth devote most of his energies to southern Italy. He travelled to Salerno, where the Bishop of Capaccio crowned him Duke of Apulia.[52] But most Norman counts and lords on the mainland refused to recognize his authority, and they were supported in this by Pope Honorius II, who excommunicated him. In two campaigns, in 1128 and 1129, Roger defeated the rebel barons, and Honorius was forced to recognize him and invest him with the Duchy of Apulia.

The situation would change totally, however, with the death of Honorius in 1130. Two competing popes were elected, Anacletus II and Innocent II, each by a section of the cardinals. This was the beginning of a schism that would last for eight years and tear apart the whole of the West. For their contemporaries, it must have been very difficult to make a choice between the two popes. Most monarchs therefore sided with one or other of the popes for political rather than religious reasons. Although Innocent was probably not most people's choice, he received powerful support from Abbot Bernard of Clairvaux, who managed to rally most Western monarchs to his cause, especially the King Louis VI of France and the Lothair III, King of the Romans (and future emperor). Even now, the Catholic Church recognizes Innocent II as the only legitimate pope of that time. Anacletus II is considered an anti-pope.

Roger II would draw as much advantage as he could from this situation. Almost alone, he came out for Anacletus II. Obviously, Anacletus was grateful and wanted to reward him. Roger asked for the title of king, which was granted to him on 27 September 1130. The first King of Sicily was crowned in the cathedral of Palermo on Christmas Day of the same year. The inhabitants of Sicily were happy enough to recognize the new king. They may well have been secretly flattered to be a kingdom for the first time in their history. So far they had mostly been ruled by foreign powers. On the other hand, this sudden increase in Roger's power, symbolic though it may have been, was unacceptable to his enemies, the barons of Apulia and Pope Innocent II. The pope appealed to his followers in the West, but only the King of the Romans responded.

Once again, Roger had no difficulty in defeating his rebel barons, at Nocera, on 25 July 1132. The expected German expedition was a much riskier proposition. Lothair arrived in Rome at the end of spring 1133. On 4 June, he was crowned emperor by Innocent II in San Giovanni Laterano, the cathedral of Rome (Anacletus II held the basilica of St Peter's). Lothair's prestige was greatly increased by this title of Holy Roman Emperor which only the pope could confer on him. This time, he did not enter the lands of the King of Sicily, but promised to return. In 1136–7 a new imperial expedition took place. Lothair invaded Roger's possessions and seized the city of Salerno. The barons took advantage of this godsend to rebel again. Roger took care not to confront the powerful German army directly. He refused to join battle, waiting instead for the heat of southern Italy to bring illness and death to the German ranks. He also knew that the emperor could not linger too long in Italy: his vassals would only accept a short campaign. In the event, Lothair left again without any decisive battle having taken place. Roger now only had to subjugate his usual rebels.

A few months later, Anacletus II died and Innocent II became the only pope. He seized the opportunity to resume hostilities, at the same time excommunicating Roger again. The King of Sicily was not looking for a confrontation, but he was forced to resist this invasion. Battle was joined on the river Garigliano, south of Gaeta, on 22 July 1139; Roger's troops won a great victory over the papal army. Innocent II found himself in the same situation as Leo IX three-quarters of a century earlier. Like his predecessor, he was forced to lift the excommunication and recognize Roger as King of Sicily, Duke of Apulia and Prince of Capua.[53] Roger accepted papal sovereignty over his states, symbolized by the annual payment of a sum of 600 *schifati*. In other words, Innocent II found himself obliged to confirm, term by term, the concession which had been made by Anacletus nine years earlier. It was obviously a great moral victory for Roger, who was now recognised incontrovertibly by the sole legitimate pope. In fact, his authority would no longer be questioned, whether from outside or from within, during the remaining fifteen years of his reign.

It was at this time, in 1140, that the king promulgated the rulings of the famous Assizes of Ariano, probably at an assembly held in Ariano Irpino.[54] This corpus of law established a centralized state, which was quite new for the region. Having been constantly rebellious, the barons were excluded from government. The king relied for support on capable men often recruited from abroad, such as Christodoulos, a former Muslim who was given the offices of *protobilissime* then 'emir', or George of Antioch, called either 'Emir of Emirs' (in Arabic) or *archonte of archontes* (in Greek). Palermo became a true administrative capital, where the kingdom was governed from offices called, in a curious Arabic-Latin pidgin, *dohana de secretis* (financial service) or *dohana de baronum* (service controlling the judges who represented the king in the towns and regions).

Innocent II, however, could not forgive Roger his relations with the Muslims, at a time when the Crusades had greatly increased mistrust and hostility between the followers of the two religions. In this respect, Sicily was a remarkable exception to the general rule. The king had no hesitation, as we have seen, in sending Muslim troops to fight Christians. In addition, he was extremely tolerant towards Islam, allowing it to be practised freely in the kingdom, especially in Sicily. On the other hand, Roger could also act as a good Christian and make gestures of goodwill towards the Church. He supported the monasteries, both Greek and Latin, and encouraged the establishment of new ones, in particular those of the Cistercians, then expanding rapidly. This policy earned him the gratitude of

Saint Bernard, who changed his attitude towards him in a spectacular fashion. However, not everything was perfect in the eyes of the ecclesiastical authorities. The king kept a tight control over the appointments of bishops and abbots, which contravened one of the essential tenets of the Gregorian reform. He benefited from an extraordinary privilege, the so-called Sicilian Legateship, which had been granted to his father, Roger I, by Pope Urban II in 1098. Under the terms of this agreement, the pope could not send legates to Sicily, and the count (later the king) himself fulfilled the function of legate. The legateship did not, however, apply to the king's possessions on the mainland. This exceptional dispensation made the application of reform more difficult in Sicily. Constantly challenged by the popes, the privilege was ardently defended by Roger II.[55]

The king's sexual morals also left a lot to be desired. Of course Roger was legitimately married to a Christian queen. In fact, he had had three Christian queens: Elvira of Castille, Sybilla of Burgundy and Beatrice of Rethel. But, at the same time, he kept a genuine harem in his palace, just like an Arab sultan. It was guarded by eunuchs led by a former Muslim, the 'great eunuch' Philip of Mahdiyya. The harem was composed entirely of Muslim women,[56] who were kept busy in the palace workshop, the *Tiraz*. It was this workshop that had produced Roger's splendid coronation cloak, which is now in Vienna.[57]

As we have seen, Roger II was the second Norman, after William the Conqueror, to found a new Norman kingdom. The two men were very different, but they had qualities in common. Good warriors and excellent strategists, they were above all great politicians and good organizers. Both ruled over mixed populations which somehow had to live together. In southern Italy, and especially in Sicily, Roger II encouraged harmonious cohabitation between communities – Latin, Greek, Jewish and Muslim – which elsewhere were in conflict at this time of Crusades. Both Roger and William appear to us less as adventurers than as builders of states.

Their successors inherited these two kingdoms without having had to conquer them. Some proved unworthy of their predecessors. Others, on the contrary, were able to maintain a heritage which, because of marriages and succession crises, was often no longer uniquely Norman. The heirs of the Norman kings were also Angevins, in England and Normandy, or Germans, in southern Italy. The most remarkable were, on the one side, Henry I Beauclerc and Richard Lionheart, and on the other, William I and Frederick II, King of Sicily and Holy Roman Emperor.

8

GREATNESS AND DECLINE

It is always difficult to succeed a great man. The Normans were no exception. The sons of the founders had a great deal of difficulty in being accepted by their new subjects, since their power was not based on personal merit but only on a right of inheritance which could be challenged and often was. In many cases, the successions provoked crisis, and even civil war. That is what happened in Normandy and in England after the death of William the Conqueror in 1087, and again after the death of his youngest son, Henry I Beauclerc, in 1135. The period known as the Anarchy which followed, from 1135 to 1154, was the result of the succession of a woman, Matilda the Empress, who was unable to take possession of the whole of her inheritance. This crisis led to the emergence of a new dynasty, the Plantagenets, which to a large extent was able to take up the torch of the Norman adventure, with Kings Henry II and Richard Lionheart.

In southern Italy, too, the barons were loath to accept the authority of young Roger Borsa, who succeeded Robert

Guiscard in 1085. Excluded from the succession in Apulia, Robert's eldest son, Bohemond, had to conquer his own principality in Antioch, during the First Crusade, gaining a reputation there which extended throughout the West. He was the true heir of Robert Guiscard. In Italy itself, as we have seen, power finally reverted to Roger II, son of the Great Count and first King of Sicily. His succession led to a period of unrest, but his son William I was quickly recognized. The real problems would arise some decades later, again because of the succession of a woman. The only legitimate heir to the Kingdom of Sicily was Constance, who was married to the Holy Roman Emperor, Henry VI, a fact which was to prove disastrous for the kingdom in the years 1189 to 1194. Nevertheless, the marriage of Henry VI and Constance would produce Frederick II, an extraordinary figure who would prolong the Norman adventure until the very middle of the thirteenth century.

By this time, Normandy had long been part of the domain of the King of France – since 1204, in fact. The Kingdom of Sicily, founded by the Normans, survived much longer then the Anglo-Norman kingdom and its continuation, the Plantagenet state. William the Conqueror had founded a royal dynasty which would rule England for centuries, but the union between the kingdom and the duchy was only to survive him with difficulty, since his sons immediately disputed the entire inheritance.

A disputed inheritance
Duke William's eldest son, Robert Curthose, was betrothed at a very young age to Margaret, heir to the County of Maine, but she died prematurely. When Robert reached adulthood, he was unable to exert any power over Maine, even though theoretically he was still the count, because it was firmly under his father's authority. That was one of the reasons, among many others, which led him to rebel against William.[1]

Relations had apparently never been good between father and son. More than a classic conflict of generations, it was the opposition of two fundamentally different personalities.

Unlike his austere, demanding father, Robert claimed the right to live a life of luxury and pleasure. He was not, however, devoid of qualities and proved himself a good war leader when the opportunity arose. On the other hand, he was a very poor administrator of his duchy. Overall, he appears to have been an unstable, indecisive figure, easily influenced and unable to impose his authority.

As the eldest son, Robert inherited the Duchy of Normandy, but not the Kingdom of England, which went to his younger brother, William Rufus. Deprived of the conquered kingdom – and the title of king – by his father, he must surely have felt as though he had been robbed. On William's death, he had the greatest difficulty asserting his authority within his duchy. The barons and lords expelled the ducal garrisons and took over their castles. Robert also had to reckon with the ambitions of his two brothers, who had also not accepted the conditions of the succession. It was not long before he was in conflict with William Rufus. Soon short of money, he was reduced to begging his youngest brother, Henry Beauclerc, who had received a large sum of money from his father.[2] In return, Henry was granted a vast estate in Normandy comprising most of Cotentin and Avranchin. But Henry was soon considered a traitor, since he had travelled to England without authorization to see William Rufus. On his return, he was imprisoned along with Robert of Bellême, which led to a virtual civil war in 1088. The fight against Robert Curthose was led by Roger of Montgommery, King William's former companion and the father of Robert of Bellême. The military campaign ended with negotiations and the two illustrious prisoners were released. Subsequently, Robert Curthose would be reconciled with Robert of Bellême and they would jointly undertake the siege of the castle of Courcy.[3] A few years later, in 1091, King William II himself landed in Normandy, but the promised confrontation did not take place. The two elder brothers, Robert and William, came to an understanding against the youngest, Henry, who had to flee Normandy.[4]

In the end, Robert never managed to establish his authority over Normandy. Instead of playing the arbiter, he took sides in the conflicts between the barons and participated in their private wars. The true arbiter was the King of England, who intervened more and more in the affairs of the duchy. Robert would have his hour of glory, however, thanks to happenings outside the Anglo-Norman world. In November 1095, at the Council of Clermont, Pope Urban II called for a Crusade. Among those present was Robert's uncle, Odo of Conteville, Bishop of Bayeux, who returned to Normandy accompanied by Jarenton, Abbot of Sainte-Bénigne de Dijon. A convinced supporter of the Crusade and a skilful preacher, Jarenton managed to persuade both uncle and nephew to become Crusaders. Odo was elderly and was to die on the journey, on his way through the Norman territories in Italy. He was buried in Palermo, the capital of the Great Count Roger I, in 1097.[5]

Duke Robert again negotiated with his brother, William Rufus. He mortgaged his duchy for five years for the sum of 10,000 silver marks.[6] Robert Curthose would become one of the leaders of the First Crusade, with Godfrey of Bouillon and Raymond IV of Saint-Gilles, Count of Toulouse. He would fight alongside members of his own family: his first cousin, Robert II, Count of Flanders,[7] and his brother-in-law Stephen Henry, Count of Blois.[8] In addition, he would rub shoulders with Normans from southern Italy, especially the fiery Bohemond, already wreathed in glory from his exploits against the Byzantine Empire. Leaving in 1096, Robert Curthose was present at all the important events of the Crusade. Passing through Rome, he crossed the Duchy of Apulia and embarked at Brindisi, along with the Count of Blois. They arrived together in Constantinople in May 1097 and agreed to the oath of loyalty demanded by Emperor Alexius Comnenus. Robert took part in both the siege of Antioch (1097–8) and the capture of Jerusalem on 15 July 1099. He returned through Italy and married the daughter of a Norman count from Apulia, Sybilla of Conversano. By September 1100, he was back in Normandy.

In the meantime the duchy had been ruled with a rod of iron by William Rufus.[9] William does not have a good reputation, because of his supposed morals and his bad relations with the Church. Of course, our information comes, as usual at this period, from clerics, in this case William of Malmesbury[10] and Orderic Vitalis.[11] Orderic reproaches William for wearing a beard and long hair, which was contrary to the dictates of Saint Paul.[12] In fact, he was not alone in this. It was the new fashion adopted by the whole of the Anglo-Norman aristocracy, following the example set by the English nobles. But there are more serious allegations. Orderic Vitalis writes: 'He had no lawful wife. But he gave himself insatiably to obscene fornications and frequent adulteries. Soiled by his sins, he set a guilty example of shameful debauchery to his subjects.'[13] Orderic seems to be making a veiled allusion to the king's probable homosexuality or, at least, bisexuality. Among his companions in 'debauchery', we also find overt heterosexuals, such as Ranulf Flambard, the not very worthy Bishop of Durham. Given this situation, it is not surprising that William Rufus found himself in conflict with the Archbishop of Canterbury, whom he had had to accept as Lanfranc's successor, Anselm of Le Bec (the future Saint Anselm).[14]

The king's morals were not the ecclesiastical authorities' only grievance against him. William deliberately gave bishops and abbots long holidays so that he and his favourites could make use of properties belonging to the Church.[15] He had also appointed some dubious characters to ecclesiastical office, Ranulf Flambard being the archetypal example.[16] The conflict with the Archbishop of Canterbury broke out as soon as he was chosen, and relations continued to deteriorate until the prelate's exile in 1098.[17]

William Rufus remains one of the few Christian rulers who refused to marry, and therefore to have children. He died without an heir, in a hunting accident in the New Forest on 2 August 1100. This was too early for Robert Curthose, who did not return from the Crusade until the following month. In the meantime his brother Henry Beauclerc had seized the English throne.[18]

Henry, by chance in England at the time of his brother's death, did not waste any time. Immediately, he took possession of the royal treasury, deposited in Winchester, and two days later, on 5 August 1100, he was crowned King of England in Westminster Abbey. Robert Curthose returned a month later to a *fait accompli*. A new conflict was inevitable between William the Conqueror's two surviving sons.[19]

The new king owed his nickname of Beauclerc to the fact that he had received a literary education. Such an education was not common in the eleventh century for the sons of kings and barons unless they were destined for an ecclesiastical career, which is likely to have been the case with Henry. He was William's third son, and William had no territory to give him. When his father died, he was only nineteen and had not yet been appointed to ecclesiastical office. This made it possible when the time came, in 1100, to accede to the throne without any problems: this would have been more difficult, if not impossible, had he been a cleric.

Henry was a good horseman: he was able to fight in battle and lead his armies to victory. He proved to be a better politician than his brother Robert and gained the upper hand over him as much through diplomacy as through war. He was also able to negotiate skilfully with the various popes, especially Calixtus II,[20] as well as with the King of France, his contemporary Louis VI the Fat. Henry could also be pitiless towards his enemies, particularly those he regarded as rebels. When his own illegitimate daughter, Juliane, rebelled against him with her husband Eustace of Breteuil, Henri took out his anger on his own granddaughters, having them mutilated by way of reprisal.[21] Whenever a town refused to surrender, he would have no hesitation in burning it to the ground, an effective method on a military level but a cruel blow to the inhabitants. Such methods allowed Henry to assert his authority over Norman lords who, disputing his legitimacy, were constantly tempted to rebel. Henry possessed both the qualities and the defects of his father, William the Conqueror. He was a genuine statesman and was able, like him, to unite and rule both Normandy and England. To do so, he had to crush his brother Robert, who would probably not have succeeded as well as he did. In a way, he was a worthy successor to William I, but also to William II, who had managed to rule England and Normandy without any problems during Robert's absence between 1096 and 1100.

Robert's return led to unrest in England. Many of the Anglo-Norman barons would have preferred him to Henry as king. For his part, Robert, who was William the Conqueror's eldest son, believed, with some justice, that he had been deprived of his rightful inheritance for the second time. Responding to an appeal from the English barons, he landed in England in 1101. Henry, however, was not yet ready for a fight, and an agreement was reached. Once again ruled by Robert, Normandy nevertheless fell back into anarchy. In their turn, a number of Norman barons asked Henry to intervene. After a first attempt, in 1104, he embarked in 1105 on a veritable campaign of conquest.

Landing at Barfleur in April 1105, he seized Bayeux, which was loyal to its duke, and burned down the town and the cathedral.[22] Most other places surrendered without a fight, except for the Abbey of Saint-Pierre-sur-Dives, which was also burned down in 1106. At this stage, only a great battle ('God's judgement') could settle matters between the two brothers. It took place at Tinchebray [23]on 28 September 1106, and was won by Henry.[24] Robert's life was spared, but he was imprisoned in England, first at Wareham in Dorset, then in Cardiff Castle. Not only was Robert still alive, he also had a legitimate son, William Clito, born in 1102 from his marriage to Sybilla of Conversano. To many barons, he remained the rightful duke. This situation led to many rebellions during the rest of Henry's reign.

The years 1106–13 were devoted to establishing peace. One of the principal rebels, Robert of Bellême, was arrested, tried and imprisoned in 1112.[25] Orderic Vitalis notes, with surprise, that the Anglo-Norman kingdom was able to enjoy five years of peace, from 1113 to 1118.[26] However, the fundamental questions had not been resolved, especially that of the legitimacy of Henry as Duke of Normandy. In addition, young William Clito had managed to escape: [27] he would find refuge with the Count of Flanders, Baldwin VII, then with King Louis VI of France. By 1119, he was seventeen, almost of age, and many barons would rally to him.[28]

The civil war resumed on the death of Count William of Évreux in April 1119. As he had no direct heir, Henry seized his lands. William's nephew, Amaury III of Montfort, a baron from the Île de France, complained to Louis VI, who granted him Évreux. Henry laid siege to the town. He was now in the same position as he had been in at Bayeux a few years earlier. This time, Audin, Bishop of Évreux, was on his side. Henry asked the bishop for authorization to burn down his town and his cathedral. Audin agreed when Henry and all the barons present promised to finance the rebuilding of the cathedral.[29] In the same summer of 1119, Louis VI tried to intervene to help the rebels, but was defeated by Henry at Bremule.[30] The King of England might have believed that he had finally succeeded in asserting his authority, but a great family tragedy was to occur, which would have far-reaching political consequences.

Unlike his brother William Rufus, Henry I loved women. He had many mistresses and is known to have had at least a dozen illegitimate children. One of the most famous was Robert of Gloucester,[31] also known as Robert of Caen.[32] Once he became King of England, Henri made a lawful marriage to Edith, the daughter of the King of Scotland, Malcolm III. Edith changed her name to Matilda, the name of Henry's mother. This marriage produced two children: a daughter, born in 1102, also called Matilda, and a son, William, born in 1103. The succession was ensured. William was even nicknamed Adelin (from the Old English *Aetheling*), which means Crown Prince. But everything changed when, on a routine crossing of the Channel to England from Barfleur in 1120, the vessel the *White Ship* sank with William Adelin and another of Henry's sons, Richard, on board, as well as 300 young members of the Norman aristocracy.[33] This disaster led to a new rebellion by a number of Norman barons between 1122 and 1124. But the most serious consequence was the problem of succession. Henry, now a widower, contracted a second marriage with Adeliza, daughter of Godfrey, Duke of Brabant. No son was born of this union.[34] His only heir, therefore, was his daughter Matilda, who had married the Holy Roman Emperor Henri V. Widowed in 1125, Matilda the 'Empress' married again in 1128. Her new husband was Geoffrey Plantagenet, the heir of Fulk V, Count of Anjou.[35]

All things considered, Henry I was a great king. He may have acceded to the kingdom by luck, but he also had a will of iron. He succeeded in appropriating the two halves – England and Normandy – of his father's heritage, neither of which was intended for him, and thus reuniting the 'Anglo-Norman kingdom' founded by William the Conqueror. Admittedly, in order to do so he had to trample on the rights of his elder brother, Robert Curthose, who remained in prison in Cardiff Castle until his death in 1134. As for William Clito, he met his death in 1128 fighting to conquer the County of Flanders which had been granted him by King Louis VI.[36] Henry demonstrated great authority: it was the only way he could maintain the Anglo-Norman entity. A bald narration of the events may give the impression that he was constantly at war with rebellious barons. That is not entirely true. In the first place, these rebellions occurred only in Normandy; England almost always remained loyal to him. Secondly, the rebellions were restricted to certain regions, especially the estate of Bellême and the County of Évreux. They were quickly contained and put down by the king. Overall, Henry I Beauclerc can be considered a worthy successor to his father, William the Conqueror. He made it possible for the Norman adventure to continue in England, while treating the English much more tactfully than his two predecessors had done. There is no doubt that he was the first truly popular Norman king in England.[37]

On Henry's death in 1135, the absence of a male heir would unleash a period of anarchy, both in Normandy and in England, until the new dynasty of the Plantagenets asserted its authority.[38]

Matilda or Adela?

In 1127, Henry I had made the English barons take an oath of loyalty to Matilda. Nevertheless, immediately after the king's death, another candidate came forward, Stephen of Blois. He was the son of Stephen II Henry, Count of Blois, and William the Conqueror's daughter Adela.[39] If succession through the female line was allowed, then his claim was as good as Matilda's, since they were both grandchildren of William the Conqueror. Stephen quickly had himself crowned, on 22 December 1135.[40] This seizure of power unleashed a civil war, which was to last nine years in Normandy and eighteen in England. Matilda's cause was supported militarily by her husband, Geoffrey Plantagenet, now Count of Anjou. On either side of the Channel, the barons divided into two camps. The strongest support for Matilda in either England or Normandy came from her half-brother, Robert of Gloucester.[41]

King Stephen managed to gain the overall advantage in England, but was unable to overcome every pocket of resistance. One great battle took place, at Lincoln on 2 April 1141. It was won by the army of Robert of Gloucester and lost by the king, who was captured. But on 14 September of the same year, Robert was also taken prisoner, and the two illustrious captives were exchanged. It was a 'draw', and a state of anarchy was to continu in England until Stephen's death.[42]

In Normandy, matters were settled more quickly. During the years 1136 and 1137, King Stephen and Count Geoffrey of Anjou entered Normandy in turn, but neither gained any decisive advantage. The unrest continued until 1141. In that year, Geoffrey Plantagenet felt strong enough to undertake the systematic conquest of Normandy.[43] The situation was more favourable now. King Stephen had been weakened by the battle of Lincoln, and Geoffrey now put forward his son Henry, born in 1133. The boy (the future Henry II) was the legitimate grandson of Henry I, and the Normans were more willing to rally to him than to the Count of Anjou, who was often regarded as a 'hereditary enemy'. The conquest culminated in the capture of Rouen on 19 January 1144. In 1150, Geoffrey cleverly ceded the duchy to his son Henry, then aged seventeen. He himself died in 1151, before the age of forty.[44] In 1153, the young duke, now twenty, set out in his turn to conquer England. Stephen did not dare confront him directly, preferring to negotiate. Discouraged by the death of his eldest son, Eustace, he agreed to consider Henry Plantagenet as his adopted son and heir. Stephen died on 25 October 1154,[45] and Henry II was crowned King of England on 19 December at Westminster.[46] He was twenty-one, and was also Duke of Normandy and Count of Anjou and Maine. In 1152, he was lucky enough to be chosen as a husband by Eleanor of Aquitaine, who had just been repudiated by her first husband, King Louis VII of France. To his existing French estate, he added his wife's heritage, Aquitaine, a large area which stretched all the way from the banks of the Loire to the Pyrenees. He now controlled nearly half the Kingdom of France. Although he was still the vassal of the King of France as far as these French fiefdoms were concerned, as King of England he was his equal. Conflict was inevitable between the two kings, and between the two dynasties of the Capetians and the Plantagenets. It was a conflict that would last for several generations.[47]

The Plantagenet state was vast and disparate. Although Henry had a strong grip on England and Normandy, he had much more difficulty in asserting his authority in Aquitaine, where many barons jealously guarded their autonomy. He also had to reckon with the King of France, who seized every possible opportunity to weaken his powerful vassal. In addition, Henry II clashed with the Church, which he had hoped to keep under his control, as his Anglo-Norman predecessors had done. This policy became increasingly difficult to sustain at a time when the spirit of reform was abroad in the Church. The conflict between Henry and Thomas Becket, whom he himself had appointed Archbishop of Canterbury, is well known. The murder of Becket on 29 December 1170 had probably not been explicitly ordered by the king; but Henry was forced to assume responsibility and perform a humiliating public penance before the cathedral of Avranches on 21 May 1172.[48]

Henry was half Norman and his policies follow directly from those of William the Conqueror and Henry I. Normandy was the fulcrum of his state. Anyone travelling from Aquitaine to England had to go through the duchy, making Rouen the *de facto* capital of the whole Plantagenet entity. This became clear during the rebellion of Henry II's eldest son, known as Henry the Young King, in 1173–4, a rebellion supported by his mother Eleanor and by King Louis VII. Henry II retaliated by conducting a remarkable campaign in Normandy between June 1173 and July 1174, leading an army mainly composed of mercenaries from Brabant against the rebel barons supported by Louis VII. Once Normandy had been recaptured, the rest of the state fell into line.[49]

Henry the Young King was pardoned, but died in 1183. The new heir was the impetuous Richard, who had been granted the Duchy of Aquitaine. He, too, would rebel, with the support of the new King of France, Philip Augustus. Henry II's last years were difficult ones. Defeated by Philip and Richard, he was forced to accept the humiliating treaty of Azay-le-Rideau and died two days later, on 6 July 1189.[50] Richard, who was already known as Lionheart, succeeded him and inherited the whole of the Plantagenet state. He would show his true mettle during the Third Crusade.

The last Anglo-Norman kings

Richard was crowned Duke of Normandy at Rouen on 20 July 1189 and King of England at Westminster on 3 September.[51] The West at that time was reeling from the disastrous battle of Hattin and the recapture of Jerusalem by the Muslims in 1187. Philip Augustus and Richard had both taken the cross and sworn to fulfil their Crusader vows as soon as possible, under pain of ecclesiastical censure. This Third Crusade was known as the Crusade of the kings. The two kings, who were friends at the time, decided to leave together. The understanding between them did not last for long and conflict arose in the winter of 1190/1, which they spent in Messina, in the Norman Kingdom of Sicily.[52] In the spring, they set sail for the Holy Land. On the way, Richard seized the island of Cyprus. The two kings met up again at the siege of Acre. The capture of the town, on 12 July 1191, was the main feat of arms of the Crusade.[53]

Philip was then twenty-five years old and Richard thirty-three. In the course of the Crusade Richard proved himself a chivalrous king, gaining the admiration of his allies, and even of his Muslim enemies. Philip Augustus did not benefit from the same aura, but proved to be a better politician. Immediately after the capture of Acre, he returned to France, considering that he had fulfilled his vow. Richard continued to wage war, but did not succeed in retaking Jerusalem. Apart from Philip Augustus, the King of England had made many enemies among the Crusaders, especially Duke Leopold of Austria, whom he had gravely offended.[54] Now he was imprudent enough to return by the land route, passing through Germany. In December 1192, he was taken prisoner by the Duke of Austria, who handed him over to the Emperor, Henry VI.[55]

In the meantime, Philip Augustus had taken advantage of the situation. In defiance of the protection due to Crusaders, he had seized many border fortresses in the east of Normandy, in collaboration with Richard's brother, John Lackland. In addition, he sent the emperor many envoys laden with gifts to dissuade him from freeing his illustrious prisoner. These efforts proved vain. Queen Eleanor did everything possible to free her son. The subjects of the Kingdom of England and all the Plantagenet states were taxed to pay the enormous ransom demanded by the Germans (100,000 silver marks, weighing some 34 tons). Thanks to Eleanor, Richard was freed and returned to England on 20 March 1194. He immediately regained the upper hand over the King of France and was able to recover all the lost territory without difficulty. John hastened to make honourable amends. The two former allies waged war on each other: Richard defeated Philip twice, at Fréteval in 1194 and Courcelles in 1198. In order to secure the Norman borders, the King of England began the construction of a formidable fortress at Château-Gaillard, which was built in record time between1197 and 1198.[56]

Richard Lionheart, now at the height of his prestige, had managed to maintain the Plantagenet state established by his father, but still had to deal with the indiscipline of his Aquitaine vassals. He met his death on 6 April 1199, while laying siege to a small fortress belonging to one of these rebel barons, the castle of Châlus.[57] This was an unexpected piece of luck for the King Philip, who would be confronting a distinctly inferior successor.

John Lackland, Henry II's youngest son,[58] was thirty-two years old at the time of his accession. In order to succeed Richard, he had first to deal with his nephew Arthur of Brittany, who had a stronger claim to the throne.[59] Arthur was only twelve, but in August 1202, when Arthur became a real threat to John, the king took him prisoner and in April 1203 killed him, possibly with his own hands.

John was no match for that skillful politician Philip Augustus, who was able to deploy all the resources of feudal law against him. Like his predecessor, John had difficulty in controlling his Aquitainian barons. His anxiety at the prospect of a marriage between Isabella, heir of the Count of Angoulême, and Hugh IX of Lusignan, the new Count of La Marche – a union which might have led to the establishment of a powerful principality in the heart of Aquitaine – led him into a spectacular but risky operation. He had just had his own marriage to Isabel of Gloucester annulled, because she had given him no children.[60] Realizing the danger, while the guest of Hugh IX in Lusignan on 5 July 1200,[61] he travelled to Angoulême and abducted young Isabella, who was twelve years old, and married her soon afterwards.[62] This audacious coup was to have disastrous consequences for him.

Philip Augustus now had the opportunity he had been waiting for. His first reaction, however, was to attempt to negotiate. He was urged to take action by the Lusignans, who rebelled against John in 1201. Hugh of Lusignan and his brother Raoul of Exoudun, Count of Eu, considered themselves released from their feudal obligations towards John, who was their suzerain lord, and appealed to their monarch, the King of France. Philip waited another year, then summoned John to appear before the royal court, which assembled in Paris on 28 April 1202.[63] Failing to appear, John was sentenced in his absence to a *commise*, that is, the confiscation of all his French fiefdoms.

But the sentence still had to be carried out, and John had the means to defend himself. Philip Augustus had first to seize John's many fortresses, beginning with Château-Gaillard. The siege began in September 1203 and continued for five months. John did not react in any way, abandoning the defenders to their fate. On 6 March, the symbolic fortress was captured. After that, Normandy was conquered in less than four months by the combined armies of the king and his ally, Guy of Thouars, Count of Brittany.[64] On 24 June 1204, Rouen, the capital, surrendered. The conquest of Normandy was followed by that of Maine, Anjou, Touraine and Pouitou (the latter occupied only temporarily). Philip Augustus did not, however, have the means to pursue his advantage to the end, and most of Aquitaine was still in John's hands.[65]

But John had well and truly lost Normandy. He was the last King of England who could be regarded as Norman,[66] a king who had made no serious attempt to defend one of the finest jewels in his territory. This was the end of the Norman adventure in England. At the same time, or almost, the Norman kings were also disappearing from the Italian scene.

Unrealized dreams

In southern Italy, only the offspring of Robert Guiscard's second marriage had been recognized as his heirs. Roger Borsa became Duke of Apulia and Calabria in 1085, and on his death in 1111 was succeeded by his son William. In 1127, the principality was recovered by Roger II.[67] Robert Guiscard's legitimate successors were not in any way notable for either their personalities or their exploits. The same could not be said of his other son, Bohemond, or his grandson, Tancred.

Bohemond, one of Robert Guiscard's sons from his first marriage, was baptized with the name Mark, but is known to posterity by the name his father gave him when he was a child.[68] His story is closely bound up with that of his nephew, Tancred, the son of his sister Emma and Odo the Good Marquis.[69] Bohemond is one of the few figures of this period of whom we have a detailed description. This was written by Anna Comnena, the daughter of the Byzantine emperor, who did not like him but had seen him at close quarters in Constantinople. Bohemond was tall and strong. His fair hair was cut short, which had ceased to be the fashion among Western knights. Similarly, he did not have a beard. 'His blue eyes expressed both courage and dignity.'[70] After his father's death, Bohemond had to negotiate with his brother Roger Borsa for the establishment of an estate in the heel of the Italian boot, around Taranto and Otranto.[71] Reduced to being the vassal of a second-rate brother, Bohemond felt as though he were stagnating in Italy. The First Crusade would provide him with the opportunity to manifest his military skills and realize his ambitions – or at least he hoped it would.

Bohemond took command of a modest but well-trained contingent of southern Italians, accustomed to fighting both the Byzantines and the Saracens, and soon asserted himself as one of the leaders of the Crusade. He had experience of navigation and naval war in the Mediterranean, something the other Crusaders lacked. His force arrived in Constantinople on 9 April 1097. In the days that followed, Bohemond readily agreed to make the Byzantine emperor Alexius Comnenus the required oath of loyalty. He certainly had no intention of respecting it, which the emperor knew: in fact, he considered Bohemond 'a most villainous individual'.[72] Bohemond's nephew Tancred, who was more honest, refrained from passing through Constantinople, thus avoiding having to make the oath.[73]

In reality, Bohemond's intention was not to liberate Jerusalem, but to carve out a principality or kingdom for himself from Saracen or Byzantine territory. The opportunity was provided by the siege of Antioch, which began in October 1097. Antioch was a great Greek city, recently captured by the Turks.[74] Bohemond played a vital role in the siege and in the final battle of 28 June 1098. Immediately the city was taken he decided not to continue with the others to Jerusalem. He would stay in Antioch and make it the capital of the principality he so desired. Naturally, he refused to restore it to the Byzantine emperor. As for Tancred, he fulfilled his Crusader vow and took part in the capture of Jerusalem in July 1099.[75] He was granted Galilee, including the town of Tiberias, while also remaining Bohemond's loyal second-in-command in Antioch.

In his first years in Antioch, Bohemond tried to assert his authority in the region. He had determined enemies, Byzantine and Muslim, to deal with. In 1100, he was taken prisoner by Emir Malik Ghazi and remained in captivity for nearly three years. The regency of the Principality of Antioch was ensured during this time by the ever-loyal Tancred, who managed to capture many fortresses from the Byzantines.[76] Bohemond realized that he and the other Frankish princes could not preserve their possessions without another intervention by westerners. In 1104, therefore, at the height of his prestige, he left for Europe. The message he wanted to convey was this: the chief enemies of the Franks were not the Saracens, but the Byzantines. He was well received by Pope Paschal II and King Philip I of France, who gave Bohemond his legitimate daughter Constance in marriage,[77] and Tancred his illegitimate daughter Cecilia.[78] It was a magnificent show of gratitude by the king to the two Norman heroes who had seized the opportunities presented them by the Crusade.

Returning to the Mediterranean, Bohemond attacked the Byzantine Empire and laid siege to the symbolic fortress of Durazzo. But the siege ended in failure: he was forced to surrender to Alexius Comnenus and accept a humiliating treaty. Bohemond appears to have been profoundly discouraged, feeling that all his hopes had been dashed. He would never be able to defeat Alexis, nor seize his empire. Leaving the Principality of Antioch to Tancred, he withdrew to Apulia, where he died in 1111. He was buried in the cathedral of Canosa.[79] Tancred succeeded him as Prince of Antioch, but died soon afterwards, in 1112.[80] From his marriage to Constance, Bohemond had had a son, Bohemond II, who was still very young at this time. This was the beginning of a dynasty which would survive in the East until 1287.[81]

Bohemond and Tancred are brilliant exceptions. The lineage of Robert Guiscard in Italy died out in 1127. The dynasty of the Norman kings in Sicily issued from the Great Count Roger I. For most of the twelfth century, it was the successors of Roger II who would reign over this kingdom.

The last lights of Norman Sicliy

The son and successor of Roger II bore the name William, an illustrious name among the Normans since the Conqueror. He is traditionally called 'the Bad', a nickname he owes to the chronicler Hugo Falcandus, who considered him an indolent womanizer.[82] William I relied greatly on his favourite, Maio of Bari, who was given the title of Emir of Emirs. The power wielded by Maio was regarded as excessive by many of the barons, and even by the clerics, and led to many rebellions. Maio was finally assassinated in 1161. William renounced his father's adventurous policies towards the Byzantines and abandoned his African conquests. At the same time, he tried to maintain a difficult balance between the two powers which threatened his kingdom: the Byzantine Empire and the Holy Roman Empire of Frederick Barbarossa. In 1158, he signed a thirty-year peace treaty with Emperor Manuel Comnenius. In 1165, he repelled a German expedition led by Christian of Mainz and restored the legitimate Pope Alexander III to the papacy, thus ending his reign with a real diplomatic success.[83]

When he died in 1166, his son William II was only thirteen. The regency was ensured by his mother, Margaret of Navarre. This was a period of unrest. But once he reached adulthood, the young king's authority was not challenged. His reign was peaceful, which earned him his nickname of William 'the Good'. Like his father, he had to deal with the problem of the great quarrel between Pope Alexander and Emperor Frederick. He played a vital role in the negotiations for the Treaty of Venice in 1177. One of the terms of this treaty was a fifteen-year truce between the Holy Roman Empire and the Kingdom of Sicily. The peace was sealed by the betrothal of Prince Henry, the heir to the empire, and William II's aunt Constance of Sicily, the daughter of Roger II, born to him posthumously.[84] No one could have foreseen the disastrous consequences of this marriage for the kingdom. William II now had his hands free to resume his grandfather's audacious foreign policy. Possessing a good fleet, he embarked on expeditions against two Muslim powers, the Ayyubids in Eygpt in 1174, and the Almohads in the Balearic Islands in 1180–2. But the main target of his attacks was the Byzantine emperor. Landing in Durazzo, his army penetrated deep into the empire, while his fleet appeared off Constantinople. This adventure ended in a fiasco, when the Normans were defeated by the Greeks on the Strymon in 1185.[85] After the Muslim recapture of

Jerusalem, William was involved in the preparations for the Third Crusade, but died prematurely on 18 November 1189, at the age of thirty-three, before he could take part in the Crusade. Because he died without children, a serious succession crisis ensued.[86]

The only legitimate heir to William II was Constance, wife of the German Prince Henry. The barons of the kingdom could not accept this, and they chose as king Tancred, the Count of Lecce, the illegitimate son of Roger, Duke of Apulia.[87] It was Tancred who welcomed the Kings of France and England on their way to the Crusade in the winter of 1190/1. Not long before, Emperor Frederick Barbarossa had also set off, taking the land route through Anatolia, where he died in an accident on 10 June 1190. This made Constance's husband the King of the Romans. He was crowned Emperor Henry VI in Rome in 1191. But he had no desire to let his wife's Sicilian heritage out of his hands. When he learned of Tancred's death on 20 February 1194, he decided to intervene immediately. He had no difficulty in having himself recognized, and was crowned King of Sicily in Palermo Cathedral on Christmas Day 1194.[88] Young William III, the son of Tancred and Sybil of Acerra, renounced the throne. The very next day, 26 December, Henry ordered most of the kingdom's barons, who had come to the capital for the ceremony, to be arrested. Many of them were tortured and executed in Palermo. Others were deported to Germany, including William III, who was blinded and castrated. With the convoy of prisoners went a substantial amount of booty, including Roger II's famous coronation cloak.[89]

A few years later, in 1197, an unsuccessful rebellion broke out against German domination, led by lords who had managed to escape the purge of 1194. A furious Henry took his revenge on his prisoners, ordering their eyes to be gouged out. Now master of both Germany and the Kingdom of Sicily, Henry VI had his sights set on the East. He was about to set sail, disguising his expedition as a Crusade, when he died on 28 September 1197.[90] His marriage to Constance had produced a son, born on 26 December 1194. Aged three at the time of his father's death, Frederick Roger, the future Frederick II, inherited his father's vast territories.

After Henry's death, young Frederick was taken to Palermo by his mother. But Constance herself died in 1198, placing her son under the guardianship of the new pope, the dynamic Innocent III. Innocent would fulfil his guardianship from a distance and regard the young prince as a pawn in the great game of Western politics. As an orphan, Frederick was brought up with a good deal of freedom in Palermo. He would nevertheless receive a solid literary education and be able to express himself in all the languages spoken in that polyglot island, including Latin, Greek and Arabic, as well as Provençal. On the other hand, we do not know if he spoke German, even though he was to become ruler of Germany.[91]

Frederick had an unusual personality. He displayed great intellectual curiosity in the most diverse fields, such as medicine or hunting.[92] He was also a harsh man, who could treat his enemies without pity. A fine Arabic scholar, capable of writing poetry in the language of Muhammad, he nevertheless deported a large number of Muslims from Sicily after rebellions in 1224 to 1225.[93] He was acutely aware of his role, especially after becoming emperor, and had no hesitation in clashing with successive Popes: Honorius III, Gregory IX and Innocent IV. He continued and even intensified the 'struggle of the priesthood and the empire' which had been poisoning relations between the emperors and the popes for more than a century.[94]

This exceptional ruler also had a taste for adventure. As early as 1211, at the age of seventeen, he left Sicily with a small escort on a hazardous journey to Germany, with a view to having himself recognized as King of the Romans.[95] The imperial throne was then occupied by Otto IV of Brunswick, whom Pope Innocent II had lost no time in crowning in 1209. Otto was a member of the Welf family, the great rivals of the Hohenstaufens. Frederick's daring was rewarded. He was crowned king in Mainz in 1212, and again at Aachen (traditionally the town for coronations) in 1215. Defeated at Bouvines by Philip Augustus in 1214, Otto was forced to give way to Frederick, who finally received the imperial crown from the hands of Pope Honorius III in 1220. But, in the enthusiasm of his royal coronation in 1215, he had vowed to go on a Crusade. The situation of the Christian possessions in the Holy Land being particularly difficult at that time, the pope urged to him to fulfil his commitment.[96]

Frederick prevaricated for such a long time that he was excommunicated by Pope Gregory IX in 1227. He finally went on his strange Crusade from 1228 to 1229. Instead of fighting the Muslims, he negotiated with the Ayyubid Sultan of Cairo, Malik al-Khamil. The two princes had much in common, and were able to discuss Arabic philosophy and poetry. Through these somewhat unorthodox methods, the emperor succeeded where since 1187 all his predecessors had failed. He peacefully obtained the restitution of Jerusalem to the Christians, the establishment of a permanent corridor between Jaffa and Jerusalem and a ten-year truce between the Franks and the Saracens.[97]

A few years later, Frederick made his peace with Gregory IX and signed the treaty of San Germano in 1230. This return to favour did not last, and the emperor was again excommunicated in 1239. The conflict became even worse under Innocent IV, who had the emperor condemned and deposed by the Council of Lyons in 1245. An anti-king was chosen in Germany, and rebellions took place as far as Sicily. Frederick was beginning to settle the situation of his lands, at least in Italy, when he died on 7 December 1250, at the age of fifty-six.[98]

Innocent IV and his successors were determined that no more of the Hohenstaufens should reign. Frederick II's legitimate son, Conrad IV, succeeded him, but died in 1254. Frederick's illegitimate son, Manfred, temporarily succeeded in asserting his authority. But the popes were looking for a prince willing to accept the crown, provided he was able to conquer the territory. The choice finally fell on Charles of Anjou, brother of the King of France, Louis IX (Saint Louis), who defeated and killed Manfred at the battle of Benevento in 1266. Two years later, in 1268, he defeated Conrad's seventeen-year-old son Conradin at the battle of Tagliacozzo[99] and had him executed in the market square of Naples, an act which marked the end of the Hohenstaufen dynasty.[100] Manfred was the last King of Sicily of Norman, or rather Norman and Swabian, descent. With him, the Norman adventure in southern Italy came to an end.

Overall, following the era of the founders, especially the founders of kingdoms, the era of the successors leaves us with a rather mixed impression. In England, the Normans were to leave a lasting imprint, but from the beginning the coexistence of the Kingdom of England and the Duchy of Normandy proved problematic. The entity thus created could only be maintained by exceptional figures such as Henry I Beauclerc, Henry II Plantagenet and Richard Lionheart. It only took a weak king, John, to destroy the fine structure inherited from William the Conqueror and Henry II. By 1204, it was all over. In southern Italy and Sicily, the Kingdom of Sicily founded by Roger II slipped away from the Norman kings in 1194, not because of their personalities but, quite simply, because of the absence of an heir old enough to reign. When Frederick II reached adulthood, he was able to give a last burst of splendour to the Norman Kingdom of Sicily, which lasted until the middle of the thirteenth century.

Many of these rulers of Norman origin had played an important role in the great collective adventure of the Crusades. This was true of Bohemond of Taranto, who seized the opportunity to establish the state that he lacked. It was also true of Robert Curthose, Duke of Normandy, who was recognized as a true war leader. And it was true, finally, of two other kings who have passed into legend, Richrad Lionheart and Frederick II.

Epilogue
THE TEST OF TIME

What is there in common between a Viking chief and a Danish or Norwegian king of the sea on the one hand, and, on the other, William, duke of a principality within the Kingdom of France and conqueror of England, and Roger II, creator of a new Mediterranean kingdom in Sicily? Whatever it is cannot be explained by heredity. There is no biological connection between the Scandinavians of the eighth century and the Normans of the eleventh century. Some Scandinavians did indeed settle in Normandy, but we now know, thanks to archaeological excavations, that there were not many of them. They merged into the surrounding population, marrying local women, and were quickly 'gallicized', even abandoning the use of their language after the middle of the tenth century.

We should not lose sight of the chronology. The Norman adventure stretched over four centuries: this book has described the various phases. They are separated by long intervals, when nothing particularly adventurous took place. This is even the case during the period of the Viking migration. Fifty years (almost two generations) separate the two waves of this migration (930–980). The second wave took place during the eleventh century, not long before the conquest of England by the Normans of Normandy. Admittedly, there is a link between the two conquests of England, the Danish one of 1014–6 and the Norman one of 1066–9. Nevertheless, they were carried out by two very different peoples. The Norman Conquest was a 'Frankish' conquest, as was very clear to contemporary witnesses.

At the other end of Western Europe, the conquest of southern Italy took place over a considerably longer period, throughout the eleventh century. From 1066 onwards, England would absorb many Normans, at least those with an adventurous spirit. Fewer chose the more exotic but more far-flung route southwards. In Italy, power was seized by ordinary men, not of royal or princely descent, but who asserted themselves by their own merits. A family from the minor aristocracy, the Hautevilles, particularly distinguished itself through figures such as William Ironarm, Robert Guiscard and the Great Count Roger, and gave birth to a new royal dynasty. In this case, there was obviously no direct connection with Scandinavia, except to a very isolated extent. We have seen how Harald Hardrada and the Normans of Italy both found themselves in the service of the Byzantine emperor in Sicily in the 1040s. This same Harald, having become King of Norway, was both accomplice and rival of William of Normandy in England in 1066. He lost and William gained the upper hand – that was the luck of history. But it demonstrates the breadth of the vistas opened up by the Vikings and their successors, who spread throughout the known world and even beyond.

What truly unites these 'Norman' protagonists, in the broadest sense, is the spirit of adventure. It took daring for the first Vikings to embark on such hazardous expeditions. There were many reasons for them to do so, principally, no doubt, the desire to procure wealth, a desire common to all mankind. The means used were not traditional, and they made it possible for the Scandinavians to live through an extraordinary collective adventure.

The Vikings were not only pillagers but also good organizers. Without towns themselves, they created them where they needed to, in both Russia and Ireland. They founded states, in England and Germania, but their most lasting success was Normandy. Thanks to its dukes, Normandy was for a long time the best governed principality in the Kingdom of France. These dukes were of Scandinavian origin, and yet, in order to establish their authority, they used means borrowed from the Franks.

The conquest of England is primarily the personal adventure of one man, William the Bastard. From his difficult childhood, when his very life was often in danger, he drew uncommon reserves of energy. He conceived the absurd ambition of conquering a kingdom. The remarkable thing is that he managed to communicate this ambition to his people, or at least to its aristocracy. Similarly, he was able to call on a network of alliances stretching to the other end of the Kingdom of France. England was captured by Bretons, Flemings and Frenchmen as much as by native Normans.

Once conquered and tamed, England was remarkably well administered, as was the Duchy of Normandy. The same is true of the Kingdom of Sicily, which Roger II and his successors would make the strongest state in Italy. This was still the case until the middle of the thirteenth century, under Frederick II. This 'good governance' remains without any doubt one of the most lasting legacies of the Normans. It was adopted by many states. The model of the Duchy of Normandy was first applied in England after the conquest, although the influences were mutual. From there, it spread to the Plantagenet state and finally to the Kingdom of France. Well before 1204, but especially after the conquest of Normandy, King Philip Augustus was greatly inspired by the Norman example, and the Kingdom of France in the thirteenth century seems to have been the best administered country in the whole of Western Europe. Paradoxically, this French model would be applied in its turn in the Scandinavian kingdoms, as well as in the Kingdom of Sicily after its conquest by Charles of Anjou.

The Normans who conquered England and Sicily were only distant descendants of the Vikings. Naturally, they remained proud of these prestigious origins. But they never considered themselves a superior race. They were determined to respect the conquered populations. William wanted at first to be a king to everyone, English and Franks alike. He only established a brutal domination over the Saxons after the many rebellions of the early years: this was certainly not his original intention. In spite of everything, over the years and decades, many links were forged between the Normans and the English. In the 1070s, William recruited Englishmen into his army to fight the rebels in Maine. On the institutional level, the king gladly made use of the more advanced elements of the English administration, such as the royal chancellery. Common institutions would soon appear on both sides of the Channel – the Exchequer, for example. Economic links would develop rapidly, especially between London and Rouen. But it was above all on the cultural level that the links went deepest. Of course, the conquerors kept their own language, a French dialect (Anglo-Norman), although they were unable to impose it on the people. After several centuries, English eventually triumphed, but by then it was a language totally transformed by its long contact with Norman French. Modern English is the fruit of this cohabitation.

In Italy, the Normans lacked the means to assert their authority by force, as they had been able to do in England. They had to show more consideration towards the local populations, who were of very different origins: Greeks, Arabs and Berbers, Lombards and northern Italians. It is interesting to note that the Kingdom of Sicily had three official languages, Greek, Arabic and Latin. Few in number and far from home, the Normans of Italy blended in perfectly with their environment. They often married local women. Robert Guiscard set an example by repudiating the Norman Alberada and marrying the Lombard Sykelgaita.

In the last analysis, the success of the Normans, in both England and Italy, was the result of a process of crossbreeding which was much more cultural than purely physical. Modern English civilization is largely the product of a fusion between Norman and Anglo-Saxon elements. Even today, many English people are unwilling to admit this reality, considering themselves heirs only of the Saxons who were conquered in 1066. In southern Italy, too, the success of the Normans can be explained by this crossbreeding. The Norman legacy is less evident there, its traces having been partly covered over by many subsequent conquerors. It has nevertheless remained alive in people's minds. The Normans were the only invaders who were generally accepted by the local populations in southern Italy and Sicily. The same cannot be said of the others. To be convinced of this, we need only consider the French under Charles of Anjou, who conquered the Kingdom of Sicily in 1266, and who were so hated by the population that they were slaughtered during the 'Sicilian vespers' of 1282.

A mere adventure cannot have lasting consequences. One of the principal merits of the Normans is that they made the most of their military adventures, establishing strong, well-administered states. It was in this way that they left a deep imprint on vast regions of the West, from England to southern Italy. More than adventurers, they proved to be builders, carving out structures which have stood the test of time.

CHRONOLOGY

Events in England are in italics.

I: The Viking migrations: Normandy and England

The Vikings in England and Neustria: 790–911

790–800	First Viking raids in the Frankish kingdom
820	First incursion into the Seine estuary (repulsed by shore guards)
841	Second incursion. Jumièges and Rouen are burned down.
845	First expedition to Paris (later repeated almost every year). First tribute (Danegeld).
851	Viking force winters in the Lower Seine for the first time.
852	Vikings winter again in Lower Seine.
853	New Scandinavian invasions on the Seine (and the Loire).
856–62	A Scandinavian 'great army' settles in the Seine estuary. Raids on the interior of the kingdom (especially Paris).

860–1	King Charles the Bald reacts by paying Danegeld. Robert the Strong is appointed the head of a great command in Neustria, to defend territory against both Vikings and Bretons.
862	Construction of a fortified bridge at Pîtres (Pont-de-l'Arche).
866	Robert the Strong dies while fighting the Vikings. 876 The Viking chief Rollo arrives at the mouth of the Seine (according to Dudo of St-Quentin).
876	*Conquest of the north-eastern parts of England by the Vikings (Danelaw). Foundation of several states, including the Kingdom of York.*
878–99	*Effective resistance by the Anglo-Saxon King of Wessex, Alfred the Great.*
885–6	The Vikings besiege Paris. The city is defended by Count Odo, the son of Robert the Strong. Emperor Charles the Fat buys their departure.
886–90	Rollo seizes Bayeux. Marriage *more danico* with Popa (who probably gives birth to William Longsword).
888–98	Odo reigns as King of France (first king from the Robertian family, the future Capetians).
898–923	Charles the Simple reigns as (Carolingian) King of France.

The first dukes of Normandy: 911–1035

911 (20 July)	Battle of Chartres. Rollo is defeated by Marquis Robert of Neustria (Odo's brother), Richard the Justiciar, Duke of Burgundy, and Count Manasses of Dijon.
911	Treaty of Saint-Clair-sur-Epte. The King of France, Charles the Simple, cedes the County of Rouen to Rollo. Birth of Normandy.
912	Rollo is baptized by the Archbishop of Rouen.
924	Rollo obtains Bessin and Maine (according to Flodoard).
927	William Longsword succeeds Rollo.
933	William Longsword obtains Cotentin and Avranchin (to the detriment of the Bretons).
937	*The Saxon king Athelstan defeats the Scandinavians at the Battle of Brunanburh and gains control of the whole of England.*

942 (17 Dec.)	William Longsword is assassinated at Picquigny on the Somme by the men of Arnulf, Count of Flanders.
942–6	Difficult minority of Richard I. The Carolingian king Louis d'Outremer tries in vain to recapture Normandy.
946–96	Richard I establishes his authority over Normandy. Alliance with the Capetians.
954	*End of the Scandinavian Kingdom of York.*
978–1016	*Reign of Ethelred II, King of England. Further Danish invasions.*
989–90	Norman bishoprics of Lisieux, Sées and Avranches are re-established.
991	Treaty of alliance between Richard I, Duke of Normandy, and Ethelred II, King of England.
996–1001	Minority of Duke Richard II. Unrest.
996	Uprising of Norman peasants, brutally suppressed by Count Ralph of Ivry.
996–1026	Rule of Richard II. Alliance with Robert the Pious, King of France.
1001	Abbey of Fécamp founded. William of Volpiano, originally from Piedmont and already Abbot of Saint-Bénigne de Dijon, becomes first Abbot of Fécamp.
1002	*Richard II's sister Emma marries King Ethelred II of England. They have two sons: Edward (the Confessor) and Alfred.*
1014–16	*England conquered by the Danes, led first by Sven Forkbeard, then by his son Knut.*
1016	Knut the Great becomes King of Denmark and England. He marries Ethelred's widow Emma.
1026–7	Rule of Richard III. He dies in 1027, possibly assassinated.
1027	Robert the Magnificent meets Herleva (Arlette) at Falaise. Birth of William the Bastard.
1027–35	Rule of Robert the Magnificent. Abortive expedition to England.
1031	Death of King Robert the Pious of France. He is succeeded by Henry I.
1035	Death of Robert the Magnificent on the way back from the Holy Land. William the Bastard becomes Duke of Normandy at the age of eight.

William the Conqueror: 1035–87

1. The minority of William the Bastard

1035–47	Difficult minority of William the Bastard. Unrest and rebellions.
1036	*Expedition by Edward and Alfred to England after death of Cnut the Great. Alfred is killed.*
1046	Conspiracy against William the Bastard. Assassination attempt at Valognes.
1047	Battle of Val-ès-Dunes. William defeats the rebels with the help of King Henry I of France.

2. The consolidation of the Norman state: 1047–66

1049	Council of Rheims. William's plan to marry his fifth cousin Matilda of Flanders is condemned by Pope Leo IX.
1050	William marries Matilda of Flanders.
1051	Campaign in southern Normandy against Geoffrey Martel, Count of Anjou. Recapture of Alencon. Conquest of Passais (Domfront).
1054	Battle of Moretemer. French are defeated. Failed invasion of Normandy by the armies of King Henry I and Geoffrey Martel, Count of Anjou.
1057	Battle of Varaville. Forces of France and Anjou are defeated. Another failed invasion of Normandy.
1060	Deaths of Geoffrey Martel and Henry I. Philip I accedes to the throne of France, at the age of eight.

3. The Conquest of England

1042–66	*Reign of King Edward the Confessor of England. Married to Godwin's daughter Edith, Edward has no heir.*
1051	*Edward names his cousin Duke William the Bastard as his successor.*
1064	Edward sends Godwin's son Harold to Normandy to confirm to William the promise of succession.
1066 (5 Jan.)	*Death of Edward the Confessor.*
1066 (Jan.–April)	*Harold is crowned King of England.*
1066 (20 Sept.)	*Harald Hardrada, King of Norway, lands in the north of England.*
1066 (25 Sept.)	*Battle of Stamford Bridge. Harold defeats Harald Hardrada, who is killed.*
1066 (29 Sept.)	*William's army lands at Pevensey, in the south of England.*

1066 (14 Oct.)	*Battle of Hastings. William the Conqueror defeats Harold, who is killed.*

4. William the Conqueror, King of England

1066 (25 Dec.)	*William the Conqueror is crowned King of England in Westminster Abbey.*
1067–8	*Uprising in Exeter.*
1068 (11 May)	*Matilda is crowned Queen of England in Westminster Abbey.*
1069	*Uprising in Yorkshire. York is recaptured by William. Rebellion harshly suppressed.*
1070	*Council of Winchester. Stigant is deposed. Lanfranc appointed Archbishop of Canterbury.*
1075–6	*Rebellion of the Earls. Execution of Waltheof, Anglo-Saxon Earl of Northampton. Ralph of Gael, Earl of East Anglia, takes refuge in Brittany and seizes Dol. Failure of last Danish invasion in Yorkshire.*
1076	Failure of William's expedition to Brittany (siege of Dol).
1077	Rebellion led by William's eldest son, Robert Curthose, with the support of King Philip I of France.
1080	Council of Lillebonne. William reasserts his authority over the bishops, especially as regards ecclesiastical law.
1082	William's half-brother Odo of Conteville, Bishop of Bayeux and Earl of Kent, is imprisoned.
1083 (1 Nov.)	Queen Matilda dies. She is buried at La Trinité de Caen.
1086	Domesday Book is compiled.
1087 (9 Sept.)	Death of William the Conqueror at Rouen. He is buried in Saint-Etienne de Caen.

William's successors: 1087–1106

1087	Robert Curthose becomes Duke of Normandy and William Rufus becomes King of England.
1088–91	Conflict between the two brothers.
1091	Temporary reconciliation. Drawing up at Caen of the *Constitutiones et Justitie*, a text recalling the rights of the duke at the time of the Conqueror.
1096	Robert Curthose leaves for the Crusades. The duchy is entrusted to King William Rufus of England.
1100 (2 Aug.)	William Rufus is accidentally killed in the New

	Forest. Henry I Beauclerc seizes the English throne.
1100 (Sept.)	Robert Curthose returns from the Crusades.
1105	Henry I Beauclerc lands in Normandy (at Barfleur). Burning and capture of Bayeux.
1106 (28 Sept.)	Battle of Tinchebray. Robert Curthose is defeated. King Henry I of England becomes Duke of Normandy. Restoration of the 'Anglo-Norman kingdom'.

Henry I, King of England and Duke of Normandy (1106–35)

1106	Robert Curthose is imprisoned in England. His son, the young William Clito, is given refuge by the King of France.
1106–13	Peace is re-established in Normandy.
1108	Death of King Philip I of France. He is succeeded by Louis VI.
1112	Robert of Bellême is arrested.
1114	Matilda, daughter of Henry I Beauclerc, marries Henry V. She is now known as 'Matilda the Empress'.
1118–19	Rebellion of Norman barons, supported by King Louis VI.
1119 (summer)	Siege and burning of Évreux, principal stronghold of rebels.
1119 (summer)	Battle of Brémule. Henry I defeats Louis VI.
1119 (Oct.)	Council of Rheims. Meeting of King Henry I and Pope Calixtus II.
1120 (Nov.)	The *White Ship* sinks, claiming 300 victims, including William Adelin, only legitimate son of Henry I.
1122–4	New rebellion by Norman barons.
1125	Death of Emperor Henry V.
1128	The Empress Matilda marries Geoffrey Plantagenet, heir to the Count of Anjou.
1128 (28 July)	William Clito is killed at Alost (Flanders).
1131	Geoffrey Plantagenet becomes Count of Anjou.
1133 (5 March)	Birth of Henry Plantagenet (the future Henry II)
1133 (2 Aug.)	The barons take an oath recognizing the Empress Matilda and her son Henry Plantagenet as the heirs of Henry I.
1135 (1 Dec.)	Death of Henry I at Lyons-la-Forêt.

The war between Stephen and Matilda: 1135–54

1135 (22 Dec.)   Stephen of Blois is crowned King of England. Matilda

	the Empress also lays claim to the throne.
1136–8	Unrest in Normandy.
1137	Death of King Louis VI of France. He is succeeded by Louis VII, who marries Eleanor of Aquitaine.
1139–41	*Matilda comes to England. She is supported by her illegitimate half-brother, Robert of Gloucester.*
1141 (2 Feb.)	*Battle of Lincoln. Stephen is defeated and taken prisoner.*
1141 (Sept.)	*Robert of Gloucester is taken prisoner at Winchester.*
1141 (1–3 Nov.)	*Exchange of prisoners. Stephen and Robert are freed.*
1141–4	Geoffrey Plantagenet conquers Normandy.
1144	Rouen surrenders. Geoffrey Plantagenet becomes Duke of Normandy (and Anjou).
1147 (30 Oct.)	*Death of Robert of Gloucester*
1147–9	*Expeditions by Henry Plantaganet to England.*
1150	Geoffrey Plantagenet cedes the title of Duke of Normandy to his son Henry (II).
1151 (7 Sept.)	Death of Geoffrey Plantagenet.
1152 (21 March)	Council of Beaugency. Marriage of Louis VII and Eleanor annulled.
1152 (18 May)	Henry Plantagenet and Eleanor of Aquitaine married at Poitiers.
1153	*Henry Plantagenet lands in England. Stephen of Blois recognizes him as his heir.*
1154 (25 Oct.)	*Death of Stephen of Blois, King of England.*

Henry II: 1154–89

1154 (19 Dec.)	*Henry II crowned King of England at Westminster.* Constitution of vast Plantagenet state stretching from Scotland to the Pyrenees and including England, Normandy, Maine, Anjou and Aquitaine.
1158 (autumn)	Campaign by Henry II in Brittany.
1159 (spring)	Campaign by Henry II against the Count of Toulouse.
1159 (Sept.)	Campaign in Beauvais.
1159 (Dec.)	Truce agreed with King Louis VII of France.
1160 (May)	Peace between Henry II and Louis VII.
1162	*Thomas Becket elected Archbishop of Canterbury, thanks to Henry II.*
1164 (30 Jan.)	*Constitutions of Clarendon, reasserting the authority of the king over the Church, especially as regards the choice of bishops and abbots.*

1164	*Thomas Becket rejects Constitutions of Clarendon and takes refuge in France.*
1166	Conquest of Brittany by Henry II. Henry's son Geoffrey is betrothed to Constance, daughter of Conan IV, Duke of Brittany.
1167	Conan IV is forced to abdicate in favour of Henry II.
1170 (14 June)	*Henry the Young King is crowned King of England (although the country remains under the guardianship of his father).*
1170 (10 Aug.)	*Testament of Henry II, arranging his succession.*
1170 (Nov.)	*Thomas Becket is authorized to return to England.*
1170 (29 Dec.)	*Thomas Becket is murdered in Canterbury Cathedral.*
1171–2	*Henry II leads a campaign in Ireland.*
1172 (21 May)	Henry II makes public penance at Avranches Cathedral.
1173 (21 Feb.)	Thomas Becket is canonized by Pope Alexander III.
1173	Henry II's sons rebel against their father (with the support of Louis VII).
1173–4	Brilliant campaign by Henry II in Normandy. Rebellion is quelled.
1180 (18 Sept.)	Death of King Louis VII of France. He is succeeded by Philip II Augustus.
1183 (11 June)	*Death of Henry the Young King. Richard Lionheart becomes Crown Prince of the Kingdom of England.*
1184	*Richard Lionheart rebels against his father.*
1186 (Aug.)	Death of Geoffrey, Duke of Britanny, son of Henry II.
1187	New rebellion by Richard, allied with Philip Augustus.
1187 (2 Oct.)	Jerusalem recaptured by the Muslims under Saladin.
1188 (Jan.)	Henry II, Philip Augustus and Richard Lionheart take Crusader vows.
1189 (June)	Henry II is defeated at Le Mans by Philip Augustus and Richard.
1189 (4 July)	Treaty of Azay-le-Rideau imposed on Henry II by Philip Augustus and Richard.
1189 (6 July)	*Death of Henry II. He is succeeded by Richard Lionheart.*

Richard Lionheart: 1189–99

1189 (3 Sept.)	*Richard Lionheart crowned at Westminster.*
1190	Vézelay. Philip Augustus and Richard leave for the Third Crusade.

1190–1	The two kings spend winter in the Norman Kingdom of Sicily (near Messina).
1191 (May)	Richard Lionheart seizes the island of Cyprus.
1191 (12 May)	Richard Lionheart marries Berengaria of Navarre in Limassol.
1191 (12 July)	Acre recaptured by the Crusaders.
1191 (31 July)	Philip Augustus leaves the Holy Land.
1192 (9 Oct.)	Richard leaves the Holy Land.
1192 (Dec.)	Richard is taken prisoner by the Duke of Austria.
1192–4	Richard is held captive in Germany.
1194 (20 Mar.)	*Richard returns to England.*
1194 (July 3)	Richard defeats Philip Augustus at Fréteval (Loir-et-Cher).
1197–8	Construction of Château-Gaillard.
1198 (28 Sept.)	Richard defeats Philip Augustus at Courcelles (near Gisors)
1199 (6 April)	Death of Richard Lionheart at Châlus, in Limousin. He is succeeded by John Lackland.

John Lackland, 1199–1216

1199 (27 May)	John Lackland crowned at Westminster.
1200 (26 Aug.)	John marries Isabella of Angoulême.
1202 (28 April)	John's French fiefdoms are confiscated.
1202 (1 Aug.)	Arthur of Brittany taken prisoner by John at Mirabeau-en-Poitou.
1203–4	Siege of Château-Gaillard by the army of Philip Augustus.
1204 (6 March)	Château-Gaillard falls.
1204 (spring)	Philip Augustus conquers Normandy.
1204 (24 June)	Rouen surrenders.
1214 (24 July)	Battle of la Roche-aux-Moines (near Angers). Prince Louis, son of Philip Augustus, defeats John.
1214 (27 July)	Battle of Bouvines (near Lille). Philip Augustus defeats Emperor Otto of Brunswick and John's other allies.
1215	*The English barons rebel against John, who is forced to grant Magna Carta.*
1216–17	Expedition by Prince Louis to England.
1216 (19 Oct.)	*Death of John. He is succeeded by Henry III.*
1217 (20 May)	*Battle of Lincoln. Prince Louis is defeated and forced to leave England.*

1223 (14 July)	Death of Philip Augustus. He is succeeded by Louis VIII.
1226 (8 Nov.)	Death of Louis VIII. He is succeeded by Louis IX.

II. THE CONQUEST OF SOUTHERN ITALY AND THE NORMAN KINGDOM OF SICILY

The first conquests

999	Forty Norman pilgrims put the Saracens besieging Salerno to flight.
1009–10	Failure of rebellion by the Lombard aristocrat Melus against the Byzantines.
1015–16	Norman pilgrims are recruited by Melus.
1017–18	Campaign in Apulia by the Normans led by Melus.
1018	(October) Battle of Cannae. The Normans are defeated.
1029	The Norman Rainulf receives the County of Aversa (in the Duchy of Naples).
1038–40	Attempted reconquest of Muslim Sicily by the Byzantines led by George Maniakes. His army contains a Norman contingent (including William Ironarm).
1040–3	The Normans conquer Byzantine Apulia, under the leadership of William Ironarm, eldest son of Tancred of Hauteville.
1045	Death of Rainulf I, Count of Aversa. He is succeeded by Ascletin, then Rainulf II.
1046	Death of William Ironarm. His brother Drogo becomes Count of Apulia.
1048	Robert Guiscard, younger brother of William Ironarm and Drogo, begins the conquest of Calabria.
1048	Leo IX becomes pope.
1048	Richard I becomes Count of Aversa.
1051 (10 Aug.)	Count Drogo of Apulia is assassinated. His brother Humphrey succeeds him.
1053 (17 June)	Battle of Civitate. The Normans defeat the coalition assembled by Pope Leo IX.
1054 (19 April)	Death of Pope Leo IX.
1057 (August)	Death of Count Humphrey of Apulia. He is succeeded by his half-brother, Robert Guiscard.
1057	Richard I of Aversa becomes Prince of Capua.

The alliance with the papacy

1058	Nicholas II becomes pope. New method of papal election (by cardinals).
1059	Synod of Melfi. Pope Nicholas II recognizes Richard I, Prince of Capua, and Robert Guiscard, Duke of Apulia, who become his vassals.
1061	Election of Pope Alexander II.
1061	Beginning of conquest of Sicily by Robert Guiscard and his younger brother, Roger.
1063	Battle of Cerami (Sicily). Norman victory.
1068	Battle of Misilmeri (Sicily). Norman victory.
1071 (16 Apr.)	The Normans seize Bari.
1072 (10 Jan.)	The Normans seize Palermo.
1073	Election of Pope Gregory VII.
1076	The Normans lay siege to Salerno. Robert Guiscard becomes Prince of Salerno.
1077	Robert Guiscard becomes Prince of Benevento.
1078	Death of Richard I, Prince of Capua. He is succeeded by Jordan I.
1081	Norman expedition against the Byzantine Empire. Conquest of Durazzo (Durrës, in Albania). Alexius Comnenius becomes Byzantine emperor and repulses the Normans.
1082	New Norman expedition against the Byzantine Empire, led by Bohemond, son of Robert Guiscard and his first wife, Alberada.
1083	Expedition by the German emperor Henry IV to Rome. Pope Gregory VII appeals to Normans for help.
1084 (May)	The Normans attack Rome. The Germans retreat. The pope is forced into exile in Salerno.
1084–5	New Norman expedition against the Byzantine Empire.
1085 (25 May)	Death of Gregory VII at Salerno.
1085 (17 July)	Death of Robert Guiscard on Cephalonia. He is succeeded by Roger Borsa, his son by his Lombard second wife, Sykelgaita.
1085–6	War between Roger Borsa, Duke of Apulia, and Bohemond, Prince of Taranto.
1090	Death of Jordan I, Prince of Capua. He is succeeded by Richard II.
1091	Conquest of Sicily completed by Normans. Roger I of

	Hauteville becomes 'Great Count' of Sicily.
1096–9	First Crusade. Bohemond and his nephew Tancred take part. Bohemond becomes Prince of Antioch and Tancred Prince of Galilee.
1101	Death of Roger I, 'Great Count' of Sicily. His young son Simon becomes Count of Sicily and Calabria.

Roger II, 'Great Count' of Sicily

1101–7	Roger I's widow Adelaide holds the reins of power as regent of the counties of Sicily and Calabria.
1105	Death of Simon, Count of Sicily and Calabria. He is succeeded by his brother Roger II, who establishes his capital in Palermo.
1106	Death of Richard II, Prince of Capua. He is succeeded by Robert I.
1111	Death of Bohemond, Prince of Antioch.
1111	Death of Roger Borsa, Duke of Apulia. He is succeeded by William II.
1112 (12 Dec.)	Death of Tancred, Prince of Galilee and Antioch.
1118	Expedition by the Sicilian Normans against Gabès (Tunisia).
1118	Expedition by the Sicilian Normans against Mahdiyya (Tunisia).
1127	Roger II seizes the island of Malta.
1127	Death of William II. Roger II seizes his possessions (in particular the Duchy of Apulia).
1128–9	Norman lords of Apulia rebel against Roger II.
1130	Election of two competing popes, Anacletus II and Innocent II. Supported by Saint Bernard, Innocent II is recognized by the King of France and the emperor.

Roger II, King of Sicily

1130 (27 Sept.)	Roger II is recognized as King of Sicily by Pope Anacletus II.
1130 (Christmas)	Roger II is crowned in Palermo Cathedral.
1131–2	New rebellion by Roger II's Norman vassals.
1132	George of Antioch is given the title of Emir of Emirs.
1132 (25 July)	Battle of Nocera. Roger II defeats his rebellious vassals.
1133 (4 June)	Lothair III crowned Emperor by Innocent II in San Giovanni Laterano.

	Expedition by Lothair to southern Italy. Salerno captured.
1138 (25 Jan.)	Death of Anacletus II. Roger II is excommunicated by Innocent II.
1139 (22 July)	Battle on the Garigliano. Roger II defeats the papal troops. Innocent II lifts the excommunication and recognizes Roger II as King of Sicily.
1140	Assizes of Ariano. Establishment of a centralised state.
1143 (24 Sept.)	Death of Pope Innocent II.
1144	Tripoli (Libya) is captured by Roger II's troops.
1147	Gabès, Susa and Mahdiyya (Tunisia) captured by the Sicilian Normans.
1147–9	Second Crusade.
1147	Corfu captured by Roger II's fleet. Attacks on the coast of Greece.
1149	Norman naval expedition to Constantinople, under the command of George of Antioch.
1151	Death of George of Antioch.
1153	Annaba (Algeria) captured by Roger II's troops.
1154 (26 Feb)	Death of Roger II, King of Sicily.

William I: 1154–66

1154	Roger II is succeeded by his son William I, known as 'the Bad'. Maio of Bari becomes Emir of Emirs.
1155–6	William's vassals rebel.
1156–60	Kingdom of Sicily loses its African possessions.
1157	Expedition against the Byzantine Empire.
1158	William signs a thirty-year peace treaty with Emperor Manuel Comnenius.
1159	Election of Pope Alexander III. Conflict between the pope and Emperor Frederick Barbarossa (of the Hohenstaufen dynasty). The King of Sicily supports the pope.
1160	Maio of Bari is assassinated. Unrest in the kingdom.
1161 (April)	William I re-establishes his authority.
1165	Expedition to Campania by Christian of Mainz, repelled by the King of Sicily. Pope Alexander III restored to the papal throne.
1166 (7 May)	Death of William I.

William II: 1166–89

| 1166 | William I is succeeded by thirteen-year-old William II, |

	known as 'the Good'.
1166–71	Minority of William II. Regency of his mother, Margaret of Navarre.
1166 (Nov.)	Stephen du Perche is appointed chancellor. He ensures the government of the kingdom.
1166–1167	Italian expedition by Frederick Barbarossa. Normans are defeated.
1167	Stephen du Perche becomes Archbishop of Palermo.
1167	Lombard League formed against Frederick Barabarossa, with the support of the Kingdom of Sicily.
1168 (summer)	Rebellion in Palermo. Stephen du Perche is forced to flee.
1169	The new Archbishop of Palermo, Walter of the Mill, seizes power.
1171	William II reaches his majority (at eighteen).
1174	Failed Norman expedition to Egypt.
1174	William II reaches an agreement with Venice.
1175	William II reaches an agreement with Genoa.
1176	Frederick Barbarossa leads a campaign in Italy. The Normans are defeated, but the Lombard League is victorious at Legnano.
1177 (13 Feb.)	William II marries Joan, daughter of Henry II, King of England.
1177 (1 Aug.)	Treaty of Venice. Frederick Barbarossa is reconciled with Pope Alexander III and Byzantine Emperor Manuel Comnenius. Fifteen-year truce between the Holy Roman Empire and the Kingdom of Sicily.
1180–2	William II's fleet launches attacks against the Balearic islands (then under the domination of the Almohads).
1181 (30 Aug.)	Death of Pope Alexander III.
1185	Normand expedition against the Byzantine Empire. Normans land in Durazzo. Capture of Thessalonika. Naval raid against Constantinople. Defeat on the Strymon.
1186	Frederick Barbarossa's son, the future Emperor Henry VI, marries Roger II's posthumously born daughter, Constance of Hauteville.
1187	Battle of Hattin. Defeat of the Franks. Saladin's troops recapture Jerusalem. William II takes Crusader vow.
1189 (18 Nov.)	William II dies at the age of thirty-six, without an heir.

Tancred of Lecce and Henry VI

1189	The Norman barons choose Tancred of Lecce, illegitimate grandson of Roger II, as king.
1190–2	Third Crusade, known as 'Crusade of the kings'.
1190 (10 June)	Death of Emperor Frederick Barbarossa in Asia Minor, on his way to the Crusade. He is succeeded by Henry VI.
1190–1191	Richard Lionheart, King of England, and Philip Augustus, King of France, winter in Sicily, on their way to the Crusade.
1191	Henry VI and Constance are crowned emperor and empress by Pope Celestine III at St Peter's in Rome. First (failed) expedition by Henry VI to Sicily.
1194 (20 Feb.)	Death of King Tancred of Lecce. He is succeeded by young William III, his son by his queen, Sybilla of Acerra.
1194	New expedition by Henry VI to Sicily.
1194 (Christmas)	Emperor Henry VI crowned King of Sicily at Palermo.
1194 (26 Dec.)	Birth of Frederick (II), son of Henry and Constance, at Iesi in the march of Ancona.
1194–5	The leading barons of the Kingdom of Sicily and young William III are arrested and deported to Germany.
1196	Young Frederick II is chosen as King of the Romans by the German princes.
1197	New rebellion by the barons, again suppressed.
1197	Death of Henry VI. He is succeeded by Frederick II.

Frederick II, King of Sicily and Holy Roman Emperor

1. The difficult youth of the King of Sicily.

1197	Frederick II becomes King of Sicily at the age of three.
1198 (8 Jan.)	Innocent III elected pope.
1198 (17 May)	Frederick II is crowned at Palermo.
1198 (27 Nov.)	Death of Frederick's mother, Constance of Hauteville. In her will, Innocent II is named as regent of the kingdom and Frederick's guardian.
1200	Markward von Annweiler, Margrave of Ancona and Duke of Romagna, captures Sicily.
1201 (Nov.)	Markward von Annweiler seizes young Philip and rules in his name.
1201–5	Walter of Brienne, second husband of Tancred of

	Lecce's widow Sybilla of Acerra, tries to seize Sicily.
1202 (Sept.)	Death of Markward von Annweiler.
1202–1206	The German captain William of Capparone gains authority over Frederick and rules in Palermo in his name. Anarchy spreads through the Kingdom of Sicily.
1206	Frederick placed under the guardianship of the chancellor, Walter of Palearia, Bishop of Troia.
1208 (25 Dec.)	Innocent III declares that Frederick has come of age (on the eve of his fifteenth birthday). Royal authority re-established in Sicily.
1209–10	Rebellion of Sicilian and Calabrian vassals, quelled by Frederick.
1209 (19 Aug)	Frederick marries Constance of Aragon at Palermo.
1209 (4 Oct.)	Otto IV, a pretender from the Welf family, is crowned emperor by Pope Innocent III at St Peter's in Rome (in disregard of the rights of Frederick II, heir of the Hohenstaufens). In Italy the followers of the rival imperial dynasties, the Welfs and the Hohenstaufens, are known respectively as Guelphs and Ghibellines.
1210 (Oct.)	The rebellious barons of the mainland part of the Kingdom of Sicily appeal to Emperor Otto IV for help. He occupies Capua, Aversa, Naples and Salerno.
1210 (18 Nov.)	Otto IV is excommunicated by Pope Innocent III, giving the emperor a pretext to invade the Kingdom of Sicily.
1211	Otto IV invades Apulia and Calabria and prepares to invade Sicily.

2. Frederick II sets out to conquer the empire.

1211 (Sept.)	Assembly of Nuremberg. The German princes again choose Frederick II as King of the Romans.
1212 (Jan.)	The German princes send envoys to Palermo to offer the imperial crown to Frederick II. Frederick accepts.
1212	(Jan.–March) Otto IV abandons idea of invading Sicily and hurriedly returns to Germany.
1212 (Feb.)	Frederick has his one-year-old son Henry crowned King of Sicily.
1212 (March)	Frederick sets sail from Messina for Rome.
1212 (March–April)	In Rome, Frederick takes an oath of loyalty to Pope Innocent II on behalf of the Kingdom of Sicily.
1212 (July–Aug.)	Frederick crosses northern Italy. He is welcomed in Ghibelline cities like Genoa, but has to avoid hostile

Guelph cities like Milan.

1212 (end Aug.)	Frederick overtakes Otto, and reaches Konstanz before him.
1212 (9 Dec.)	First royal coronation of Frederick II, at Mainz.
1212–1213	Frederick II is recognized in southern Germany (traditionally favourable to the Hohenstaufens). Northern Germany continues to favour Otto IV and the Welfs. Frederick II is supported by Philip Augustus, King of France, and Otto IV by John Lackland, King of England.
1214 (27 July)	Battle of Bouvines. Otto IV is defeated by Philip Augustus.
1215 (25 July)	Second royal coronation of Frederick II, at Aachen. Frederick takes Crusader vow.
1215 (Nov.)	Fourth Lateran Coucil. Frederick II is confirmed as emperor.
1216 (16 June)	Death of Pope Innocent III.
1216 (18 July)	Honorius III elected pope.
1218 (13 May)	Death of Otto IV.
1220 (23 April)	Assembly of Frankfurt. The German prices choose Henry (now aged nine) as King of the Romans.
1220 (22 Nov.)	Imperial coronation of Frederick II by Pope Honorius III at St Peter's in Rome.
1220 (Dec.)	Assizes of Capua. Abolition of all rights, customs and property acquired after 1198. Reorganization of the Kingdom of Sicily.
1221	Frederick II undertakes the reorganization of the tribunal of the royal court.
1222	Death of Constance of Aragon, Empress and Queen of Sicily.
1223–4	Campaigns to suppress the rebellious vassals.
1224–5	Campaigns against the Muslims of Sicily, who are deported to Lucera, in Apulia.
1224	University of Naples founded.
1225 (Feb. 1225)	First treaty of San Germano between Honorius III and Frederick II, who commits himself to leaving for the Crusade on 15 August 1227 with a thousand cavalry.
1225 (9 Nov.)	Fredrick II take as his second wife the fourteen-year-old Isabella of Brienne (also known as Yolande), heiress to the Kingdom of Jerusualem.
1227 (18 March)	Death of Pope Honorius III. Election of Gregory IX.

3. The Crusade and the conflict with the papacy

1227 (15 Aug.)	A large part of the imperial army sets sail from Brindisi.
1227 (8 Sept.)	Frederick II leaves for the Crusade, and quickly returns because of illness.
1227 (29 Sept.)	Pope Gregory IX excommunicates Fredrick for not having fulfilled his Crusader vow.
1228 (28 June)	Frederick, still excommunicate, leaves for the Crusade with about a hundred cavalry.
1228	Fredrick stops at the island of Cyprus, where he restores the imperial authority over the 'Kingdom of Cyprus'.
1228–9	Frederick fights in the Crusade.
1229 (Feb.)	Treaty of Jaffa with the Sultan of Egypt, al-Khamil. A ten-year truce is agreed, and Jerusalem is restored to the Christians.
1229 (17 March)	Fredrick is crowned King of Jerusalem at the Church of the Holy Sepulchre.
1229	A rumour spreads in Sicily that Frederick is dead. Rebellion and invasion by the papal army.
1229	Frederick returns from the Holy Land, via Cyprus.
1230	Frederick re-establishes his authority over the Kingdom of Sicily.
1230 (23 July)	Second Treaty of San Germano between Gregory IX and Frederick II.
1230 (28 Aug.)	Pope lifts the excommunication from Frederick.
1231	The pope recognizes Fredrick as King of Jerusalem.
1231 (Aug.)	Constitutions of Melfi. Reestablisment of the state in the Kingdom of Sicily.
1232 (Easter)	Diet of Aquilea. Conflict between Fredrick and his son Henry VII.
1235 (May)	Henry VII is forced to renounce the crown and is stripped of all his rights.
1235 (July)	Fredrick marries for a third time. His bride is Isabella, sister of King Henry III of England.
1237 (Feb.)	The nine-year-old Conrad, son of Frederick and Isabella of Brienne, is chosen as King of the Romans at Vienna.
1237–8	Frederick tries to subdue the Lombard cities.
1239 (Maundy) Thursday	Frederick is again excommunicated by Pope Gregory IX.
1239–40	Frederick invades the papal states.

1241 (Easter)	The pope summons a council in Rome.
1241 (4 May)	The Pisan fleet, allied with Frederick II, attacks the Genoese ships transporting the fathers of the Council. Three papal legates and a hundred bishops are taken prisoner.
1241 (21 Aug.)	Death of Pope Gregory IX.
1241 (Oct.–Nov.)	Election and death of Pape Celestine IV. Papal vacancy.
1242	Frederick II's son Henry VII dies in captivity.
1244	Peace of San Giovanni Laterano. Restitution by Frederick II of territories he occupied in the papal states. Failure of negotiations on other outstanding matters.
1244 (June)	Pope Innocent IV escapes from Rome with the help of his Genoese compatriots.
1244 (Dec.)	The pope finds refuge in Lyons.
1245 (28 June–17 July)	Council of Lyons.
1245 (17 July)	Emperor Frederick II is excommunicated and deposed.
1246–1247	Conspiracy against Frederick in the Kingdom of Sicily. Rebellion at Capaccio (Campania), harshly suppressed.
1246	The German princes choose Heinrich Raspe as King of the Romans.
1247	Death of Heinrich Raspe.
1248	The German princes choose William of Holland as King of the Romans.
1249	Frederick II returns to the Kingdom of Sicily.
1250 (13 Dec.)	Death of Frederick II at Castel Fiorentino (in Apulia) at the age of fifty-six. He is buried in Palermo Cathedral.

The last Norman-Swabian kings

1252 (January)	Conrad IV, legitimate son of Frederick II, travels to southern Italy.
1254 (21 May)	Death of Conrad IV at the age of twenty-six.
1258 (10 Aug.)	Manfred, illegitimate son of Frederick II, is crowned King of Sicily in Palermo.
1264–5	The crown of Sicily is offered to Charles of Anjou, brother of Louis IX (Saint Louis) by Popes Urban IV and Clement IV.

1266 (6 Jan.)	Charles of Anjou crowned King of Sicily at Peter's in Rome.
1266 (26 Feb.)	Battle of Benevento. Manfred is defeated and killed by Charles of Anjou.
1268	Conrad IV's son Conradin, aged sixteen, travels to Italy.
1268 (23 Aug.)	Battle of Tagliacozzo. Conradin's army is defeated by Charles of Anjou.
1268 (29 Oct.)	Conradin is executed in the market square of Naples.

NOTES

Prologue

1   According to the Premières Annales de Fontenelle: *Annalles Fontanellesensenses priores*, ed. J. Laporte. Rouen and Paris: Société de l'histore de Normandie, Mélanges, 15th series, 1951, 63–91. Cf. P. Bauduin, in E. Deniaux, C. Lorren *et al.*, *La Normandie avant les Normands*, Rennes: Éditions Ouest-France, 2002, 372.

2   The Bayeux Tapestry illustrates scene 51 with these words.

3   This is the thrust of Duke William's speech as noted by William of Poitiers. See William of Poitiers, *Gesta Guillelmi ducis Normannorum et regis Anglorum*, ed. R. Foreville, vol. 15. Paris: Les Belles Lettres, 1952, 182–85.

Chapter 1

1   We are here in the tradition established by the great French historian Lucien Musset, who passed away in 2004. See L. Musset, *Les Invasions. Le second assaut contre l'Europe chrétienne*. Paris: PUF, 3rd edn, 1984, 107–46, 253–61.

2   P. Bauduin, *Les Vikings*, Paris: PUF, 2004, 3ff.

3   L. Musset, *Introduction à la runologie*, Paris: Abier-Mongaigne, 2nd edn. 1976.

4   R. Boyer, *Les Vikings*, Paris: Plon, 1992, 369 and *passim*.

5   *Ibid.*, 31.

6   François-Xavier Fillmann, tr., Snorri Sturluson, *L'Histoire des rois de Norvège*, Paris: Gallimard, 2000.

7   Régis Boyer, tr., *La Saga de saint Olaf*, Paris: Payot, 2nd edn, 1992.

8   Boyer, *Les Vikings*, 33.

9   *Ibid.*

10 Bauduin, *Les Vikings*, 5–6.

11 E. Ridel (ed.), *L'Héritage maritime des Vikings en Europe de l'ouest*, Caen: Presses universitaires, 2002. See esp. C. Lemée, 'L'evolution du bateau en Scandinavie, de l'âge de pierre aux Vikings', 173–98; T. Dåmgard-Sørensen, 'Les bateaux de Skuldeleve (Roskilde) et leurs répliques modernes', 199–227.

12 Note in particular Hedeby, on the southern border of Denmark, with contact to the Frankish world, and Kaupang in Norway (south of Oslo), Birka then Sigtuna and Helgö in Sweden.

13 See O. Crumlin-Pedesen, Ships and Boats of the North, vol. 2: *Viking Age Ships and Shipbuilding in Hedeby/Haithabu and Shleswig*. Schleswig-Roskilde, 1997.

14 A. Nissen Jaubert, 'Peuplement et structures d'habitat en Danemark durant les III–XII siècles dans leurs contexte nord-ouest européen', EHESS thesis, Paris 1996, vol. 1, 128–212; *idem*, 'Les finanges et leurs rendements: l'exemple danois', in *Le Village mediéval et son environnemnt. Études offertes en l'honneur de Jean-Marie Pesez*. Paris: Publications de la Sorbonne, 1998, 551–70.

15 Boyer, *Les Vikings*, 23–5; L. Musset, 'Les apports anglais en Normandie de Rollon à Guillaume le Conquérant', in *Nordica et Normannica*, Paris: Société des études nordiques, 19997, 447–66.

16 Boyer, *Les Vikings*, 70–2.

17 *Ibid.*, 70; Boyer, *Les Vikings*, 281–7; M. Gravier, *Les Scandinaves*, Paris: Éditions Lidis; Turnhout: Brepols, 1984, 187–91; Bauduin, *Les Vikings*, 15–16.

18 Boyer, *Les Vikings*, 281–7; M. Gravier, *Les Scaninaves*, Paris and Turnhout, Éditions Lidis- Brepols, 1984, 187–91; Bauduin, *Les Vikings*, 15–16.

19 As has often been stated.

20 Bauduin, *Les Vikings*, 17.

21 Musset, *Les Invasions*, 133; Bauduin, *Les Vikings*, 19–21.

22 Musset, *Les Invasions*, 133, 236–7.

23 Boyer, *Les Vikings*, 374–83.

24 C.J. Clover and J. Lindow, *Old Norse-Icelandic Literature: A Critical Guide*, London: Ithaca, 1985, 94–7; Boyer, *Les Vikings*, 256.

25 Boyer, *Les Vikings*, 255ff.

26 *Ibid.*, 260–4.

27 *Ibid.*, 263.

28 *Ibid.*, 194–5, 266.

29 *Ibid.*, 267–8.

30 The first Dukes of Normandy nevertheless had much difficulty in keeping to this monogamy. See below.

31 *Ibid.*, 270–1.

32 *Ibid.*, 269.

33 *Ibid.*, 194–200. The Icelanders nevertheless recognized the distant authority of the King of Norway.

34 *Ibid.*, 273–9; Bauduin, *Les Vikings*, 23–26.

35 Between 1014 and 1016 the kings of the sea took part in engagements that led to the conquest of England. One of these was Lacman, a *jarl* from the Orkneys (?), and the future King of Norway (and saint) Olaf. F. Neveux, *La Normandie des ducs aux rois*, Rennes: Éditions Ouest-France, 1998, 69–71.

36 Boyer, *Les Vikings*, 274.

37 *La Saga de saint Olaf*; Boyer, *Les Vikings*, 275

38 E. Kantorowicz, *Les Deux Corps du roi*, 1957.

39 Boyer, *Les Vikings*, 276–7.

40 Bauduin, *Les Vikings*, 27.

41 Vestfold is situated on the western shores of Oslo fjord.

42 This battle took place in about 885, not far from Stavenger, in the south-west of Norway.

43 Bauduin, *Les Vikings*, 28–9.

44 Boyer, *Les Vikings*, 374–83. See above.

45 J. Renaud, *Les Dieux des Vikings*, Rennes: Éditions Ouest-France, 1996; Boyer, *Les Vikings*, 334–52.

46 Boyer, *Les Vikings*, 353–6.

47 Bauduin, *Les Vikings*, 34–5.

48 Ibn Fadlân, *Voyage chez les Bulgares de la Volga*, trans. M. Canard, Paris: Sinbad, 1988, 80.
49 Boyer, *Les Vikings*, 354–5.

Chapter 2
1   See Musset, *Les Invasions*, 206–9.
2   Jordanes, *Getica*, ed. T. Mommsen, Berlin: MGH, 1882.
3   Boyer, *Les Vikings*, 77.
4   Bauduin, *Les Vikings*, 48; A. Nissen-Jaubert, 'Habitats ruraux et communautes rurales', *Ruralia*, 2 1998, 213–25.
5   Musset, *Les Invasions*, 206; Boyer, *Les Vikings*, 76–7.
6   See below.
7   Musset, *Les Invasions*, 160, 219.
8   Sauscourt-en-Vimeu, commune of Nibas, canton of Friville-Escarbotin, Abbeville *arrondissement*, the Somme.
9   *Rithmus Teutonicus de piae memoriae Hluduico rege filio Hluduici aeque Regis* [Ludwigslied], in *Althochdeutches Lesebuch*, ed. W. Braune and E. A. Ebbinghaus, Tübingen, 1979, 136–8. Cf. J. Schneider, 'Les *Northmanni* en Francie ocidentale au IX siècle, le Chant de Lous', *Annales de Normandie*, 53rd year, no. 4, September 2003, 291–315.
10 Musset, *Les Invasions*, 119–20, 246–8. For English sources on Alfred the Great, seee S. Keynes and M. Lapidge (eds), *Alfred the Great, Asser's Life of King Alfrd and Other Contemporary Sources*, Penguin, 1983 (repr. 2004).
11 Cf. *L'Héritage maritime des Vikings*, esp. 171–359,
12 The Gokstad ship was discovered in 1880 and the Oseberg ship in 1904.
13 This site near Schleswig was was Danish. Since 1864 it is sited in Germany (today in Schleswig-Holstein).
14 Cf. *L'Héritage maritime des Vikings*, esp. 199–227. Specialists have been reconstructing Viking ships for years now using ancient techniques, which has proven very useful for historians.
15 C. Lemée, 'L'évolution du bateau en Scandinavie: de l'âge de Pierre aux Vikings', in *L'Héritage maritime des Vikings*, 173–98. The discovery dates from 1921–2.
16 *Ibid.*, 180–1. For technical explanations see below.
17 *Ibid.*, 184–6 and T. Damgard-Sørensen, 'Les bateaux de Skuldelev (Roskilde) et leurs répliques modernes', 214–15.

18   É. Ridel, 'Bateaux de types scandinave en Normandie', in *L'Héritage maritime des Vikings*, 289–320.

19   *Ibid.*, 290, 297. The first mention of the word *isnechia* in Normandy was in *Les Miracles de saint Vulfranni*; cf. *Miracula sancti Vulfranni episcopi*, in *Acta Sanctorum*, March, III, vol. 9, 152.

20   Cf. J. Renaud, 'La mer et les bateaux dans les sagas', in *L'Héritage maritime des Vikings*, 229–46.

21   Ridel, 'Bateaux de types scandinave en Normandie', 297.

22   Renaud, 'La mer et les bateaux dans les sagas', 230–1.

23   Musset, *Les Invasions*, 210.

24   *Ibid.* An excellent depiction of their axes and their effects can be seen in the Bayeux Tapestry: during the Battle of Hastings, *housecarls* (*huskarlar*), warriors of Scandinavian origin, fight on the English side (scenes 51 to 57).

25   Bauduin, *Les Vikings*, 44–7.

26   *Ibid.*, 45.

27   J. Renaud, *Les Vikings et les Celtes*, Rennes: Éditions Ouest-France, 1992.

28   Musset, *Les Invasions*, 121–4.

29   Bauduin, *Les Vikings*, 77–83; Boyer, *Les Vikings*, 186–200.

30   Musset, *Les Invasions*, 137–8, 146, 208.

31   Boyer, *Les Vikings*, 224–28; F. Durand, 'L'Anse aux Meadows, porte océane de l'Amerique norroise', *Proxima Thulé*, vol. 4, Spring 2000, 9–33; Bauduin, *Les Vikings*, 84–6.

32   S. Lebecq, 'Aux origines du phénomene viking. Quelques réflexions sur la part de responsabilités des Occidentaux', in *La Progression des Vikings, des raids à la colonisation*, ed. Anne-Marie Flambard-Hericher, Rouen: Rouen University, 2003, 15–25.

33   *Ibid.*, 15 n. 1.

34   *Ibid.*, 21–2.

35   Bauduin, *Les Vikings*, 50–5.

36   *Ibid.*, 45.

37   There are, however, exceptions, the most notable being that of the Kingdom of Wessex under Alfred the Great (871–99). See Keynes and Lapidge, 'Introduction', in *Alfred the Great*, 9–58.

38   Musset, *Les Invasions*, 127–9.

39   'Miracles of saint Philibert', in *Monuments de l'histoire des abbayes de saint Philibert*, ed. R. Pourpardin, Paris, 1905, Book 2, 60–3.

40   Saint-Philibert-de-Grand-Lieu, *chef-lieu* (principal town), canton of Loire-Atlantique.

41   Cunault, canton of Gennes, Maine-et-Loire. A fine eleventh–twelfth-century priory church still survives at Cunault today.

42   Messais, canton of Moncontour, Vienne.

43   Tournus, *chef-lieu*, canton of Saône-et-Loire. This region was soon victim to Hungarian invasions. The monks of Noirmoutier remained, however, and Tournus today has a magnificent romanesque abbey church.

44   Musset, *Les Invasions*, 127–8.

45   *Ibid.*, 129; Bauduin, *Les Vikings*, 56.

46   In the Carolingian era, the benefice was equivalent to a fief. The 'privilege' (Fr. *apanage*) is land granted by the king to a younger brother to compensate for his exclusion from the throne. This term appeared in France in the thirteenth century.

47   Bauduin, *Les Vikings*, 59–60.

48   *Ibid.*, 67–8.

49   Boyer, *Les Vikings*, 156–9. Cf. Keynes and Lapidge, *Alfred the Great*.

50   Bauduin, *Les Vikings*, 57.

51   I return to this in the next chapter.

52   Bauduin, Les Vikings, 59; Musset, *Les Invasions*, 129, 166–7.

53   Musset, *Les Invasions*, 59–72, 147–57.

Chapter 3

1   L. Halphen, *Charlemagne et l'Empire carolingien*, Paris: Albin Miche, 1947; rev. edn. 1968; P. Richer, *Les Carolingiens, une famille qui fit l'Europe*, Paris: Hachette, 1983; J. Davier, *Charlemagne*, Paris: Fayard, 1999.

2   The Abbey of Fontenelle was founded in 649 by Saint Wandrille; hence it is also called Saint-Wandrille.

3   The Abbey of Jumiegès was founded in 654 by Saint Philibert.

4   Einhard, *Vie de Charlemagne*, ed. and trans. L. Halphen, Paris: Les Belles Lettes, 1947. Einhard stayed at the Abbey of Fontenelle from 816 to 823.

5   The term *missus dominicus* ('sent by the lord') is often used in the plural (*missi dominici*) because the *missi* were sent on inspections in teams of two or more. See below.

6   L. Musset, in M. de Boüard, *Histoire de la Normandie*, Toulouse: Privat, 1970, 88. C. Lorren in Deniaux, Lorren *et al.*, *La Normandie avant les Normands*, 284–86.

7   Fulda is situated in present-day Hesse, in Germany. Raban Maur lived from about 780 to 856; he ended his career as Archbishop of Mainz.

8   Cf. *crire l'histoire au Moyen Âge. 1. Autour de Freculf de Lisieux*, Actes de la table ronde tenue à Lisieux, 26 April 2003, *Tabularia*, 'Études', no. 4, 2004; M.I. Allen, 'A past for the present: Frechulf's Histories in context and Medieval Alterlife', Ph.D. thesis, Toronto, 1994 (forthcoming); P. Depreux, *Prosopographie de l'entourage de Louis le Pieux* (781–840), Sigmaringen: Thorbecke, 1997.

9   *Pagi* is the plural of *pagus*. The French word *pays* comes from this Latin term.

10   The *pagus* of Hiémois was vast: it extended south of the current deparment of the Orne to the Channel (between the Orne and Dives esturaries). The capital was Exmes, currently *chef-lieu*, canton of the Orne.

11   The term Cotentin has now changed meaning. It no longer means the region of Coutances but only the island of Cotentin, that is, north of the present deparment of the Manche.

12   C. Lorren in Deniaux, Lorren *et al.*, *La Normandie avant les Normands*, 288; Bauduin, in Deniaux, Lorren *et al.*, *La Normandie avant les Normands*, 388.

13   C. Lorren in Deniaux, Lorren *et al.*, *La Normandie avant les Normands*, 276–80, 288–90; Bauduin, in Deniaux, Lorren *et al.*, *La Normandie avant les Normands*, 366.

14   A. Chedeville and H. Guillotel, *La Bretagne des saints et des rois*, Rennes: Éditions Ouest-France, 1984, 21–49.

15   *Ibid.*, 224–78.

16   *Ibid.*, 313–21.

17   At this time, the Kings of Brittany were in conflict with the papacy. The argument focused on the question of the deposition of the simoniacal bishops and the so-called Breton schism: the Bretons did not recognize the primacy of the Archbishop of Tours, and wanted to create an archbishopric at Dol.

18   L. Musset, in M. de Boüard, *Histoire de la Normandie*, 96.

19   Bauduin, in Deniaux, Lorren *et al.*, *La Normandie avant les Normands*, 367–70.

20   *Annales Regni Francorum*, ed. F. Kurze, MGH, *Scriptores rerum germanicarum*, vol. 6; *Annales de Saint Bertin*, ed. F. Grat, J. Viellard, S. Clémencet, Paris: Societe de l'Histoire de France, 1964; *The Annals of St. Bertin*, trans. Janet Nelson, Manchester: Manchester University Press, 1991; *Annales Fontanellenses priores*, 63–91.

21   Bauduin, in Deniaux, Lorren *et al.*, *La Normandie avant les Normands*, 372.

22   Hoseri was already famous for his earlier exploits; *Annales Fontanellenses priores*, 86–8.

23   Saint-Germer-de-Fly, canton of Coudray-Sainte-Germer, Oise.

24   Bauduin, in Deniaux, Lorren *et al.*, *La Normandie avant les Normands*, 373.

25   Doubtless at Port-Villez (canton of Bonnières-sur-Seine, Yvelines), not far from Vernon.

26   Jeufosse, canton of Bonnières-sur-Seine, Yvelines.

27   Bauduin, in Deniaux, Lorren *et al.*, *La Normandie avant les Normands*, 374.

28   Saint-Maur-des-Fosses, *chef-lieu*, canton du Val-de-Marne.

29   F. Lot, 'La grande invasion normande de 856–852', *Bibliothèque de l'Ecole des Chartes*, 69, 1908, 1–62; Bauduin, in Deniaux, Lorren *et al.*, *La Normandie avant les Normands*, 374–5.

30   Trilbardou, *arrondissement* of Meaux, Seine-et-Marne.

31   Charenton-le-Pont, *chef-lieu*, canton of Val-de-Marne. Auvers-sur-Oise, *chef-lieu*, canton of Val-d'Oise.

32   Pîtres, canton of Pont-de-l'Arche, Eures.

33   B. Dearden, 'Charles the Bald's fortifed bridge at Pîtres: recent archaological investigations', *Anglo-Norman Studies*, 11, 1988, Woodbridge 1989, 107–12; C. Gilmore, 'The logistic of fortified bridge-building on the Seine under Charles the Bald', *Ibid.* 87–106.

34   Igoville, canton of Pont-de-l'Arche, Eure.

35   P. Bauduin, *La Première Normandie*, Caen: Presses universitaires de Caen, 2004, 107–9; *idem*, in Deniaux, Lorren *et al.*, *La Normandie avant les Normands*, 383–6.

36   This demolition was due especially to bishops and chapters wanting to rebuild their cathedrals and its environs.

37 Bauduin, in Deniaux, Lorren *et al.*, *La Normandie avant les Normands*, 386.

38 Flodoard, *Annales*, ed. P. Oauer, Paris: Picard, 1905 (for the year 925).

39 J. Le Maho, 'Châteaux d'époque franque en Normandie', *Archéologie médiévale*, 10, 1980, 153–65. Quettehou, *chef-lieu*, canton of la Manche; Radicatel, commune of Saint-Jean-de-Folleville, canton of Lillebonne, Seine-Maritime; Beaubec-la-Rosière, canton of Forges-les-Eaux, Seine Maritime

40 J. P. Brunterc'h, 'Le duchéé du Maine et la marche de Bretagne', in *La Neustrie*, 1989, vol. 1, 29–127.

41 *Ibid.*, 82–7.

42 Bauduin, in Deniaux, Lorren *et al.*, *La Normandie avant les Normands*, 387–8.

43 Brunterc'h, 'Le duchéé du Maine et la marche de Bretagne', 42–9.

44 Bauduin, *La Première Normandie*, 103.

45 In 856–866.

46 Brissarthe, canton of Châteauneuf-sur-Sarthe, Maine-et-Loire.

47 F. Lot, 'La Loire, l'Aquitaine et la seine, Robert le Fort', *Bibliothèque de l'Ecole des Chartes*, 76, 1915, 473–510.

48 In 867; see above.

49 Schneider, 'Les *Northmanni* en Francie occidentale', 291–315.

50 Bauduin, *La Première Normandie*, 104. Rénaud was killed while defending the Seine valley, in 885; Henry was killed near Paris, at the time of the siege (in 886).

51 As the Nivelonides, who keep the counties of Vexin and Madrie; *ibid.*, 119–21.

52 J. Le Maho, 'Les prèmieres installations normandes dans la basse vallée de la Seine (fin du IX siècle)', in *La Progression des Vikings; des raids à la colonisation, Cahiers du GRHIS*, Rouen 2003, 153–69; *idem*, 'Les Normands de la Seine à la fin du IX siècle', in *Les Fondations scandinaves en Occident*, 161–79.

53 The Abbey of Saint-Ouen was then situated outside the city walls.

54 See above.

55 Boulogne and Montreuil-sur-Mer, *sous-préfectures* of Pas-de-Calais.

56 Saint-Riquier, canton of Ailly-le-Haut-Clocher, Abbeville *arrondissement*, Somme.

57   Haspres, Cambrai *arrondissement*, Nord.

58   Gasny, canton of Ecos, Eure.

59   Condé-sur-Aisne, canton of Vailly-sur-Aisen, Soissons *arrondissement*, Aisne.

60   Le Maho, 'Les prèmieres installations normandes', 156–7.

61   Les Andelys, *sous-préfecture* of the Eure (in the Vexin).

62   Braine, cl of the canton, Soissons *arrondissement*, Aisne (near Condé-sur-Aisne, where the monks of Saint-Ouen took refuge).

63   Deux-Jumeaux, canton of Isigny-sur-Mer, Bayeux *arrondissement*, Calvados.

64   Today Saint-Marcouf, canton of Montebourg, Manche.

65   Émendrevile or Émentruville, ancient locality today within the commune of Rouen, in the Saint-Sever district.

66   Le Maho, 'Les prèmieres installations normandes', 157–9; *idem*, 'Les Normands de la Seine à la fin du IX siècle', 169–73' *idem*, 'Coup d'il sur la ville de Rouen autour de l'an mil', in *La Normandie, ver l'an mil*, Rouen: Societe de l'histoire de Normandie, 2000, 175–8; and 'Regard archéologique sur l'habitat rouennais vers l'an mil: le quartier de la cathédrale', in *La Normandie, ver l'an mil*, 179–84.

67   This was not true of the other towns mentioned.

68   Le Maho, 'Les prèmieres installations normandes', 159–61.

69   Saint-Paul, *lieu-dit* ('locality'), commune of Duclair, *chef-lieu*, canton of Seine-Maritime.

70   Saint-Vaast, *lieu-dit*, commune of Heurteauville, canton of Duclair, Seine-Maritime

71   Le Maho, 'Les prèmieres installations normandes', 161–2.

72   L. Musset, 'Les problèmes e la colonisation normande sur l'estuaire de la Seine', *Annuaire des cinq départments de la Normandie*, 137, 1980 (pub. 1981), 75–8.

73   Le Maho, 'Les Normands de la Seine à la fin du IX siècle', 175 (with map of Scandinavian place-names in the Seine valley); J. Renaud, *Les Vikings et la Normandie*, Rennes: Éditions Ouest-France, 1989, 185 (Scandinavian place-names in the Caux and Basse-Seine).

74   Renaud, *Les Vikings et la Normandie*, 157–98.

75   Scandinavian toponyms are here given in italics. R. Lepelley, *Dictionnaire étymologique des noms de communes de Normandie*, Caen/Condé-sur-Noireau: Presses universitaires de Caen/Corlet, 1993.

76　Sanvic, commune of Havre, Seine-Maritime.

77　Harfleur, canton of Gonfréville-l'Orcher; Montivilliers, *chef-lieu* of the canton, Seine-Maritime.

78　Villequier, canton of Caudebec-en-Caux, Seine-Maritime.

79　Conihout, commune of Jumièges, canton of Duclair, Seine-Maritime.

80　Sahurs, canton of Grand-Couronne, Seine-Maritime. This estate is not recorded as belonging to the church of Bayeux until the eleventh century, though it did belong well before then.

81　Crémanfleur, canton of Honfleur, Calvados: Fiquefleur, canton of Beuzeville, Eure.

82　Risleclif, commune of Saint-Samson-de-la-Roque, canton of Quillebeuf, Eure.

83　Quillebeuf, *chef-lieu* of the canton of Eure. This estate was restored to the Abbey of Jumièges in 940.

84　Vieux-Port, canton of Pont-Audremer, Eure.

85　Bliquetuit, commune of Notre-Dame and Saint-Nicholas de Bliquetuit, canton of Caudebec-en-Caux, Seine-Maritime.

86　Brotonne, commune of Vatteville-la-Rue, canton of Caudebec-en-Caux; Couronne, commune of Grand-Couronne, *chef-lieu* of the canton; Caudebec-lès-Elbeuf, canton of Elbeuf, Seine-Maritime.

87　D. Bates, *Normandy before 1066*, London and New York: Longman, 1982, 18.

88　Le Maho, 'Les prèmieres installations normandes', 162–4.

89　Under Richard II, Dudo was appointed ducal chaplain.

90　Books 1 to 4.

91　Bauduin, *La Prèmiere Normandie*, 63–8.

92　Esp. H. Prentout, *Étude critique sur Dudon de Saint-Quentin et son histoire des premiers ducs de Normandie*, Paris: Picard, 1916.

93　Bauduin, *La Prèmiere Normandie*, 63.

94　P. Bouet, 'Dudon de Saint-Quentin and Virgil: *l'Énéide* au service de la cause normande', in *Recueil d'études en hommage à Lucien Musset, Cahier des Annales de Normandies*, no 23, Caen, 1990, 215–36; *idem*, 'Dudon de Saint-Quentin et le martyre de Guillaume Longue Épée', in *Les Saints dans la Normandie médiévale*, ed. P. Bouet and F. Neveux, Caen: Presses universitaires de Caen, 37–58.

95　L. Musset, 'L'origine de Rollon', 1981; repr. in *Nordica et Normannica*, 383–7.

96   Rollo and his followers may have taken part in the siege of Saint-Lô.

97   Bauduin, *La Prèmiere Normandie*, 128–9; *idem*, in Deniaux, Lorren *et al.*, *La Normandie avant les Normands*, 375–6.

98   Bauduin, *La Prèmiere Normandie*, 99, 111; *idem*, in Deniaux, Lorren *et al.*, *La Normandie avant les Normands*, 375–6.

99   Dudo de Saint-Quentin, ed. J. Lair, vol. 2, 151–3.

100   Le Maho, 'Les prèmieres installations normandes', 164–7; *idem*, 'Les Normands de la Seine à la fin du IX siècle', 176–9.

101   Corbény, canton of Craonne, Aisne.

102   Bauduin, *La Prèmiere Normandie*, 129–32; *idem*, 'L'Insertion des Normands dans le monde franc, fin IX–début X siècle': l'exemple des pratiques matrimoniales', in *La Progression des Vikings*, 105–17; *idem*, 'Chefs normands et élites franques, fin IX–début X siècle', in *Les Fondations scandinaves en Occident*, 181–94.

103   Dudo de Saint-Quentin, ed. J. Lair, 157; F. Neveux, 'La fondation de la Normandie et les Bretons (911–933)', in *Mondes de l'Ouest et villes du monde*, 297–309.

104   R. Merlet, 'Origines de la famille des Bérenger, comtes de Rennes et ducs de Bretagne', in *Mélanges d'histoire offerts à M. Ferdinand Lot*, 1925, 549–56; A. Chédeville and H. Guillotel, *La Bretagne des saints et des rois, V–X siècle*, Rennes: Éditions Ouest-Frace, 1984, 393–5; Neveux, 'La fondation de la Normandie et les Bretons', 304.

105   Katharine Keats-Rohan, 'Poppa de Bayeux et sa famille', in *Onomastique et Parenté dans l'Occident médiéval*, ed. K. Keats Rohan and C. Settipani, Oxford: Occasional Publications of the Unit for Prosopographical Research, Lineacre College, 2000, 140–53.

106   Chédeville and Guillotel, *La Bretagne des saints et des rois*, 391–5; H. Guillotel, 'Une autre marche de Neustrie', in *Onomastique et Parenté dans l'Occident médiéval*, ed. Keats Rohan and Settipani, 7–13.

107   *Annales de l'abbaye Saint-Pierre de Jumièges. Chronique universelle des origines au XIII siècle*, ed. J. Laporte, Rouen: Lecerf, 1954, 51; Bauduin, *La Prèmiere Normandie*, 130.

108   Dudo de Saint-Quentin, ed. J. Lair, 187, 189.

109 This term was used by several members of the jury during Bauduin's *viva-voce* thesis presentation at the University of Caen in 1998.

110 K. Keats-Rohan, 'Poppa of Bayeux and her family', *The American Genealogist*, 92, July-October 1997, 187–204; *eadem*, 'Poppa de Bayeux et sa famille', 140–53.

111 According to the *Complainte de la mort de Guillaume Longue Épée*; cf. Prentout, *Étude critique sur Dudon de Saint-Quentin*, 178–9.

112 Le Maho, 'Les prèmieres installations normandes', 164–7; *idem*, 'Les Normands de la Seine à la fin du IX siècle', 176–9. The date of 976 was upheld by Jacques Le Maho, because a count of Rouen was mentioned for this year, which shows that royal authority had not completely disappeared in the region. On the 'pact of Jumièges', see above.

113 Dudo de Saint-Quentin, ed. J. Lair, 162–5.

114 Bauduin, *La Prèmiere Normandie*, 132–5 ('The enigma of Chartres').

115 L. Musset, 'Pour l'étude comparative de deux fondations politiques des Vikings: le royaume d'York et le duché de Rouen' (1975). repr. in *Nordica et Normannica*, 157–72.

116 Text note

117 Bauduin, *La Prèmiere Normandie*, 133 and n. 171.

118 Dudo de Saint-Quentin, ed. J. Lair, 25–30, 165–71.

119 L'Andelle is a tributary of the Seine, which runs near Forges-les-Eaux (Seine-Maritime) to Pîtres (Eure), where it joins the river. This river marks the western boundary of the ancient County of Vexin.

120 P. Bouet, 'Les négotiations du traité de Saint-Clair-sur-Epte selon Dudon de Saint-Quentin', 92.

121 Dudo de Saint-Quentin, ed. J. Lair, 25–27, 165–8.

122 Saint-Clair-sur-Epte, canton of Magny-en-Vexin, Val-d'Oise.

123 The Epte is a tributary of the Seine which flows around Gournay-en-Bray (Seine-Maritime) to Limetz-Villez (Yvelines), where it joins the Seine. This river ran through the ancient county of the Vexin. After 911, it beame the frontier of the new Normandy; henceforth it separated the Norman Vexin from the French Vexin.

124 Dudo de Saint-Quentin, ed. J. Lair, 29, 168–9.

125 *Ibid.*, 169.

126 *Ibid.*

127 *Ibid.*, 170. The date of Rollo's baptism is one of the rare dates Dudo provides.

128 Dudo de Saint-Quentin, ed. J. Lair, 30, 170–1.

129 M. Fauroux, *Receuil des actes des ducs de Normandie*, Mémoires de la Société des antiquaires de Normandie, 36, Caen: Caron, 1961, 20 n. 5. Longpaon was situated on the outskirts of Rouen (today Darnétal, *chef-lieu*, canton of Seine-Maritime).

130 *Ibid.*, 20 n. 6. Berneval-le-Grand, canton of Dieppe, Seine-Maritime.

131 Bauduin, *La Prèmiere Normandie*, 135–41 ('the territory conceded to Rollo').

132 Founded by Saint Leufroy, the Abbey of la Croix-Saint-Ouen was restored in the eleventh century as La Croix-Saint-Leufroy. Today the commune of La Croix-Saint-Leufroy is in the canton of Gaillon (Eure).

133 P. Lauer, *Receuil des actes de Charles III le Simple*, no. 92, vol. 1, 209–12.

134 *Ibid.*, no. 94, vol. 1, 214–16.

135 Suresnes, *chef-lieu*, canton of Hauts-de-Seine.

136 Bouafle, canton of Aubergenville, Yvelines.

137 Thiverny, canton of Montataire, Oise.

138 Sérifontaine, canton of Coudray-Saint-Germer, Oise.

139 An 'honnour' is a group of fiefs held by a great kingdom.

140 Bauduin, *La Prèmiere Normandie*, 137.

141 Flodoard, *Annales*, year 923, 16.

142 *Ibid.*, year 925, 31.

143 Flodoard, *Historia Ecclesiae Remensis*, 577.

144 Flodoard, *Annales*, year 924, 24. Cf. Bauduin, *La Prèmiere Normandie*, 140–1. We return to this point in the next chapter.

Chapter 4

1 Bauduin, *La Prèmiere Normandie*, 112–13.

2 K. F. Werner, 'Quelques observations au sujet des débuts du "duché" de Normandie'. *Droit privé et institutions régionales*, in *Études historiques offertes à Jean Yver*, Paris: PUF, 1976, 691–709. Werner has been criticized by R. Helmerichs,

'Princeps, comes, Dux Normannorum: early Rollonid designators and their significance', *Haskins Society Journal*, 9, 1997, 57–77. See also Bauduin, *La Prèmiere Normandie*, 192–3.

3   See below.

4   Dudo de Saint-Quentin, ed. J. Lair, II, 31, 171.

5   This is particularly important for maritime law. F. Neveux, 'L'héritage maritime des Vikings dans la Normandie ducale', in *'L'Héritage maritime des Vikings en Europe de l'Ouest*, Caen: Presses universitaires de Caen, 102, 101–18.

6   Longpaon was a rural estate situated in present-day commune of Darnétal, which today is on the outskirts of Rouen and largely urbanized.

7   Dudo de Saint-Quentin, ed. J. Lair, II, 32, 172.

8   See below.

9   Dudo de Saint-Quentin, ed. J. Lair, III, 39–46, 182–91.

10   Orderic Vitalis, *Historia ecclesiastica*, ed. Chibnall, vol. 1, 154.

11   Bauduin, *La Prèmiere Normandie*, 162–73.

12   L. Musset, in M. de Boüard, *Histoire de la Normandie*, 109.

13   Bauduin, *La Prèmiere Normandie*, 145.

14   Longueville was situated along the banks of the Seine. Coudres, canton of Saint-André de l'Eure; Illiers-l'Évêque, canton of Nonancourt, Eure.

15   L. Musset, 'Actes inédits du XI siècle, III', 23, 29. See also A. Lemoine-Descourtieux, 'La frontière normade de l'Avre de la fin du X siècle au début du XIII siècle: la défense et les structures de peuplement', thesis, University of Caen, 2003.

16   Montreuil-sur-Mer, *sous-préfecture*, Pas-de-Calais. See below.

17   Picquigny, *chef-lieu* of the canton of the Somme, near Amiens. Cf. Dudo de Saint-Quentin, ed. J. Lair, III, 59–64, pp. 203–9.

18   Dudo de Saint-Quentin, ed. J. Lair, IV, 68, pp. 221–2

19   Bauduin, *La Prèmiere Normandie*, 166–72. See below.

20   See below.

21   M. Fauroux, no. 3, 70–2.

22   M. Arnoux, 'Classe agricole, pouvoir seigneurial et autorité ducale. L'évolution de la Normandie féodale d'apres le témoignage des chroniqueurs', *Le Moyen Âge*, 98, no. 1, 1992, 36–60; *idem*, 'Les paysans et le duc: autour de la révolte de 996', in *La Normandie vers l'an mil*, 105–11.

23   Bauduin, *La Prèmiere Normandie*, 17–210.

24   Especially towards the south, with the conquest of Passais, which belonged to the diocese of Le Mans.

25   These Roman boundaries corresponded to the ecclesiastical province of Rouen. Passais never formed part of this province.

26   Bauduin, *La Prèmiere Normandie*.

27   M. Arnoux, 'Disparition ou conservation des sources et abandon de l'acte écrit: quelques observations sur les actes de Jumièges', *Tabularia, Études*, no.1, 2001, 1–10.

28   Dudo de Saint-Quentin, ed. J. Lair, II, 28, p. 168.

29   Flodoard, *Annales*, year 924, 24.

30   L. Musset, in M. de Boüard, *Histoire de la Normandie*, 98.

31   Chédeville and Guillotel, *La Bretagne des saints et des rois*, 393–5. Cf. see above.

32   R. Fossier, *La Terre et les hommes en Picardie jusqu'a la fin du XIII siècle*, 2 vols, Paris and Louvain: Nauwelaerts, 1968, vol. 1, 176–8; vol. 2, 477–80. Cf. Bauduin, *La Prèmiere Normandie*, 147.

33   Bauduin, *La Prèmiere Normandie*, 145–61.

34   Flodoard, *Annales*, year 923, 16–17.

35   Flodoard, *Annales*, year 925, 29–30. Cf. Bauduin, *La Prèmiere Normandie*, 146.

36   Eu, *chef-lieu* of the canton of Seine-Maritime. Situated on the Bresle, Eu is the northernmost place in Normandy. For Montreuil, see above.

37   Richer, Histoire de France, I, 50, vol. 1, 100–2. Cf. Bauduin, *La Prèmiere Normandie*, 146.

38   Bauduin, *La Prèmiere Normandie*, 155–6.

39   Flodoard, *Annales*, year 931, 50. This Breton rebellion, with hat of the Norman Riouf, momentarily challenged the power of the Count of Rouen. See above.

40   Chédeville and Guillotel, *La Bretagne des saints et des rois*, 393–5.

41   *Ibid.*, 395–6. The Latin text: *Willeim[us] Dux Bri[tonum]*. Cf. L. Musset, 'Considérations sur la genèse et le tracé des frontières de la Normandie', in *Nordica et Normannica*, 403–13.

42   Flodoard, *Annales*, year 927, 39–40.

43   Flodoard, *Annales*, year 933, 55.

44   Bauduin, *La Prèmiere Normandie*, 161.

45   *Ibid.*, 157–8. Cf. Dudo de Saint-Quentin, ed. J. Lair, III, 59–62, pp. 203–8.

46 G. Louise, *La Seigneurie de Bellême (X–XII siècle)*, 2 vols, Flers: Le Pays Bas-Normand, no. 199–202, 1990–91, vol. 1, 139, 150. The Lords of Bellême amassed a huge estate on the borders of Normandy and Maine. They were only brought to heel by King Henry I of England in the twelfth century. Certain place-names refer to this frontier position, such as Moulins-la-Marche (*chef-lieu* of the canton on the Orne).

47 Bauduin, *La Prèmiere Normandie*, 163.

48 *Ibid.*, 166–72.

49 C. Maneuvrier, 'Paysages et sociétés rurales au Moyen Âge: le pays d'Auge jusqu'à la fin du XIII siècle', Ph.D. thesis, 1999–2000, vol. 1, 89. According to Maneuvrier, it is not possible to say when precisely the *pagus* of Lisieux was integrated into Normandy.

50 It should not be forgotten these ecclesiastical provinces were founded on Roman provincial administrative units of the Late Empire, and had long ceased to correspond to any political reality.

51 F. Lifshitz, 'La Normandie carolingienne. Essai sur la continuité, avec utilisation de sources négligée', *Annales de Normandie*, 48/5 (1998), 505–24. According to Lifshitz, the Normans of the Seine, led by Rollo, were baptized several times towards the end of the 880s by Francon de Rouen, then again after 892, by Witton de Roune and Hervé of Reims. After each baptism they returned to paganism. This is a complex issue and the texts are not entirely clear. It is perhaps best to remain cautious on this issue.

52 Dudo de Saint-Quentin, ed. J. Lair, II, 30, 170–1.

53 We know of a bishop of Bayeux in 927, but no other from 876. The bishopric must therefore have been restored after a gap of almost half a century. See below.

54 Adhémar de Chabannes, *Chronicon*, ed. J. Chavanon, Paris: Les Belles Lettres, 1987, 139.

55 Robert subsequently became King Robert 1 (922–3). See Bauduin, *La Prèmiere Normandie*, 145.

56 Dudo de Saint-Quentin, ed. J. Lair, III, 58, 200–3.

57 Dudo de Saint-Quentin, ed. J. Lair, III, 42–6, 185–91.

58 Flodoard, *Annales*, year 943, 88. Cf. Bauduin, *La Prèmiere Normandie*, 164.

59   Renaud, *Les Vikings et la Normandie*, 12—2. Réville, canton of Quettehou, Manche.

60   *Ibid.*, 123. The tomb on the island of Groix dates from the tenth century.

61   P. Bouet, 'Dudon de Saint-Quentin et le martyre de Guillaume Longue Épée', in *Les Saints dans la Normandie médiévale*, ed. P. Bouet and F. Neveux, Caen: Presses universitaires de Caen, 2000, 237–58. Cf. Dudo de Saint-Quentin, ed. J. Lair, III, 59–64, 203–9.

62   Le Maho, 'Les prèmieres installations normandes', 157, 166. See also above, Chapter 3.

63   *Les Évêques normands du XI siècle*, Colloque de Cerisy-la-Salle (1993), ed. P. Bouet and F. Neveux, Caen: Presses universitaires de Caen, 1995, esp. P. Bouet and M. Dosdat, 'Les évêques normands de 985 à 1150', 19–35.

64   J. Decaëns, 'L'évêque Yves de Sées', in *Les Évêques normands du XI siècle*, 117–37.

65   L. Musset, 'La satiriste Garnier de Rouen et son milieu (début du XI siècle)', *Revue du Moyen Âge latin,* 19 (1954), 237–66.

66   Archbishop Robert died in 1037. He was initially replaced by his son, Raoul of Gacé. See below, Chapter 6.

67   D. Bates, 'Notes sur l'aristocratie normande. 1: Hughes de Bayeux (1011–v.1049)', *Annales de Normandie*, 23/1 (1973), 7–21; V. Gazeau, 'Le patrimoine d'Hughes de Bayeux (*c.* 1011–49)', in *Les Évêques normands du XI siècle*, 139–47.

68   Bouet and Dosdat, 'Les évêques normands de 985 à 1150', 19, 20, 23, 24, 25.

69   William of Jumièges, *Gesta Normannorum Ducum*, ed. J. Marx, Rouen and Paris: Picard, 1914. See also Decaëns, 'L'évêque Yves de Sées', 125–9.

70   M. Chibnall, 'La carrière de Geoffroi de Montbray', in *Les Évêques normands du XI siècle*, 179–93.

71   This last ill is obviously relative. It only became an issue because the reforming popes of the eleventh and twelfth centuries aimed to make the secular clergy follow the example of monastic celibacy; the Eastern, Orthodox, Church did not insist on the celibacy of priests.

72   The Abbey of Saint-Vanne was situated in the town of Verdun

73   L. Musset, in M. de Boüard, *Histoire de la Normandie*, 111.

74   William of Jumièges, *Gesta Normannorum Ducum*, VII, 10, ed.
      J. Marx, 129. See also O. Guillot, 'La libération de l'Église par le
      duc Guillaume avant la conquête', in *Histoire religieuse de la
      Normandie*, ed. N.-J. Chaline, Chambray: CLD, 1981, 77, 84 n.
      20. Guillot dates the Council of Lisieux to 1054.

75   V. Gazeau, 'Recherches sur l'histoire de la principauté
      normande', thesis, Paris I, 2002, vol. 2, 193.

76   P. Bouet, 'Le premier millénaire', in *Le Mont-Saint-Michel,
      Histoire et Imaginaire*, Paris: Anthese/Éditions due Patrimoine,
      1998, 21–6; *idem*, 'La *reuelatio* et les origins du culte a saint
      Michel sur le mont Tombe', in *Culte et pèlerinages à saint Michel
      en Occident. Les trois monts dédié à l'archange*, Rome: École
      française de Rome, 2003, 65–90; K. Keats-Rohan, 'L'histoire
      secrète d'un santuaire célèbre. La reforme du Mont-Saint-
      Michel d'après l'analyse de son cartulaire et de ses nécrologues',
      ibid., 139–59.

77   Keats-Rohan, *Ibid*. 146–7. Katharine Keats-Rohan denies that
      Mainard I was a disciple of the reforming Gérard of Brogne.

78   F. Neveus, 'L'abbaye benedictine a la periode ducale (966–1024),
      in *Le Mont-Saint-Michel, Histoire et Imaginaire*, 30–4.

79   A. Renoux, *Fécamp: du palais dical au palais de Dieu*, Paris:
      Éditions du CNRS, 1991.

80   P. Bouet, 'Dudon de Saint-Quentin. Construction de la
      nouvelle collégiale de Fécamp (990), in *La Normandie ver l'an
      mil*, 123–9.[4]

81   The Abbey of Cluny demanded that the duke cede all rights of
      apanage throughout the Normandy forests. These conditions
      were inacceptable for the duke.

82   V. Gazeau, 'William of Volpiano et le monachisme normand. Vie
      de saint Guillaume abbé de Dijon, in *La Normandie ver l'an mil*,
      132–6.

83   L. Musset, 'La contribution de Fécamp à la reconquête monas-
      tique de la Basse-Normandie (90–1066), in *L'Abbaye béné-
      dictine de Fécamp, ouvrage scientifique du XIII centenaire*,
      Fécamp, 1959–60, vol. 1, 57–66, 341–3.

84   *Ibid*. See also Gazeau, 'Recherches sur l'histoire de la princi-
      pauté normande', vol. 2, 25–6 (Bernay), 122–3 (Jumièges), 166–8
      (Mont-Saint-Michel).

85   *Ibid.*, vol. 2, 84–7.

86 *Ibid.*, 107. M. Fauroux, no. 61, 185–7.

87 Gazeau, 'Recherches sur l'histoire de la principauté normande', vol. 2, 184 (Saint-Pierre de Préaux). Saint-Pierre is a monastery, Saint-Leger a nunnery. Both were sited in Les Préaux, commune in the canton of Pont-Audermer, Eure.

88 *Ibid.*, 233–7. The nunnery was replaced at Saint-Pierre–sur-Dives by a monastery. The Abbey of Notre-Dame-du-Pré at Lisieux, founded in 1050, continued until 1994, when the monks left for Valmont (*chef-lieu* of the canton of Seine-Maritime).

89 *Ibid.*, 64 (Cormeilles), 149 (Lyre). Cormeilles, *chef-lieu*, canton of Eure; Lyre, commune of Vieille-Lyre, canton of Rugles, Eure.

90 *Ibid.* 8–12. Lanfranc became Abbot of Saint-Étienne of Caen (1063–70), then Archbishop of Canterbury (1070–89). Anselm was Abbot of Bec (1078–93), then succeeded Lanfranc as Archbishop of Canterbury (1089–1109). He is considered a saint as well as one of the great philosophers of the Middle Ages.

91 Bauduin, *La Prèmiere Normandie*, 145, 167.

92 The death of Herbert II of Vermandois led to the breaking up of his principality.

93 The primacy of Hughes le Grand was essentially in the reign of Louis IV d'Outremer (936–54).

94 Bauduin, *La Prèmiere Normandie*, 166–70.

95 *Ibid.*, 169.

96 *Ibid.*, 180–5. William of Jumièges, *Gesta Normannorum Ducum*, V, 9–12, ed. J. Marx, 82–7. Cf. L. Musset, 'Actes inédits du XI siècle, III', 44 n. 138.

97 Bauduin, *La Prèmiere Normandie*, 181–5.

98 D. Barthélemy, *L'Ordre seigneurial*, Paris: Seuil, 1990, appendix 2, table 8.

99 William of Jumièges, *Gesta Normannorum Ducum*, II, 6 (Popa), III, 2 (Sprota), ed. J. Marx, 24, 33.

100 Bauduin, *La Prèmiere Normandie*, 20–1 (genealogical charts of the ducal family).

101 This is no doubt why he designated his elder son, Hughes, as Bishop of Bayeux in about 1011.

102 Bauduin, *La Prèmiere Normandie*, 197–210.

103 *Ibid.*, 20–21, 292 n. 37.

104 The County of Exmes (Hiémois) was conferred to William, son of Richard I, then Robert (the Magnificent), second son of

Richard II, and the County of Mortain to Robert, half-brother of William the Bastard.

105 William of Jumièges, *Gesta Normannorum Ducum*, V, 13, ed. J. Marx, 88.

106 Bauduin, *La Prèmiere Normandie*, 152–4.

107 *Ibid.*, 153, 156.

108 With this singular name Dudo describes all the Anglo-Saxon kings. According to the context, *Alstemus* can refer to Alfred the Great (871–899), Edward the Elder (899–925) or Athelstan (925–39).

109 Dudo de Saint-Quentin, ed. J. Lair, II, 17–18, pp. 158–9. See also Bauduin, *La Prèmiere Normandie*, 154 n. 53. Dudo gives an idealized view of events, where Alstemus goes as far as to promise Rollo half his kingdom.

110 *Complainte de Guillaume Longue Épée*, ed. Philippe Lauer, in *Le Règne de Louis IV d'Outremer*, Paris: Bouillon, 1900, 319–23.

111 Bauduin, *La Prèmiere Normandie*, 153–4.

112 F. Neveux, *La Normandie des ducs aux rois*, Rennes: Éditions Ouest-France, 1998, 512.

113 Musset, *Les Invasions*, vol. 2, 134–5.

114 This can partly be explained by the weakening of the Normans during the minority of Richard II.

115 William of Jumièges, *Gesta Normannorum Ducum*, V, 4, ed. J. Marx, 76–7. According to this author, Elthelred's objective was to seize Duke Richard II, this is hard to believe considering that the English landed in the Val-de-Saire, far from Rouen and Fécamp.

116 William of Jumièges, *Gesta Normannorum Ducum*, IV, 18, ed. J. Marx, 68–9.

117 William of Jumièges, *Gesta Normannorum Ducum*, V, 7–9 ed. J. Marx, 79–83.

118 William of Jumièges, *Gesta Normannorum Ducum*, V, 8, ed. J. Marx, 80–2. William of Jumièges states that Lacman and Olaf came to Cnut's aid. This is extremely doubtful, since Olaf II Haraldsson appears to have been an enemy of the Danes, at least from his accession to the Norwegian throne in 1015. In fact he was killed in fighting Norwegian magnates, who were supported by Cnut, in 1030 at Stiklestad (near Trondheim).

Alleged to have been killed fighting pagans, in Norway he was considered a saint, even a martyr. See also L. Musset, *Les Peuples scandinaves au Moyen Âge*, Paris: PUF, 1951, 128–9, 159–60.

119 Ethelred died on 23 April 1016, in London. His son Edmund Ironside succeeded him. Although he had to divide the kingdom with Cnut, it was agreed that whoever of the two survived would inherit the whole kingdom. Shortly after this agreement, Edmund died in mysterious circmstances, probably assassinated (30 November 1016).

Chapter 5

1   William of Jumièges, *Gesta Normannorum Ducum*, ed. J. Marx; ed. Elizabeth van Houts, 2 vols, Oxford: Clarendon Press, 1992–5.

2   Wace, *Le Roman de Rou*, ed. A. J. Holen, Paris: Picard, 3 vols, 1970–3. 'Roman' here refers to a text written in the 'Roman' language, i.e. Old French.

3   Benoît de Sainte-Maure, *Chronique des ducs de Normandie*, ed. Carin Fahlin, vols 1 and 2, Uppsala, 1951–4; vol. 3 (Glossary), ™sten Södergard, Uppsala, 1967; vol. 4 (notes), by Sven Sandqvist, Stockholm, 1979.

4   There was only one other duke of this name: Robert II Curthose, Duke of Normandy from 1087 to 1106. He was the youngest son of William the Bastard, who, in thus naming his son, was paying homage to his father, Robert the Magnificent.

5   Robert the Devil is described by thirteenth-century preachers as a debauched adventurer.The confusion with this legendary character began towards the end of the Middle Ages and is current even today even in some serious publications such as the *Encyclopaedia Britannica*. Se M. de Boüard, *Guillaume le Conquérant*, Paris: Fayard, 1984, 77–8.

6   If Richard III had effective control of the Norman army, this campaign should be placed in 1025–6. Richard was eighteen in 1026.

7   The County of Burgundy corresponds to present-day Franche-Comté. It then belonged to the Kingdom of Burgundy, which was soon (1032) incorporated into the Holy Roman Empire.

8   Chalon-sur-Saône, prefecture of Saône-et-Loire.

9   Mimande, canton of Chagny, Saône-et-Loire.

10 M. Fauoux, no. 58, 180–2.

11 This document is particularly important for the history of the town, and is one of the first written records of the town.

12 This was not because of the premature death of the duke or Adele's remarriage to the son of the Count of Flanders.

13 The County of Hiémois straddled present-day departments of the Orne and Calvados.

14 Exmes, *chef-lieu*, canton of the Orne.

15 See above, Chapter 2, note 46.

16 Thirty years earlier, the County of Hiémois was granted to William, a brother of Richard II, who had already revolted. Much the same thing seems to be happening again here.

17 Falaise, *chef-lieu* of the canton of Calvados.

18 The rebellion of Robert was not so far-reaching as that of his uncle, William, also Count of Hiémois, who gathered behind him the majority of local lords.

19 Thirty years earlier, William was deprived of the County of Hiémois, but shortly after received the County of Eu in compensation.

20 William of Jumièges, *Gesta Normannorum Ducum*, VI, 2, ed. J. Marx, 99–100.[4]

21 William of Malmesbury, *Gesta regum Anglorum* (The History of the English Kings), ed. and trans. R.A.B. Minor, R.M. Thompson and M. Winterbottom, II, 178, vol. 1, 304–9.

22 William of Jumièges, *Gesta Normannorum Ducum*, VI, ed. J. Marx, 102–3.

23 Fulbert, Bishop of Chartres (1006–28). A famous thinker and theologian, he played an important part in theological debates and political affairs of his day.

24 William of Jumièges, *Gesta Normannorum Ducum*, VI, 3, ed. J. Marx, 100.

25 Argences, canton of Troarn, Calvados (near Caen).

26 Heudebouville, canton of Louviers, Eure (on the Seine).

27 Maromme, *chef-lieu* of the canton of Seine-Maritime (near Rouen).

28 Fauroux, no. 70, 206–7.[4]

29 The ancient Montgommery estate straddled the present-day communes of Sainte-Foy-de-Montgommery and Saint-Germain-de-Montgommery (canton of Livarot, Calvados).

30 Vimoutiers, *chef-lieu*, canton of the Orne. Fauroux, no. 74, 214–16.

31 Fauroux, nos 66–7, 197–203; no. 71, 207–9. See below.

32 Orderic Vitalis, interpolations of William of Jumièges, *Gesta Normannorum Ducum*, VII, 3, ed. J. Marx, 157–8.

33 The dead were often buried in a leather shroud.

34 Soon, as part of the Gregorian reforms, the Church would rule more severely on the sexual life of clerics.

35 Wace, *Le Roman de Rou*, Pt. 3, v. 2823–2922, vol. 1, 266–70.

36 Benoît de Sainte-Maure, *Chronique des ducs de Normandie*, v. 33445–34008, 15–22.

37 The Ante is a tributary of the Dives, which runs below the castle of Falaise.

38 A daughter of Robert the Magnificent is also known, doubtless the child of another concubine. See Bauduin, *La Première Normandie*, 20–1, 288, 304, 306 n. 118. This information comes from Robert of Torigni, *Chronique*, vol. 1, 34.

39 He provided her with a husband.

40 William of Jumièges, *Gesta Normannorum Ducum*, VI, 3, ed. J. Marx, 100–1.

41 Marie Fauroux has edited some thirty charters of Robert the Magnificent. See Fauroux, nos 60–91, 184–242.

42 L. Musset, 'Actes inédits du xi siècle', 144–5.

43 This was always the case in this period under similar circumstances; as, for example, in the minority of William the Bastard over the whole duchy or during Odo's disgrace (1082) in the Bayeux diocese.

44 Fauroux, nos 66–7, 197–203.

45 Pierreval, canton of Buchy, Seine-Maritime.

46 According to Marie Fauroux, this is Vicq, canton of Montfort-l'Amaury, Yvelines. But this is situated south of the Seine, not in the French Vexin, whereas the text says explicitly '*in Vilassino Francico, unam villam Vy vocitatam*'. Cf. Fauroux no. 66, 200.

47 It is significant that there were a number of restituions in the *pagus* of Évreux. See Fauroux no. 66, 197–201.

48 This monastery, dedicated to the Trinity, was situated on the 'Mont-Sainte-Catherine', on the outskirts of Rouen. In 1042 Gosselin and Emmeline established a nunnery, Saint-Amand, in the heart of the city.

49 Fauroux nos 60–1, (1030), 184–7.

50 Fauroux nos 63, 189–92 (Jumièges); no. 65, 195–7; no. 73, 210–14 (Mont-Saint-Michel); nos 78–9, 218 (Saint-Ouen). etc.

51 Fauroux no. 70, 206–7.

52 Fauroux no. 71, 207–9.

53 The guests were temporary tenants, who could be settled, for example, on land for deforestation.

54 Fauroux no. 64, 192–5.

55 Cerisy-la-Forêt, canton of Saint-Clair-sur-l'Elle, Manche.

56 Le Molay-Littry, canton of Balleroy, Calvados.

57 Le-Bois-d'Elle, an ancient wood in the commune of Cerisy-la-Forêt.

58 Maupertuis, commune of Torteval, canton of Caumont-l'Éventé, Calvados.

59 Lyons-la-Forêt, *chef-lieu*, canton of the Eure, in the Norman Vexin.

60 Épinay-sur-Odon, canton of Villers-Bocage, Calvados.

61 Vienne-en-Bessin, canton of Bayeux, Calvados.

62 The Argences vineyard (canton of Troarn, Calvados) was situated on the slopes above the Muance, tributary of the Dives. Famous in the Middle Ages, it continued in production until the nineteenth century.

63 Only after 1050 did laymen found abbeys in the Cotentin.

64 Fauroux no. 90, 231–5. Cf. L. Musset, 'Les premier temps de l'abbaye de Montivilliers', in *Histoire d'une ville et de son abbaye*, 8–12.

65 Harfleur, canton of Gonfréville-l'Orcher; Saint-Martin-du-Manoir, canton of Montivilliers, Seine-Maritime. Musset, 'Les premier temps de l'abbaye de Montivilliers', 9.

66 We know nothing about her precise position in the ducal genealogy. More likely a daughter of Richard I than Richard II, she should be described as Robert's great-aunt.

67 Montivilliers was founded before Saint-Amand of Rouen (1042) and Saint-Léger de Préaux (1050).

68 Fauroux no. 87, 228–9. The Abbey of Fécamp did not lose out from this exchange.

69 Chiffreville, commune of Sévigny, canton of Argentan, Orne.

70 La Haye-du-Theil, canton of Amfreville-la-Campagne, Eure.

71 Le Bec-Hellouin, canton of Brionne, Eure. This abbey was founded by Herluin, a simple knight, vassal of Count Gilbert of Brionne.

72 *Gallia Christiana*, vol. 11, *instrumenta*, col. 199 E.

73 Toutainville, canton of Pont-Audemer, Eure.

74 Fauroux no. 89, 230–1.

75 Herluin of Conteville.

76 William of Jumièges, *Gesta Normannorum Ducum*, VI, 7, ed. J. Marx, 104–5. Mauger was the son of Richard I and Gonnor.

77 Villeneuve-Saint-Georges, *chef-lieu* of the canton of Val-de-Marne.

78 Baldwin IV, a widower, married Alienor, sister of Robert the Magnificent, thus sealing their alliance.

79 Chocques, canton of Béthune, Pas-de-Calais.

80 William of Jumièges, *Gesta Normannorum Ducum*, VI, 6, ed. J. Marx, 103–5.

81 We will see again how Robert the Magnificent intervenes in Brittany. See below.

82 See above, Chapter 4.

83 William of Jumièges, *Gesta Normannorum Ducum*, VI, 9, ed. J. Marx, 109–10.

84 Of course Jersey was then a Norman island and did not depend on England.

85 William of Jumièges, *Gesta Normannorum Ducum*, VI, 8, ed. J. Marx, 105–6. William of Jumièges, says that this fortress is called Carrucae and is not far from Couesnon. Robert of Torigni's interpolations suggest this is Carrues; however, one should remain caution about its exact location, which could be either in Brittany or Normandy.

86 William of Jumièges, *Gesta Normannorum Ducum*, VI, 10, ed. J. Marx, 110.

87 William of Jumièges, *Gesta Normannorum Ducum*, VI, 11, ed. J. Marx, 111.[4]

88 The situation in the Holy Land would change with the arrival of the Seljuk Turks: this is the origin of the crusading movement.

89 Fauroux, no. 60, 184; no. 66, 197–201; no. 68, 204; no. 88, 229–30.

90 *Ibid.*, no. 90, 231–5.

91 William of Jumièges, *Gesta Normannorum Ducum*, VI, 11, ed. J. Marx, 111–12.

92 Wace, *Le Roman de Rou*, vol. 1, Pt. 3, v.2987–3240, 272–81.

93 Benedict IX enjoyed a bad reputation. He belonged to the great Roman Theophylacte family.

94 Wace adds other details, largely legendary, which cannot be recounted here.

Chapter 6

1 During the assembly of 13 January 1035, before the departure of Robert the Magnificent. See above, Chapter 5.

2 We should not forget that he seized Church possessions, following the example of the duke: in particular he destroyed the market of the monks of Jumièges, at Vimoutiers. See above, Chapter 5.

3 Louise, *La Seigneurie de Bellême*. Roger and Mable were married in about 1050.

4 William of Jumièges, *Gesta Normannorum Ducum*, VI, ed. J. Marx; ed. van Houts.

5 William of Poitiers, *Gesta Guillelmi ducis Nomannorum et Regis Anglorum*, ed. R. Foreville, Paris: Les Belles Letters, 1952; ed. R.C.H. Davis and M. Chibnall, Oxford: Clarendon Press, 1998.

6 Saint-Evroult-Notre Dame-des-Bois, canton of La Ferté-Frênel, Orne. This abbey was also called the Abbey of Ouche.

7 Orderic Vitalis, interpolations of William of Jumièges, ed. J. Marx, 151–98. Orderic Vitalis, *Historia ecclesiastica*, ed. M. Chibnall, 6 vols, Oxford: Clarendon Press, 1969–80.

8 Orderic Vitalis died after 1142.

9 Suger, *Vita Ludovici Grossi Regis*, ed. H. Waquet, Paris: Les Belles Lettres, 1964, 178–9. Suger was of course describing the châteaux constructed without warrant in the royal domain under Louis VI; but the expression equally fits the reign of young William in the previous century.

10 Tillières-sur-Avre, canton of Verneuil-sur-Avre, Eure.

11 Gilbert Crespin was reluctant to deliver the château without combat.

12 Argentan was put to the torch by the royal army.

13 William of Jumièges, *Gesta Normannorum Ducum*, VII, 2, ed. J. Marx, 117–18.

14 A. Chédeville and Y.-N. Tonnerre, *La Bretagne féodale, XI–XIII siècle*, Rennes: Éditions Ouest-Frane, 1987, 41. Vimoutiers, *chef-lieu* of the canton of the Orne.

15 William of Jumièges, *Gesta Normannorum Ducum*, VII, 3, ed. J. Marx, 118 with interpolations by Orderic Vitalis, *ibid.*, 160.

16 Creully, *chef-lieu* of the canton of Calvados.

17 Today Thury-Harcourt, *chef-lieu*, canton of Calvados.

18 Le Plessis-Grimoult, canton of Aunay-sur-Odon, Calvados. The lordship of Grimoult du Plessis was vast. See de Boüard, *Guillaume le Conquérant*, 122.

19 William of Jumièges, *Gesta Normannorum Ducum*, VII, 7, ed. J. Marx, 122–4. William of Poitiers, 1, 7–9, ed. Foreville, 14–21. Grimoult du Plessis was the only rebel for whom William would not grant a pardon.

20 Wace, Pt, 3, v.3585–4226, vol. 2, 19–44.

21 Wace, Pt, 3, v.3881–3886, vol. 2, 31.

22 The forest of Brix was at this time vast, occupying a large part of the north Cotentin. It has since been largely deforested, especially in the eighteenth and nineteenth centuries.

23 Today there are no traces of the medieval castle of Valognes.

24 Saint-Clement, commune of Osmanville, canton of Isigny-sur-Mer, Calvados.

25 Ryes, *chef-lieu*, canton of Calvados.

26 The sons of Hubert of Ryes were rewarded by William.

27 Wace, Pt, 3, v.3641–3736, vol.2, 22–5.

28 Bellengreville, canton of Bourguébus, Calvados.

29 Two monuments record this battle: the first is on the N13 at Vimont, the other on the D41.

30 Wace, Pt, 3, v.3801–4162, vol.2, 28–42.

31 Henry I attended Mass at Valmeray (ancient parish, commune of Airan, canton of Bourguébus, Calvados).

32 Wace, Pt, 3, v.4203–4220, vol.2, 28–42.

33 Wace, Pt, 3, v.4221–4225, vol.2, 44. The Bishop of Bayeux was then Odo of Conteville, the duke's half-brother. In 1074 the Conqueror gave him the land of Plessis; see *Antiquus Cartularius Ecclesie Baiocensis*, d. abbé Victor Bourienne, vol. 1, no. 3 (1074).

34 Wace, Pt, 3, v.5343–5396, vol.2, 85–7. The date of the council has been disputed; it should be situated just after the battle of Val-ès-Dunes in 1047: see de Boüard, *Guillaume le Conquérant*, 136–9.

35 The Abbot of Saint-Ouen de Rouen was then Nicolas, illegitimate son of Richard III. He ruled the abbey for over fifty years, until his death in 1092. Gazeau, 'Recherches sur l'histoire de la principauté normande', vol. 2, 195–8.

36 It is, however, likely that Hughes of Bayeux was not among the rebels.

37 Gazeau, 'Le patrimoine d'Hughes de Bayeux (*c*.1011–49)', 141–2.

38 Wace, Pt, 3, v.5357–5372, vol. 2, 85–6.

39 The Romanesque chapel of Sainte-Paix is situated on the right bank of the Orne, in the Vaucelles district, in former times in a semi-rural zone, now amid industrial developments.

40 Although married to Herluin of Conteville, Herleva was never fully recognized by the top echelons of the aristocracy.

41 William of Poitiers, I, 21, ed. Foreville, 44–7

42 Wace, Pt, 3, v.4496–4500, vol. 2, 54.

43 See above, Chapter 5.

44 Orderic Vitalis, interpolations by William of Jumièges, ed. J. Marx, 181–3.

45 Gerloc, sister of William Longsword, was an ancestor of Matilda.

46 The Count of Flanders is vassal of the emperor for certain fiefs. In this period they were in conflict: in 1047 the count burnt down the imperial palace. In 1049 Baldwin concluded a favourable peace with Henry II in the Treaty of Aix-la-Chapelle.

47 Orderic Vitalis, interpolations by William of Jumièges, ed. J. Marx, 165–8. Cf. Decaëns, 'L'évêque Yves de Sées', 125–9. This episode can doubtless be explained by internal rivalry among the Bellême family.

48 William of Jumièges, *Gesta Normannorum Ducum*, VII, 9, ed. J. Marx, 127–8.

49 *Vita Lanfranci*, in J. P. Migne, *Patrologie latine*, vol. 40, col. 29–58.

50 Wace, Pt, 3, v.4519–4524, vol. 2, 55. According to Wace, Archbishop Mauger excommunicated William and Matilda and put the duchy under an interdict.

51 Orderic Vitalis, interpolations by William of Jumièges, ed. J. Marx, 181–3; Wace, Pt, 3, v.4525–4540, vol. 2, 55. According to Wace, other than the two abbeys, William founded a hundred prebendary chapels for the poor and sick of Rouen, Caen, Bayeux and Cherbourg.

52 C. Collet, P. Leroux and J.-Y. Marin, *Caen, cité médiévale. Bilan d'archaéologie et d'histoire*, Caen: Service départementale d'Archéologie du Calvados, 1996, no. 32–62, 26–31. This is the site of the original Abbaye-aux-Hommes, today Caen's Hôtel de Ville.

53 Fauroux, no. 32, 120–2 (1021–25). Richard II gave the Abbey Saint-Père de Chartres a house in Caen; *Ibid.*, no. 34, 124–31 (1025); the same duke gave property to the Abbey of Fécamp. For Caen, see L. Jean-Marie, *Caen aux XI et XII siècles. Espace urbain, pouvoirs et société*, Caen: Éditions La Mandragore, 2000, 27–36.

54 Fauroux, no. 58, 180–2. See above, Chapter 4.

55 Robert the Magnificent acted in the same way in founding the Abbey of Cerisy (1032).

56 In 1105 Bayeux remained loyal to Robert Curthose, Duke of Normandy. Hence the town was burnt by Henry I of England. see below, Chapter 8.

57 This wall was not easy to defend, unlike the castle. See Jean-Marie, *Caen aux XI et XII siècles*, 103–11.

58 Fauroux, no. 231, 442–6 (1066); donations from William and Matilda to the abbaye-aux-Dames.

59 *Ibid*. William chose this date to take advantage of the gathering of all the Norman lords in view of the conquest of England.

60 The resources made available from the conquest of England meant that work could progress apace.

61 L. Musset, *Normandie romane*, vol. 1, La Pierre-Qui-Vire, Zodiaque, 1967, 49–104.

62 I.e. about the same time as his marriage (celebrated at the same place).

63 Orderic Vitalis, interpolations by William of Jumièges, ed. J. Marx, 171–3.

64 William of Jumièges, *Gesta Normannorum Ducum*, VII, 4, ed. J. Marx, 119–20. William of Poitiers, I, 23–5, ed. Foreville, 50–9.

65 Archbishop Mauger was also the son of Richard II and Papia.

66 This nomination coincided with the transfer to Lisieux of the nunnery founded several years earlier.

67 Mouliherne, canton of Longué, Maine-et-Loire.

68 For the help Henry I had afforded him at Val-ès-Dunes.

69 William of Poitiers, 1, 11–12, ed. Foreville, 22–7. The castle was finally taken by the besiegers.

70 Orderic Vitalis, interpolations by William of Jumièges, ed. J. Marx, 161–5.

71 William of Poitiers, 1, 16–19, ed. Foreville, 34–45.

72 In this region, the Sarthe provides the boundary between Normandy and Maine.

73 William of Poitiers, 1, 19, ed. Foreville, 42–3.

74 Wace, Pt, 3, v.4227–4371, vol. 2, 44–9.

75 Wace, Pt, 3, v.4319–4320, vol. 2, 47.

76 Orderic Vitalis, interpolations by William of Jumièges, ed. J. Marx, 171; Wace, Pt, 3, v.4347–4354, vol. 2, 49.

77 William of Poitiers, 1, 26–28, ed. Foreville, 56–65. Moulins-la-Marche, *chef-lieu*, canton of the Orne. Guimond, the Lord of Moulins himself, returned the fortress to the king.

78 Mortemer, canton of Neufchâtel-en-Bray, Seine-Maritime.

79 William of Jumièges, *Gesta Normannorum Ducum*, VII, 10, ed. J. Marx, 129–30 ; William of Poitiers, 1, 30–31, ed. Foreville, 68–75.

80 Varaville, canton of Cabourg, Calvados.

81 There was a large estuarine bay at Dives, which has since disappeared. The present-day D27 follows the same route as the old road but inside the properties.

82 William of Jumièges, *Gesta Normannorum Ducum*, VII, 12, ed. J. Marx, 131–2; William of Poitiers, 1, 34, ed. Foreville, 80–83.

83 Bassebourg, commune of Brucourt, canton of Dozulé, Calvados.

84 The marriage of these children was never consummated because Margaret died around 1063. This notwithstanding, William held on to Maine, which he was in the process of conquering.

85 William of Poitiers, 1, 39–40, ed. Foreville, 92–101. William of Poitiers describes a 'crafty plan' used by William to set light to

the castle of Mayenne; Orderic Vitalis reveals the nature of this plan (the use of two children); see Orderic Vitalis, interpolations by William of Jumièges, ed. J. Marx, 184.

86 William of Poitiers, 1, 43–45, ed. Foreville, 106–13.

87 Bayeux Tapestry, scenes 16–20.

88 The attack on Dinan is only mentioned in the tapestry (scene 19).

89 Rennes was then capital of the Duchy of Brittany. It is represented on the tapestry after the scene that depicts Conan's flight (scene 18).

90 Chédeville and Tonnerre, *La Bretagne féodale*, 45. Chateau-Gontier, *sous-prefecture* of Mayenne (i.e. a town of Maine).

91 This 'party' consisted of numerous aristocrats of Scandinavian origin established in the kingdom in the time of Cnut.

92 Judith was therefore Matilda's aunt.

93 Stigant could not receive the pallium, symbol of the archiepiscopal office, except from the anti-pope Benedict X (1058–9).

94 William of Poitiers, I, 41–4s, ed. Foreville, 101–7.

95 Bayeux Tapestry, scenes 1–24.

96 Bayeux Tapestry, scene 17.

97 William of Jumièges, *Gesta Normannorum Ducum*, VII, 13, ed. J. Marx, 132–3.

98 Scene 23.

99 William of Poitiers, I, 42, ed. Foreville, 103–5. Bonneville-sur-Touques, canton of Pont-l'Évêque, Calvados.

100 *Ibid.*

101 On the coronation of Harold, see B. English, 'Le couronnement d'Harold dans la Tapisserie de Bayeux', in *La Tapisserie de Bayeux: l'art de broder l'histoire*, Caen: Presses universitaires de Caen, 2004, 347–81. The date of the coronation is unknown: possibly 6 January or in Paril. Easter fell on 16 April and Halley's comet appeared in England on 24 April. In the tapestry, the comet is linked to the cornonation (scenes 29–32).

102 William of Poitiers, II, 1, ed. Foreville, 146–7.

103 Harald Hardrada (the Severe or Pitiless), King of Norway (1047–66). See above, Chapter 7.

104 Bayeux Tapestry, scene 53, depicting a battle scnee with the legend '*Hic ceciderunt simul Angli et Franci in prelio*' (Here died together in combat English and French).

105 E.M.C. van Houts, 'L'écho de la conquête dans les sources latines', in *La Tapisserie de Bayeux: l'art de broder l'histoire*, 135–54.

106 Cf. especially the Bayeux Tapestry, scene 38.

107 Wace, Pt, 3, v.6423–6432, vol. 2, 123. Wace emphasizes the father's testimony. William of Jumièges, on the other hand, mentions 3,000 ships, which seems exaggerated. William of Jumièges, *Gesta Normannorum Ducum*, VII, 14, ed. J. Marx, 134; Wace, *Ibid*.

108 List of ships, Oxford, Bodleian Library. E.M.C. van Houts, 'The ship list of William the Conqueror', *Anglo-Norman Studies*, 10 (1987), Woodbridge: Boydell Press, 1988, 159–83.

109 William of Poitiers, II, 1, ed. Foreville, 148–9.

110 Bayeux Tapestry, scene 44. Odo certainly commissioned this work.

111 The horses on board are depicted in lively fashion; it seems that the draftsman (or woman) was passionate about horses (and boats). See scenes 38–39.

112 Pope from 1061 to 1073, Alexander II was a former pupil of Lanfranc at Bec. He favoured reform, was in conflict with the emperor but was inclined to support the Normans, in southern Italy, in Normandy and in England.

113 William of Poitiers, II, 3, ed. Foreville, 152–5

114 William of Poitiers, II, 6, ed. Foreville, 158–60.

115 By way of comparison, the Allied landing in Normandy in June 1944 was delayed by twenty-four hours because of poor weather conditions.

116 The bay of the Somme still retains its semi-maritime character today, although the bay of Dives has disappeared. Saint-Valéry-sur-Somme, *chef-lieu*, canton of the Somme, Abbeville *arrondissement*.

117 William of Poitiers, II, 7, ed. Foreville, 160–5.

118 P. Bouet, 'Hastings, le triomphe de la ruse normande', in *L'Invasion de l'Angleterre. Guillaume le Conquérant*, 46–57.

119 *Ibid.*, 54–5.

120 Cf. M. W. Campbell, 'Note sur les deplacements de Tostig Godwinson en 1066', *Annales de Normandie*, 22/1 (1972), 3–9.

121 Bouet, 'Hastings, le triomphe de la ruse normande', 54–5.

122 On the Norwegian invasion of England, see K. DeVries, *The Norwegian Invasion of England*, Woodbridge: Boydell Press, 1999.

123 Stamford Bridge is situated on the river Derwent, a tributary of the Humber, on the border between Yorkshire and Humberside. DeVries, *The Norwegian Invasion of England*, 262–91.

124 William of Poitiers, II, 8, ed. Foreville, 164–9.

125 Pevensy, in East Sussex, between Eastbourne and Bexhill. The ancient Roman fortress on the site was later used by the Normans. In the eleventh century, the fortress was on the shore; today the sea has receded from the ancient shoreline.

126 William of Jumièges, *Gesta Normannorum Ducum*, VII, 14–15, ed. J. Marx, 134–5 (summary account, completed by Orderic Vitalis in his interpolations, 196–7); William of Poitiers, II, 15–25, ed. Foreville, 182–209; Wace, Pt, 3, v.7699–8972, vol. 2, 171–219 (epic narration). One can add to these accounts the more sober Orderic Vitalis, *Historia eccelsiastica*, ed. M. Chibnall, vol. 2, 172–9.

127 *Carmen de Hastingae Proelio*, ed. C. Morton and H. Muntz, Oxford Medieval Texts, Oxford: Clarendon Press, 1972.

128 The Anglo-Saxon Chronicle (Version D) devotes only a dozen lines to the battle. See *The Anglo-Saxon Chronicles*, trans. M. Swanton, 199.

129 E.g. C. H. Lemmon, *The Battle of Hastings, St. Leonards-on-Sea*, 1964; R. Allen Brown, 'The Battle of Hastings', *Anglo-Norman Studies*, 3 (1980), Woodbridge: Boydell Press, 1981, 1–21, 197–201; S. Morillo, 'Warfare under the Anglo-Norman kings, 1066–1135', *Anglo-Norman Studies*, 14 (1993, 1994), 150–63; M. Strickland, 'Military technology and conquest: the anomaly of Anglo-Saxon England', *Anglo-Norman Studies*, 19 (1996, 1997), 353–82; J. France, 'L'apport de la Tapisserie de Bayeux àl'histoire de la guerre', in *La Tapisserie de Bayeux: l'art de broder l'histoire*, 289–300.

130 P. Bouet and F. Neveux, 'La bataille d'Hastings', in *Guillaume le Conquérant et son temps*, exhibition catalogue, *Art de Basse Normandie*, no. 97, 38–49; Bouet, 'Hastings, le triomphe de la ruse normande', 47–57; P. Bouet, *Guillaume le Conquérant et les Normands au XI siècle*, CRDP de Basse Normandie/Éditions Corlet, 2003, 39–46,

131 It is Orderic Vitalis who gives us this place-name (Senlac). See Orderic Vitalis, *Historia eccelsiastica*, ed. M. Chibnall, vol. 2, 172–3. In 1067, William founded Battle Abbey on the site of the battle.

132 Bayeux Tapestry, scenes 51–2. The English shields were sometimes round, sometimes oblong; the Norman shields were always oblong, which better suited the cavalry.

133 The English, and especially the *housecarls*, were alone in using the battle-axe, originally a Scandinavian weapon.

134 Bayeux Tapestry, scene 53.

135 This was a very different from the Hundred Years War, when the English won many battles against the French on account of the efficiency of their archers.

136 Bouet, 'Hastings, le triomphe de la ruse normande', 57.

137 Bayeux Tapestry, scene 51.

138 This change of tactic can clearly be seen in the tapestry (scenes 56–7). See Bouet, *Guillaume le Conquérant et les Normands au XI siècle*, 44; and *idem*, 'Hastings, le triomphe de la ruse normande', 57.

139 Bayeux Tapestry, scene 57. Harold's wound to the eye was also mentioned by Aimé of Mont-Cassin (around 1080), by Baudri of Bourgueil (at the turn of the twelfth century) and, of course, by Wace (about 1170), who had certainly seen the tapestry at Bayeux.

140 *Carmen de Hastingae Proelio*, ed. C. Morton and H. Muntz, v. 532–551. Cf. Bouet, *Guillaume le Conquérant et les Normands au XI siècle*, 45.

141 William of Jumièges, *Gesta Normannorum Ducum*, VII, 16, ed. J. Marx, 135–6; William of Poitiers, II, 30, ed. Foreville, 220–3; Orderic Vitalis, *Historia eccelsiastica*, III, ed. M. Chibnall, vol. 2, 182–5.

142 This is the origin of a long controversy between the archbishops of Canterbury and York about the primacy within the English Church.

143 *The Anglo-Saxon Chronicles*, trans. M. Swanton, 199.

144 D. Bates, ed. *Regesta Regum Anglo-Normannorum. The Acta of William I (1066–1087)*, Oxford: Clarendon Press, 1998, Introduction, 44–50 *et passim*. We know of thirty-two acts of William in Old English. Orderic Vitalis, *Historia eccelsiastica*, III, ed. M. Chibnall, vol. 2, 256–7.

145 Bayeux Tapestry, scenes 30, 50, 57. Bates, ed. *Regesta Regum Anglo-Normannorum*, nos 223, 286; in these acts Harold is called king (*rex*). In all the others in which he is named, he is generally called count (*comes*): e.g. 290, 291, 300, 317, 320, 322 and 324.

146 Bayeux Tapestry, scene 17: Harold saves a Norman and an Englishman in the quicksands of the bay of Mont-Saint-Michel.

147 P. Bouet, 'La Tapisserie de Bayeux, une oeuvre pro-anglaise?', in *La Tapisserie de Bayeux: l'art de broder l'histoire*, 197–215.

148 Exeter, capital of Devon.

149 This revolt took place primarily in Yorkshire.

150 This island is surrounded by several arms of the Ouse. Ely is north of Cambridge.

151 On these rebellions, see de Boüard, *Guillaume le Conquérant*, 359–76.

152 E.g. those of Rochester, Norwich and York.

153 Waltheof remained in office until 1075, at which time he took part in the plot of the earls (largely Normans and Bretons). De Boüard, *Guillaume le Conquérant*, 374–6, 392–402.

154 In Anglo-Norman England, the term *manor* both the seigneurial dwelling and the lordship.

155 Michel de Boüard has rightly described this situation with the neat phrase, 'King and duke; impossible ubiquity'. See de Boüard, *Guillaume le Conquérant*, 386.

156 *Ibid.*, 386–92, 423–4.

157 Winchester was as much a capital as London; it was here that the royal treasury was stored.

158 Orderic Vitalis, *Historia ecclesiastica*, IV, ed. M. Chibnall, vol. 2, 236–9.

159 Thus, the siege of Old Sarum was transferred to Salisbury; that of Selsey to Chichester, and Elmham to Norwich.

160 There were seven, or perhaps nine of these commissions.

161 *Domesday Book*, 4 vols, ed. A. Farley, 1793 (parts 1 and 2); E. Ellis, London, 1816 (parts 3 and 4). See de Boüard, *Guillaume le Conquérant*, 424–9.

162 These were the lands north of the Tees, the Counties of Durham, Northumberland and Cumbria.

163 One finds nevertheless more detailed reports in the *Little Domesday*, which have not been reworked. The same is true of

the *Exon Domesday*, in relation to the five counties of the south-west.

164 Orderic Vitalis, *Historia eccelsiastica*, IV, ed. M. Chibnall, vol. 2, 202–3.

165 Orderic Vitalis, *Historia eccelsiastica*, VII, 8, ed. M. Chibnall, vol. 4, 38–45. See also de Boüard, *Guillaume le Conquérant*, 416–20.

166 Her tomb in black marble, with a decorative epitaph, survives to this day. Her body has recently been identified by Professors Dastugue and de Boüard.

167 De Boüard, *Guillaume le Conquérant*, 405–12.

168 Phillip I granted to Robert Curthose the command of the fortress of Gerberoy (canton of Songeons, Oise). William besieged it and the garrison effected a sortie. The duke-king was wounded, perhaps by his son.

169 Simon of Crépy, Count of Vexin, had granted the county to Phillip I in 1077.

170 One should remember however that Henry I had granted the suzerainty of the Vexin to Robert the Magnificent (see above, Chapter 5). This grant proved to be short lived, however, because of troubles issuing from the minority and conflict between William and the King of France.

171 This was more an accident that a war wound; he was wounded in the stomach by the crown of his saddle.

172 The third son, Henry Beauclerc, received only the sum of 5,000 *livres* from the royal treasury.

173 *De obitu Willelmi, ducis Normannorum regisque Anglorum, qui sanctam Ecclsiam in pace vivere fecit*, in William of Jumièges, *Gesta Normannorum Ducum*, ed. J. Marx, 145–9; de Boüard, *Guillaume le Conquérant*, 429–39. William's tomb was ransacked in the sixteenth century. Only a single bone remains of his body.

174 Orderic Vitalis himself was from a mixed marriage. His father was French (from the Orléans region), his mother English.

175 The English Exchequer was based at Winchester, the Norman in Caen castle, where the twelfth-century Exchequer chamber still exists to this day.

176 The Normans are certainly ancestors of the Royal Family and good part of the aristocracy. Unlike most English people, the modern aristocracy is generally proud of its Norman ancestry.

Chapter 7

1   Aimé du Mont-Cassin, *Historia Normannorum* ed. V. de Bartholomaeis, *Storia de Normanni di Amato di Montecassino, volgarizata in antico francese*, Rome: Tipographia del Senato, 1935.

2   William of Apulia, *Gesta Robert Wiscardi.*

3   Geoffrey Malaterra, *Historia sicula* or *De rebus gestis Rogerii Calabriae et Siciliae comitis et Roberti Guiscardi ducis, fratris eius*, ed. E. Pontieri, 2 vols, Bologna: Nicola Zanichelli, 1927–8.

4   The papal states did not exist before 756. However, in Rome at the beginning of the ninth century a false document was drawn up, the donation of Constantine, according to which the Emperor Constantine gave Italy and the whole of the West to the pope in 330, when he established his new capital in Constantinople.

5   Lombardy corresponded to Apulia.

6   The conquest lasted fifty years, from 827 to 878 (when Syracuse, the Byzantine capital, was taken). A final Greek revolt took place in 910.

7   According to tradition, the archangel appeared in a cave in Mont Gargano in 490, 492 and 493. See G. Otranto, 'Genesi, cartteri e diffusione del culto micaelico del Gargano', in *Culte et pèlerinages à saint Michel en Occident*, 43–64.

8   F. Neveux, 'Quelques aspects de l'imperialisme normand au XI siècle en Italie et en Angleterre', in *Les Normands en Méditerranée*, coloque de Cerisy, 51–62.

9   H. Bresc, 'Les Normands, constructeurs de châteaux', in *Les Normands en Méditerranée*, 63–77.

10 Harald Hardrada became King of Norway in 1046–7 and died while invading England, at Stamford Bridge on 25 September 1066. See above, Chapter 6.

11 From 1060.

12 See J.-M. Martin, *La Pouille du VI au XII siècle*, Rome: École française de Rome, 1993.

13 J.-M. Martin, *Italies normandes*, Paris: Hachette, 1994, 57.

14 *Comes Normannorum totius Apuliae et Calabriae*. See P. Bouet, '1000–1100: la conquéte', in *Les Normands en Méditerranée*, 11–23.

15 This Norman custom was practiced at this time but had not been formalized; it was written down only towards the end of the twelfth and beginning of the thirteenth century.

16 Hauteville-sur-Mer, canton of Montmarin-sur-Mer; Hautteville-Bocage, canton of Saint-Sauveur-le-Vicomte; Hauteville-la-Guichard, canton of Saint-Sauveur-Lendelin.

17 It has often been thought that the name 'Guichard' came from Robert 'Guiscard'. This attribution cannot be stated with any certainty.

18 P. Bouet, 'Généalogie des descendants de Tancrède', in *Les Normands en Méditerranée*, 36–7.

19 L. Musset, 'Origine et nature du pouvoir ducal en Normandie jusqu'au milieu du xi siècle', in *Nordica et Normannica*, 263–77. The word *ullac* is a transposition of the western Scandinavian *utlagi*, 'outlaw'.

20 From 1020, Roger of Tosny was present in Spain; others included Robert Crespin, Rotrou of Perche and Robert Burdet. See F. Neveux, 'L'espansione in Europa', in *I Normanni, popolo d'Europa*, Venice: Marsilio, 1994, 98–105.

21 Robert of Grandmesnil founded the Abbey of sant'Eufemia in Calabria (1061–2). Robert Guiscard granted him the Abbey of Venosa in about 1063, then the church of Saint-Michel of Mileto, in Calabria, in about 1080. See Gazeau, 'Recherches sur l'histoire de la principauté normande', vol. 2, 216–18. He later became Bishop of Troina and Messina, in Sicily. See P. Aubé, *Les Empires normands d'Orient*, 63.

22 The Normans of Italy came largely from Lower Normandy (65 per cent), especially from the departements of the Manche, Calvados and to a lesser extent the Orne. Se L. R. Ménager, 'Inventaire des familles normandes et franques émigrées en Italie meridionale et en Sicile', in *Roberto il Guiscardo e il suo tempo*, Rome: Il Centro di Recerca Editorre, 1975, 259–390.

23 P. Bouet, 'Pour quelles raisons les Normands ont-ils émigré en Italie du Sud au XI et XII siècles?', in *Les Normands en Méditerranée*, 6–10.

24 The same phenomenon can be observed in England after the conquest.

25 The ancient castle of Scribla is today called 'Il Torrione', in the commune of Spezzano Albanese. See A. M. Flambard Heriher,

'Un instrument de la conquête et du pouvoir: les châteaux normands de Calabre. L'exemple de Scribla', in *Les Normands en Méditerranée*, 38–43.

26   San Marco Argentano is situated upstream from Scribla, in the same valley, which it dominates The motte still survives, though surmounted by a round tower which is doubtless later than the time of Robert Guiscard.

27   See above, Chapter 6.

28   But he was soon replaced by his brother Onfroi.

29   F. Chalandon, *Histoire de la domination normande en Italie et en Sicile*, Paris: Picard, 1907; repr. New York: Burt Franklin, 1960, vol. 1, 136–7.

30   The pontificate of Leo IX stands out for another event, with much more lasting consequences: the definitive break between the Eastern (Orthodox) and Western Churches in 1054; this schism has lasted until the present day.

31   Didier was Abbot of Monte-Casino from 1058 to 1086, when he became Pope Victor III (1086–7). See Martin, *Italies normandes*, 246.

32   This became the traditional formula for papal election.

33   The synod is an ecclesiastical assembly. In this period the popes gathered each year a synod of the clergy province of Rome.

34   According to the synod's Latin formula, *nec gratis nec pretio*.

35   P. Bouet, 'Les étapes d'une longue et difficile conquête', 16–20.

36   See below.

37   H. Bresc, 'Une culture solide, Un État faible', in *Palerme, 1070–1492*, Paris: Éditions Autrement, 1993, 34–9,

38   See M.-A. Lucas-Avenel, 'Les populations de Sicile et les conquérants normands vus par Geoffroi Malaterra', in *De la Normandie à la Sicile: réalites, représentations, mythes*, Saint-Lô: Archives départemenales de la Manche, 2004, 49–66.

39   M.-A. Lucas-Avenel, 'Les mouvements militaries du comte Roger en Sicile de 1061 à1072', in *Les Normands en Méditerranée*, 44–9.

40   Judith was the daughter of Count William of Évreux, descendant of Duke Richard of Normandy and of Havoise, whom he took as his second wife. See Aubé, *Les Empires normands d'Orient*, 63–4. According to Pierre Bouet, Judith of Évreux is only a cousin of Robert of Grandmesnil: see P. Bouet,

'Les Grandmesnil: une famille européenne', in *Les Normands en Méditerranée*, 49.

41   Chalandon, *Histoire de la domination normande en Italie et en Sicile*, vol. 1, 186–90 (siege of Bari); 206–8 (siege of Palermo). Lucas-Avenel, 'Les mouvements militaires', 49.

42   Lucas-Avenel, 'Les populations de Sicile et les conquérants normands vus par Geoffroi Malaterra', 60–66.

43   The pope took refuge in the castle of Canossa, in the Apennines. The previous year he was deposed by Henry IV at the Council of Worms. In turn, Henry was excommunicated by Gregory VII. In January 1077, in mid-winter, Henry went to Canossa to ask for a pardon, which was granted. But he wasted no time in opposing the pope again; the pope, in turn, looked for every possible means to overturn him.

44   On 19 August 1071 the Byzantine Emperor was taken prisoner at Manzikert, in modern Turkey. The victor was the Turkish chief Arslan, who conquered Byzantine Anatolia and was soon to dominate the Near East.

45   The city built by Leo IV (847–855) corresponds more or less to the modern Vatican.

46   Chalandon, *Histoire de la domination normande en Italie et en Sicile*, vol. 1, 258–84.

47   Bouet, '1000–1100: la conquête', 20.

48   Aubrée de Buonalbergo was the daughter of a Norman who has settled in Italy.

49   Chalandon, *Histoire de la domination normande en Italie et en Sicile*, vol. 1, 285–326; P. Bouet, 'La politique d'integration par les femmes', in *Les Normands en Méditerranée*, 35.

50   Bouet, 'Généalogie des descendants de Tancrède', 36–7; F. Neveux, 'Histoire du royaume de Sicile au XII siècle', in *Les Normands en Méditerranée*, 50–7.

51   Martin, *Italies normandes*, 69.

52   *Ibid*. The Lombard princes were in effect crowned by the Bishop of Capaccio.

53   The last Norman Prince of Capua, Robert II, died in 1129. The succession reverted to Roger II.

54   O. Zecchino, 'Les assises de Roger II', in *Les Normands en Méditerranée*, 143–9; *idem*, 'Les assises des rois normands de Sicile', *ibid*., 106–11.

55 S. Fodale, 'L'Église et les Normans en Italie du Sud et en Sicile', in *Les Normands en Méditerranée*, 171–8; *idem*, 'L'alliance de Normands avec la papaute reformatrice', *ibid.*, 98–105.

56 We know this detail from Ibn Djubayr, who visited the island in 1184. He describes the situation of the Muslims, which, in this respect, had doubtless little changed since the time of Roger II. See Ibn Djubayr, 'Illusions et découverte de la vérité', in *Palerme, 1070–1492*, 77–80.

57 Roger II's cloak is now conserved in the Schatzkammer in Vienna. For Roger II and the Kingdom of Sicily, see P. Aubé, *Roger II de Sicile. Un Normand en Méditerranée*, Paris: Payot, 2001. For political and military developments, see Chalandon, *Histoire de la domination normande en Italie et en Sicile*, vol. 1, 355–403; vol. 2, 1–165.

Chapter 8

1 Our principal source for William's children is Orderic Vitalis, *Historia ecclesiastica*, ed. M. Chibnall. Orderic was a monk belonging to Saint-Évroult.

2 Henry had been granted 5,000 *livres*, but no land: see Chapter 6.

3 Courcy, canton of Morteaux-Couliboeuf, Calvados. The castle belonged to Richard of Courcy, who was in conflict with Robert of Bellême.

4 Orderic Vitalis, *Historia ecclesiastica*, VIII, 1–5, ed. M. Chibnall, vol. 4, 11 – 63. The two reconciled brothers drew up together at Caen the famous document, the *Consuetudines et Justitie*, where they recalled the rights of the Duke of Normandy in the time of their father, William the Conqueror. These rights had been flouted since the accession of Robert Curthose.

5 Orderic Vitalis, *Historia ecclesiastica*, IX, 2–4, ed. M. Chibnall, vol. 5, 8–37; X, 4, vol. 5, 206–13.

6 *Ibid.*, IX, 3, vol. 5, 26–7; X, 4, 206–13. See also J. Richard, *Histoire des croisades*, Paris: Fayard, 1996, 42. William Rufus procured this considerable sum by forcing a loan across his kingdom. The crusade was one of the 'four cases' where vassals were bound to serve their lord.

7 Robert II, Count of Flanders (1093–1111), was the son of Robert I Frison and the nephew of Queen Matilda. He was therefore second cousin of Robert Courthose.

8   Stephen Henry, Count of Blois (1089–1102) married Adela, daughter of the Conqueror and sister of Robert Courthose.

9   Orderic Vitalis, *Historia eccelsiastica*, X, 17, ed. M. Chibnall, vol. 5, 300–3.

10   William of Malmsbury, *Gesta regum Anglorum*, IV, 312, vol. 1, 554–7.

11   Orderic Vitalis, *Historia eccelsiastica*, X, 2–15, ed. M. Chibnall, vol. 5, 200–95.

12   Paul, 1st Letter to the Corinthians, 11: 14–15.

13   Orderic Vitalis, *Historia eccelsiastica*, X, 2, ed. M. Chibnall, vol. 5, 202–3.

14   Anselm's nomination dragged on. He was not confirmed as archbishop until 1092 or 1093, three or four years after Lanfranc's death.

15   The monarch had a a right to enjoy the benefices of archbishopric or abbey as long as there was a vacancy; William Rufus flagrantly abused this right.

16   Orderic Vitalis, *Historia eccelsiastica*, X, 2, ed. M. Chibnall, vol. 5, 202–3.

17   Orderic Vitalis, *Historia eccelsiastica*, X, 3, ed. M. Chibnall, vol. 5, 282–95.

18   Orderic Vitalis, *Historia eccelsiastica*, X, 14–15, ed. M. Chibnall, vol. 5, 282–95.

19   *Ibid.*

20   Callixtus II, pope from 1119 to 1124.

21   Their eyes were gouged out and their noses cut off. But their father had meted out the same treatment to his young hostage, son of the Count of Ivry. See Orderic Vitalis, *Historia eccelsiastica*, XII, 10, ed. M. Chibnall, vol. 5, 282–95.

22   There is a contemporary account of this event in Latin verse by Serlon, canon of Bayeux. Serlon, 'Versus Serlonis de capta Baiocensium civitate', *Recueil des Historiens des Gaules et de la France*, vol. 19, xciff.

23   Tinchebray, *chef-lieu* of the canton of the Orne. An international symposium took place here in September 2006, organized by the municipality to commemorate the 9th centenary of the event.

24   Orderic Vitalis, *Historia eccelsiastica*, XI, 7–20, ed. M. Chibnall, vol. 6, 78–93.

25 Robert of Bellême remained in prison from his trial, in 1112, until his death in 1130.

26 Orderic Vitalis, *Historia ecclesiastica*, XI, 45, ed. M. Chibnall, vol. 6, 182–3.

27 William Clito's tutor, Hélie of Saint-Saëns, preferred to go into exile rather than surrender his pupil. See reference in the following note.

28 Orderic Vitalis, *Historia ecclesiastica*, XI, 37, ed. M. Chibnall, vol. 6, 162–7.

29 Orderic Vitalis, *Historia ecclesiastica*, XII, 17, ed. M. Chibnall, vol. 6, 228–35.

30 Orderic Vitalis, *Historia ecclesiastica*, XII, 18, ed. M. Chibnall, vol. 6, 234–43. Brémule, commune of Gaillardbois-Cressenville, canton of Fleury-sur-Andelle, Eure.

31 He is sometimes called Robert of Caen, since his mother came from the city. See L. Musset, in G. Désert, *Histoire de Caen*, Toulouse: Privat, 1981, 30.

32 Robert received the County of Gloucester in England.

33 Orderic Vitalis, *Historia ecclesiastica*, XII, 26, ed. M. Chibnall, vol. 6, 294–307.

34 Orderic Vitalis, *Historia ecclesiastica*, XII, 28, ed. M. Chibnall, vol. 6, 308–9.

35 Orderic Vitalis, *Historia ecclesiastica*, XII, 48, ed. M. Chibnall, vol. 6, 390–1.

36 Orderic Vitalis, *Historia ecclesiastica*, XII, 45–6, ed. M. Chibnall, vol. 6, 368–81.

37 As far as one can tell from the essentially ecclesiastical sources.

38 For the Plantagenets, see M. Aurell, *L'Empire des Plantagenêt*, Paris: Perrin, 2003; J. Favier, *Les Plantagenêts. Origine et destin d'un empire, XI–XIV siècles*, Paris: Fayard, 2004.

39 Adela was an energetic woman. During the First Crusade, her husband, Stephen Henry, Count of Blois, escaped from the siege of Antioch and returned to her; she persuaded him to leave once more for Jerusalem. Orderic Vitalis, *Historia ecclesiastica*, X, 20, ed. M. Chibnall, vol. 5, 324–5.

40 He did not even wait until 25 December, the anniversary of William the Conqueror's coronation in 1066.

41 Robert was hesitant at first, because he feared losing his English estates; but in 1138 he firmly declared for Matilda (and Geoffrey

Plantagenet). He was to remain his half-sister's closest ally until his death in 1147.

42   Orderic Vitalis, *Historia eccelsiastica*, XIII, 43, ed. M. Chibnall, vol. 6, 538–47.

43   Orderic Vitalis, *Historia eccelsiastica*, XIII, 44, ed. M. Chibnall, vol. 6, 546–51.

44   Geoffrey Plantagenet died at the age of fourty.

45   Stephen of Blois died at the age of about fifty-seven.

46   Like Count Stephen of Blois nineteen years earlier, Henry II did not wait until 25 December. See Neveux, *La Normandie des ducs aux rois*, 513–24.

47   On Henry II, see J. Boussard, *Le Gouvernement d'Henri II Plantagenêt*, Paris: Librairie d'Argences, 1956.

48   R. Foreville, *L'Église et la royauté en Angleterre sous Henri Plantagenêt (1134–1189)*, Paris, 1943; P. Aubé, Thomas Becket, Paris: Fayard, 1988; M. Aurell, *L'Empire des Plantagenêt*, 240–86; Favier, *Les Plantagenêts*, 261–83.

49   Boussard, *Le Gouvernement d'Henri II Plantagenêt*, 471–88.

50   *Ibid.*, 569–81.

51   For Richard Lionheart, see R. Pernoud, *Richard Cœur de Lion*, Paris: Fayard, 1988; J. Flori, *Richard Cœur de Lion, le roi-chevalier*, Paris: Payot, 1999.

52   The King of Sicily was then Tancred of Lecce. See below.

53   Flori, *Richard Cœur de Lion*, 131–52.

54   *Ibid.*, 145–6. During the seizure of Acre, Leopold, Duke of Austria, placed his standard beside those of the three kings (of France, England and Jerusalem); Richard had the standard thrown over the city walls. Unable to gain any reparations, Leopold abandoned the crusade and returned home, full of rancour towards Richard.

55   *Ibid.*, 181–8.

56   *Ibid.*, 188–204, 205–30.

57   *Ibid.*, 201–55. Châlus, *chef-lieu* of the canton of Haute-Vienne, in the Limousin. The castle of Châlus-Chabrol belonged to Aimar of Limoges.

58   For John Lackland and Normandy, see esp. M. Powicke, *The Loss of Normandy (1189–1204). Studies in the History of the Angevin Empire*, Manchester: Manchester University Press, 1913; new edn. 1961.

59   Born in 1187, Arthur was the posthumous son of Geoffrey, third son of Henry II; John was only the fourth son.

60   Isabel was the granddaughter and heiress of Robert of Gloucester, illegimiate son of Henry I. John Lackland and Isabel were therefore both great grandchildren of Henry I. John used their consanguinity to annul the marriage.

61   Lusignan, *chef-lieu* of the canton of Vienne.

62   Favier, *Les Plantagenêts*, 662–3. The marriage took place on 26 August 1200, conducted by the Archbishop of Bordeaux, Helié of Malemort.

63   *Ibid.*, 664. This meeting may be considered a first manifestation of the *Cour des pairs*, which would develop in the course of the thirteenth century.

64   Guy of Thouars was the second husband of Constance, widow of Geoffrey and heir of Brittany. He ruled the duchy in the name of his wife and daughter, Alix.

65   J. Baldwin, Philippe Auguste, Paris: Fayard, 1991, 250–55. The fact that Aquitaine remained under English control subsequently posed major problems for the French monarchy.

66   Before he came to power, he owned much land in Normandy, notably the County of Mortain. During his reign he often stayed in Normandy and got to know the province well.

67   William, Duke of Apulia, died without heir; see above.

68   For Bohemond, see C. Cahen, *La Syrie du Nord à l'époque des croisades et la principauté franque d'Antioche*, Paris: 1940; G. Coppola, 'Bohémond 1er, prince d'Antioch', in *Les Normands en Méditerranée*, 88–97.

69   Bouet, 'Généalogie des descendants de Tancrède', 36–7.

70   Anna Comnena, *Alexiade*, ed. B. Leib, Paris: Les Belles Lettres, 1967,

71   Chalandon, *Histoire de la domination normande en Italie et en Sicile*, vol. 1, 285–326. The relationship between the brothers was always difficult; they waged war against one another twice, in 1085–6 and 1087–90.

72   Coppola, 'Bohémond 1er, prince d'Antioch', 92.

73   Richard, *Histoire des croisades*, 59.

74   Antioch had first been conquered by the Arabs in 636, then retaken by the Byzantines in 969. It was taken by the Seljuk Turks in 1084, only thirteen years before the arrival of the First Crusade. Today it is the Turkish town of Antakya.

75 Richard, *Histoire des croisades*, 63–84.

76 *Ibid.*, 140.

77 Orderic Vitalis, *Historia eccelsiastica*, XI, 12, ed. M. Chibnall, vol. 6, 68–73.

78 Coppola, 'Bohémond 1er, prince d'Antioch', 95. Cecilia was the daughter of Philippe I and Bertrade of Monfort, wife of Fulk IV, Count of Anjou, whom the king had kidnapped.

79 Coppola, 'Bohémond 1er, prince d'Antioch', 96–7. Bohemond died in the same year as his half-brother Roger Borsa. His mausoleum, in the form of a Byzantine church, is attached to the cathedral of Saint-Sabine, in Canosa in Apulia.

80 Orderic Vitalis, *Historia eccelsiastica*, XI, 25, ed. M. Chibnall, vol. 6, 104–7.

81 Bouet, 'Généalogie des descendants de Tancrède', 36–7. Richard, *Histoire des croisades*, 391, 502–7. The Principality of Antioch was restored to the County of Tripoli under Bohemond IV. Antioch was taken back by the Mamluks in 1268, under Bohemond VI. The last representative of the dynasty, Bohemond VII, died in 1287. Tripoli finally fell into Muslim hands in 1289 (two years before Acre, the last Christian stronghold in the Holy Land).

82 Hugues Falcand, *The History of the Tyrants of Sicily by 'Hugo Falcandus' (1154–69)*, ed. and trans. G.A. Loud and T. Wiedeman, Manchester and New York: Manchester University Press, 1998.

83 Chalandon, *Histoire de la domination normande en Italie et en Sicile*, vol. 2, 167–304.

84 Constance was born in 1154. Her marriage to Henry took place in 1186, when Henry was twenty and she thirty-two.

85 The Strymon flows into the Aegean Sea in northern Greece, not far from Thessalonica, which was taken by the Normans. Parallel to the landed attack, a Norman fleet turned towards Constantinople. It retired without damage after the defeat of the Strymon.

86 Chalandon, *Histoire de la domination normande en Italie et en Sicile*, vol. 2, 305–18.

87 Tancred's mother was a concubine. He died before his father.

88 Chalandon, *Histoire de la domination normande en Italie et en Sicile*, vol. 2, 419–38.

89 *Ibid.*, vol. 2, 439–91. Aubé, *Les Empires normands d'Orient*, 258–63.

90 *Ibid.*

91 For Frederick II, see E. Kantorowicz, *Kaiser Friedrich der Zweite*, Stuttgart, 1927; *Frédéric II (1194–1250) et l'héritage normand de Sicile*, Actes du colloque de Cerisy-la-Salle (1997), ed. A.-M. Flambard Héricher, Caen: Presses Universitaires de Caen, 2000. See esp. Flambard Héricher, 'Du "gamin d'Apulieö à la "splendeur du monde", les grandes étapes du règne de Frédéric II, in *Frédéric II (1194–1250) et l'héritage normand de Sicile*, 15–28; and for Frederick's childhood, Kantorowicz, *Kaiser Friedrich*, 11–40.

92 He wrote a treatise on hunting: *De arte venandi cum avibus* (On the art of hunting with birds). See S. Fodale, 'Frédéric II, savant et empereur', in *Frédéric II (1194–1250) et l'héritage normand de Sicile*, 147–56.

93 The Muslims were deported to Lucera, in Apulia (near Foggia), where the emperor had a palace and kept his menagerie. Kantorowicz, *Kaiser Friedrich*, 121–7.

94 *Ibid.*, 74–155, 412–80, 561–639.

95 *Ibid.*, 41–73. The young Frederick had already been elected King of the Romans by the German princes in 1196, when he was twelve years old.

96 *Ibid.*, 74–104.

97 *Ibid.*, 156–96. See also H. Bresc, 'Frédéric II et l'Islam', in *Frédéric II (1194–1250) et l'héritage normand de Sicile*, 79–92.

98 Kantorowicz, *Kaiser Friedrich*, 412–80, 561–639.

99 Tagliacozzo is situated east of Rome, in the Abruzzi mountains.

100 H. Bresc, 'La chute des Hohenstaufen et l'installation de Charles 1er d'Anjou', in *Les Princes angevins du xiii au xv siècle. Un destin européen*, 61–83. S. Palmieri, 'De l'Anjou à la Sicile', in *L'Europe des Anjou. Aventure des princes angevins de xiii au xv siècle*, 23–25. E.G. Léonard, *Les Angevins de Naples*, Paris: Presses universitaires de France, 1959.

BIBLIOGRAPHY

Only the principal sources are shown here, as well as a selective bibliography comprising the essential documents and works referenced in this book.

Anglo-Saxon and Norman England

Bates, D. (ed.), *Regesta Regum Anglo-Normannorum: The Acta of William I (1066–1087)*. Clarendon Press, 1998.

Farley, A. and Sir H. Ellis (eds), *Domesday Book*. 4 vols, 1783 and 1816.

Greenway, D. (ed. and trans.), Henry of Huntingdon, *Historia Anglorum (The History of the English People)*. Clarendon Press, 1996.

Griscom, A. (ed.), Geoffrey of Monmouth, *Historia Regum Britanniae*, Longmans, Green and Co., 1929.

Keynes, S. and Lapidge, M. (eds and trans.), John Asser, *Asser's Life of Alfred and Other Contemporary Sources*. Penguin, 1983 (reprint 2004).

Mynors, R.A.B., R.M. Thompson and M. Winterbottom (eds and trans.), William of Malmesbury, *Gesta regum Anglorum (The History of the English Kings)*. 2 vols. Clarendon Press, 1998–9.

Morton, C. and Muntz, H. (eds). Guy, Bishop of Amiens, *Carmen de Hastingae Proelio*, Oxford Medieval Texts. Clarendon Press, 1972.

Stubbs, W. (ed.). Benoit de Peterborough, *De vita & gestis Henrici II. et Ricardi I (The Chronicle of the Reigns of Henry II and Richard I)*. Rolls Series. 2 vols. Longman & Co., 1867.

—— Roger of Hovenden (Howden), *Chronica*. Rolls series. 4 vols. London, 1868–71.

Swanton, M. J. (trans.). *The Anglo-Saxon Chronicles*. Phoenix Press, 1996.

Southern Italy and Sicily

Loud, G.A. and Wiedemann, T. (eds and trans.). *The History of the Tyrants of Sicily by 'Hugo Falcandus'* (1154–69). Manchester University Press, 1998.

The Scandinavians and the Viking Age

Crumlin-Pedersen, O. *Ships and Boats of the North*, vol. 2 in *Viking-Age Ships and Shipbuilding in Hedeby/Haithabu and Shleswig*. Archaeölogisches Landesmuseum der Christian-Albrechts-Universität, 1997

Normandy and Anglo-Norman England

Allen Brown, R. 'The Battle of Hastings', *Anglo-Norman Studies*, 3. Boydell Press, 1980.

—— *The Normans and the Norman Conquest*. Constable, 1969.

—— *The Normans*. Boydell Press, 1984.

—— (ed.) *Anglo-Norman Studies (Proceedings of the Battle Conference)*. 27 vols. Boydell & Brewer Ltd., 1979–2005.

Bates, D. 'Notes on the Norman aristocracy. I : Hugues de Bayeux (1011–c.1049); II : Herluin de Conteville et sa famille', in *Annals of Normandy*, 23/1, 7–38. 1973.

—— *Normandy before 1066*. Longman, 1982.

—— *William the Conqueror*. Philip, 1989.

Church, S.D. (ed.), *King John: New Interpretations*. Boydell, 1999

DeVries, K. *The Norwegian Invasion of England in 1066*. Boydell Press 1999.

Dearden, B. 'Charles the Bald's fortified bridge at Pîtres (Seine): recent archaeological investigations', in *Anglo-Norman Studies*, 11, 107–12 Boydell & Brewer Ltd, 1989.

Gillingham, J., *Richard Cœur de Lion: Kingship, Chivalry and War in the Twelfth Century*. Hambledon Press, 1994.

—— *Richard the Lionheart*. Weidenfield and Nicolson, 1978 (2nd edn, 1989).

—— *The Angevin Empire*, Arnold, 1984 (2nd edn. 2001).

Gillmor, C., 'The logistics of fortified bridge building on the Seine under Charles the Bald' in *Anglo-Norman Studies*, 11, 87–106, Boydell & Brewer, 1989.

Green, J., *The Government of England under Henry I*. Cambridge University Press, 1986.

Keats-Rohan, K.S.B., *Domesday People: A Prosopography of Persons Occurring in English Documents, 1066-1166*. 2 vols. Boydell Press, 1999.

Lemmon, C.H., *The Battle of Hastings*, St-Leonards-on-Sea, 1964.

Morillo, S., 'Warfare under the Anglo-Norman Kings, 1066–1135', in *Anglo-Norman Studies, 14*, 150–163. Boydell & Brewer Ltd., 1994.

Powicke, M., 'The Loss of Normandy (1189-1204)'. *Studies in the History of the Angevin Empire*. Manchester University Press, 1913 (reprint 1961).

Strickland, 'Military technology and conquest: the anomaly of Anglo-Saxon England'. in *Anglo-Norman Studies, 19*, 353–82 Boydell & Brewer Ltd. 1997

Van Houts, E., 'The ship list of William the Conqueror' in *Anglo-Norman Studies, 10*, 159-709, Boydell & Brewer Ltd., 1988.

INDEX